JUNG

and the

ALCHEMICAL
IMAGINATION

On The Hudson
Jung
BOOK SERIES

The Jung on the Hudson Book Series was instituted by The New York Center for Jungian Studies in 1997. This ongoing series is designed to present books that will be of interest to individuals of all fields, as well as mental health professionals, who are interested in exploring the relevance of the psychology and ideas of C. G. Jung to their personal lives and professional activities.

For more information about the annual Jung on the Hudson seminars, this series and the New York Center for Jungian Studies contact: Aryeh Maidenbaum, Ph.D., 27 North Chestnut St., Suite 3, New Paltz, NY 12561, telephone (845) 256-0191, fax (845) 256-0196.

For more information about becoming part of this series, contact: Nicolas-Hays, Inc., P.O. Box 540206, Lake Worth, FL 33454-0206, telephone: (561) 798-1040, fax: (561) 798-1042, email: info@nicolashays.com.

JUNG

and the

ALCHEMICAL IMAGINATION

*The alchemical art and its allegories are the drama of
our own souls—playing out the individuation
process on the wheel of life*

JEFFREY RAFF

NICOLAS-HAYS, INC.
Lake Worth, Florida

First published in 2000 by
Nicolas-Hays, Inc.
P.O. Box 540206
Lake Worth, FL 33454-0206
www.nicolashays.com

Distributed to the trade by
Red Wheel/Weiser, LLC
Box 612
York Beach, ME 03910
www.redwheelweiser.com

Library of Congress Cataloging-in-Publication Data

Raff, Jeffrey.
    Jung and the alchemical imagination / Jeffrey Raff.
        p. cm.
    Includes bibliographical references and index.
    ISBN 0-89254-045-1 (pbk.: alk. paper)
    1. Jungian psychology. 2. Alchemy—Psychological aspects. 3. Jung, C. G. (Carl Gustav), 1875–1961. I. Title.
BF173.R18 2000
150.19'54—dc21   00–040194

EB

The author gratefully acknowledges Princeton University Press for giving him permission to quote material from the following titles: Jung, C. G., *Psychology and Alchemy*, Copyright © 1953 by Bollingen Foundation, New York, NY; © 1968 Bollingen Foundation, Reprinted by permission of Princeton University Press; Jung, C. G., *Alchemical Studies*, Copyright © 1967 by Bollingen Foundation, Princeton University Press, Reprinted by permission of Princeton University Press; Jung, C.G., *Mysterium Coniunctionis,* Copyright © 1970 by Bollingen Foundation, Princeton University Press, Reprinted by permission of Princeton University Press.

Cover design by Kathryn Sky-Peck
Typeset in 12/14 Centaur MT

Printed in the United States of America

    8   7   6   5   4   3

The paper used in this publication meets the minimum requirements of the American National Standard for Information Sciences—Permanence of Paper for Printed Library Materials Z39.48–1992 (R1997).

CONTENTS

ACKNOWLEDGMENTS

I would like to thank those individuals whose writing skills helped me through the difficult challenge of learning to put my ideas on paper and whose comments helped make this book far better than it would otherwise have been: Lydia Lennihan and Gary Hartman. My thanks to Steve Wong for getting me into writing, and to Linda Vocatura for helping me shape many ideas that appear in this work. I wish also to thank Kay Galvan for her help with the book. And my special thanks to my wife Marilyn for her patient support through the hard work and discouraging moments that accompanied this creative process and for being partner in the alchemy of relationship.

INTRODUCTION

When I was 22 years old, I experienced a spiritual awakening. Long before I ever heard of either C. G. Jung, or alchemy, a spiritual current raced through my soul and summoned me to experiences I had never imagined could exist. I was young and very ignorant, and had no way to conceptualize the experiences that I was undergoing. In my need to comprehend, I sought teachers and traditions that might help me to understand. I found none—until I came upon the writings of C. G. Jung. Though his ideas, and the complexity of his writings puzzled me, in my heart I knew I had found a kindred spirit. I could sense, long before I could understand, that Jung provided the framework in which I could decipher the visions that I experienced.

My study of Jung introduced me to earlier traditions that also spoke to my depths. Of these, the most important was alchemy. For me, alchemy was a vast cauldron of image and symbol, a chaotic mixture of the reasonable and the bizarre, the endearing and the terrifying. At the core of it all stood the fascinating image of the philosopher's stone, the magical substance with the power to transmute metals, heal the sick, reveal the mysteries of the spirit, and bestow immortality on its fortunate creator. It was the image of the stone, more than any other, that captured my imagination and moved me to the study of alchemy—a study that has continued for over twenty years.

Originally I did not seek intellectual understanding about the origins of alchemy, nor did I wish to get into the minds of the early alchemists to deduce what they might have intended in their writings. Rather, it was the symbols that they created and the imagery that they used that held my attention. I felt that if I could understand the meaning of these symbols I would gain insight into my own experiences, and the experiences that clients shared with me. I am, I suppose, a mystic. I have never been at home in organized religion, but have had to find my own path and decipher my own truths. Without either Jung or alchemy, though, my efforts would have failed.

I have continued my exploration of the inner world for over thirty years. And I still find in the symbolic language of alchemy much that is useful in understanding the inner terrain. In writing this book, it is my intention to share the keys to understanding that alchemy presents and to unlock some of the secrets of the inner world. I make no claim to being definitive, nor do I presume to argue that my understanding is the only one possible. However, I do believe that the combination of my own inner experience and my work with many others in analysis creates a unique perspective on the spiritual dimensions of alchemy, which in turn illumines the spiritual path of individuation.

There can be no hope of understanding my perspective on alchemy without considering the Jungian model that serves as my starting point. For this reason, I touch on some of the basic ideas of Jungian theory such as the self, active imagination, dream interpretation, and the transcendent function. My approach to these concepts is not that of a theoretician attempting to explicate Jung's theoretical constructs. I approach Jung as if he were an alchemist, the latest in a long tradition of spiritual teachers. For purposes of this book, I am not interested in Jung in his entirety, but only in those aspects of his work that clarify the spiritual meaning of alchemical symbols. In other words, I explore alchemical images to understand inner experience, and I explore Jung to understand the alchemical images. The reverse holds true as well. Understanding inner experiences sheds light on the meaning of alchemical images that, in turn, amplify the concepts that Jung formulated.

There are some who might object to this view of Jung, who might question his role as a spiritual teacher or as an inner alchemist. In my opinion, however, Jung's most important contribution was not that of a practicing psychologist, but of a teacher to the world, of one who reintroduced the wisdom of many ancient traditions into the contemporary Western world. Indeed, Jung was not a practicing alchemist, but he recognized and honored the alchemical imagination, the imaginative world in which many alchemists lived and worked. In the alchemical imagination, the world may be perfected, disease vanquished, matter transformed into spirit, and spirit into matter. In the imaginative universe, the opposites unite, creating a magical third, which transcends ordinary consciousness. Fundamentally, Jung's commitment to the processes of transformation and the creation of a new psychic center, which he termed the self, place him in the imaginative world of the alchemist.

To be sure, many Jungians today reject the spiritual aspect of Jung's psychology and repudiate the notion of him as a prophet of some kind. They are not completely wrong. It would be a mistake to elevate Jung to an extramundane position and make his teachings into contemporary scripture. He, himself, would abhor that! Yet, Jung was a great teacher. In the model that he presents for spiritual exploration and transformation, the world acquired a great legacy. In recent years, the Jungian world has dramatically abandoned the spiritual dimension of Jung's work, preferring to restrict its perspective to the narrowly clinical and personal field. This is a great loss. Despite the self-conscious protestations of many that they have surpassed Jung—that he is outmoded and outdated—the deeper aspects of Jung's writings have yet to be understood. I believe that the Western world is in search of a new paradigm for inner development and spiritual awakening. By probing and expanding Jung's spiritual model I hope to contribute to that search. Viewed as a spiritual teacher, Jung offers a modern path to enlightenment.

I was most fortunate to have had the late Marie-Louise von Franz as one of my teachers in Zurich. I owe much of my understanding of Jung's spiritual contribution to her. In the pages that follow, I explore that legacy and its relevance for today, as well as its usefulness in penetrating the secrets of alchemical symbols. First, however, I outline a working overview of alchemy's nature and history.

THE BEGINNINGS OF ALCHEMY

There is still considerable controversy concerning the origins and historical development of alchemy. Many questions remain unanswered as to the nature of the various alchemical schools of thought and their relationship to one another. Nevertheless, it is possible to summarize the study of alchemy so that we reflect the consensus among scholars.

The term alchemy itself comes from two roots: *al,* which is Arabic for "the," and *chemeia*. It is unclear what *chemeia* actually means. There were two forms of the term in Greek: *chemeia* and *chymia*. The former refers to the process of extracting juice, while the later has to do with deriving metals from ore. For both forms, the transmutative processes comprise the common element, the transformation of a given substance into a higher one.[1] We might, therefore, think of alchemy as the art of *transmutation*.

We could conveniently divide the history of alchemy into three main phases: Hellenistic alchemy, from approxi-

---

1. Jack Lindsay, *The Origins of Alchemy in Graeco-Roman Egypt* (New York: Barnes and Noble, 1970), p. 68.

mately 200 B.C. to A.D. 600: Arabic alchemy, extending to about A.D. 1000; and Latin alchemy, continuing from about 1100 to 1700.

The father of alchemy, as we know it, was a writer named Bolos of Mendes whose life remains shrouded in obscurity. Apparently he lived and wrote in Hellenistic Egypt, but exactly when remains unclear. Jack Lindsay, whose work on early alchemy remains unsurpassed, believed Bolos's compilations and writings united the main threads of earlier alchemy into the form in which it existed for many centuries.[2] Many believe that the roots of alchemy lay in the traditions of ancient Egypt, and Bolos certainly used images and ideas that derive from Egyptian practices. In addition, Bolos was the first to introduce the visionary element into the world of alchemy, for his discovery of the guiding principles of the alchemical work came about in a magical fashion.

Bolos, himself, wrote that he studied alchemy with a master named Ostanes, who unfortunately died before revealing the full nature of the work. Though Bolos worked at unraveling the secrets, he had little success. Rather than give up, Bolos evoked the spirit of the dead Ostanes in a magical ritual. Though he was successful in summoning the spirit of his teacher, the guardians of the dead would not let Ostanes speak. He managed to say only that the "books are in the temple."[3]

Bolos went in search of the books, but could not find them. Later he attended a banquet with Ostanes's son and one of the building's columns opened of its own accord. The son told Bolos that this column held his father's books,

---

2. Jack Lindsay, *The Origins of Alchemy in Graeco-Roman Egypt*, p. 101.
3. Jack Lindsay, *The Origins of Alchemy in Graeco-Roman Egypt*, p. 102.

but when they looked they found only a single formula: "A nature is delighted by another nature, a nature conquers another nature, a nature dominates another nature."[4] Bolos realized that all the secrets of alchemy were contained in this single formula.

Thus the famous triadic formula, one used by alchemists until the 17th century, was a revelation acquired through dialogue with a ghost. Lindsay correctly pointed out that the whole scene and its revelatory character is reminiscent of other hermetic tracts, such as the *Book of Poimandres*.[5] That Bolos portrayed the beginning of the sacred art as a visionary event demonstrates not only that alchemy was considered to be one of the magical arts, but that visionary experience was integral to it from the very beginning.

Greek or Hellenistic alchemy is not exclusively of a visionary character, for there are several tracts devoted to the practical side of the work, such as the design for building the famous "Bath of Marie," used for centuries by aspiring alchemists. But the visionary element cannot be denied. Zosimos, one of the most famous of the Greek alchemists, recorded a series of visions in which he expressed some of the essential secrets of the work. I cannot discuss these visions in detail, but they describe a series of dream-like revelations in which Zosimos gained insight into the nature of the "divine waters." He saw several personified figures who represented the arcane substance, and who both dialogued with him and underwent bloody and violent operations. These figures, both in their dialogue with Zosimos, and in the torments they underwent, revealed different aspects of

---

4. Jack Lindsay, *The Origins of Alchemy in Graeco-Roman Egypt*, p. 103.

5. Jack Lindsay, *The Origins of Alchemy in Graeco-Roman Egypt*, p. 103. For *The Book of Poimandres*, see Walter Scott, *Hermetica* (Boston: Shambhala, 1983), pp. 115–285.

the alchemical *opus*.[6] The Greek alchemists integrated both the practical and visionary aspects of alchemy, but the latter quality seemed to hold a great deal of power for them.

When the Arabs conquered the eastern provinces of the Byzantine Empire, they took over the part of the world where alchemy flourished. In Egypt and Syria they discovered alchemical writings, and soon took over the study of transmutation. There were several Arab schools of alchemy; some more devoted to physical alchemy and others to spiritual alchemy.

The most famous of the Arab alchemists, and one who attempted to unite both the spiritual and practical sides of alchemy, was Jabir Ibn Hayyan who is supposed to have died around 800. As with many of the early alchemists, there is considerable controversy about this man's life. Some question whether he existed at all, or if the works ascribed to him could have been written by one individual. His theories are complex and difficult and, at times, arcane to the extreme.

But his work is far from nonsensical; it is a sophisticated philosophy rooted in Neo-Platonic thought. Jabir rejected the notion of empirical study in favor of the view that eternal truths alone form the basis for science.[7] Jabir's system combines the mystery of numbers and letters with the processes of alchemical transmutation. For him, the secret of creating the magical stone depended upon the correct balance that is attained through insight into the inner essence of things. Clearly, his was a very complicated system, and though not overtly visionary, it is related to

---

6. For a full discussion of Zosimos and his visions, see Lindsay, chapters 15 and 16.

7. Syed Nomanul Haq, *Names, Natures and Things* (Boston: Kluwer Academic Publishers, 1994), p. 66.

the magical practices of number and letter combinations. At the same time, his system is based on the power of the mind to see into the essence of things:

> *Proceed with the understanding that this is an art which de-mands special skills; nay, it is the greatest of all arts for it [concerns] an ideal entity which exists only in the mind.*[8]

There remains a great deal to learn, not only about Jabir, but about the rest of the Arabic alchemists, as well, including the relationship between alchemy and the Islamic mysticism known as Sufism.

The Sufi mystical tradition is of great importance for it possesses an elaborate theory of the imagination, and offers a unique perspective on the meaning of alchemy. The Sufi view of alchemy unites a theory of imagination with the goal of creating subtle bodies and of seeing into the heart of the universe. For the Sufis, alchemy is primarily a spiritual operation based on visionary states and experiences. Discussing how spiritual and material bodies interact in the alchemical work, for example, one writer notes that alchemical operations would be inconceivable if they were performed on material bodies, but once we recognize that they must be applied to *spiritual* bodies, the work becomes fully intelligible.[9]

The Sufi alchemists understood that the matter on which they operated was not purely physical in nature, but belonged more to the world of Paradise. Although the union of the physical and the spiritual is a theme found in alchemy of all periods, the Sufis were the most explicit in expressing the otherworldly nature of the work. When body becomes

---

8. Syed Nomanul Haq, *Names, Natures and Things*, p. 197.
9. See Shaikh Ahmad Ahsa'i, in Henry Corbin, *Spiritual Body and Celestial Earth* (Princeton: Princeton University Press, 1989), p. 209.

spirit and spirit becomes body, we enter a new realm of experience that I call the *psychoid*. I discuss the nature of psychoidal experience in the appropriate context, but it is noteworthy that the Sufis developed this notion centuries ago.

Alchemy next migrated to Western Europe in about the 13th century, where it thrived for hundreds of years. Though it always remained an underground movement that never received official approbation, alchemy was popular with people from all walks of life. Dukes and kings, bishops and popes, all were interested in alchemy at one time or another. There were hundreds of texts, varying from the brilliant to the hackneyed, written from the 13th century through the 18th century. There were alchemists who believed in the physical nature of the enterprise and devoted themselves to laboratory work in a way that often anticipated later scientific experimentation. But there were also many who wrote about alchemy from the spiritual and visionary perspective, and many more who tried to combine the two threads.

One of the earliest published works available to us to demonstrate the inner and visionary aspect of alchemy was *Aurora Consurgens*, which was attributed to Thomas Aquinas. Marie-Louise von Franz wrote an insightful analysis of this work in which she demonstrated its ecstatic quality. In fact, she believed that the author wrote much of the work while in an ecstatic state. The text was filled with a fervor and a type of love poetry written to the feminine Wisdom. The author wove in quotes from the Bible with obvious references to alchemical procedures and declared the advent of heaven on earth for the one who weds Wisdom and creates the philosopher's stone.[10]

---

10. Marie-Louise von Franz, *Aurora Consurgens*, Bollingen Series LXXVII (New York: Pantheon, 1996), pp. 129–131.

The admixture of religious imagery and alchemical process is not atypical of alchemy in Western Europe. There are many comparisons of the philosopher's stone to Christ, and other references to the Book of Genesis, as well as to the wisdom literature of the Bible. The alchemical undertaking clearly had a religious flavor for the writers of the Middle Ages and Renaissance, for whom the creation of the stone was a miracle. Moreover, the alchemy of this period possessed distinct elements of visionary and revelatory features. One finds references to dreams and visions as well as recorded dialogues between the alchemists and alchemical spirits such as Mercury, Sulfur, and Nature. Though some of these dialogues served didactic purposes, some reflect genuine inner experiences. In addition, there are some examples of visionary material that were never meant for publication. For instance, George Starkey, an alchemist writing in the 17th century, related one of his dreams in a letter written to his patron. In this dream he was working in his laboratory when a spiritual being suddenly materialized. Recovering from his shock and assuring himself that the apparition was not evil, Starkey asked it a question about the nature of the alchemical *alchahest*, or original material. The spiritual entity revealed to him its nature, and though Starkey could not understand what he had heard intellectually, he knew it for truth.[11] The revelation of the recipe for the magical substances is a common theme in alchemical writings; alchemists frequently warned that success in the work could only come through revelation from God.

I could adduce further examples to illustrate the association of visionary states with alchemy during the three pe-

---

11. William R. Newman, *Gehennical Fire* (Cambridge, MA: Harvard University Press, 1994), p. 65.

riods of its development. The ones mentioned, however, should be sufficient to convey something of the richness of the visionary tradition associated with the Great Work from its inception.

Interest in alchemy still continues today, and is most often divided into two main branches—inner and practical. As the names indicate, the latter is concerned with work in the laboratory and the hope of creating healing potions and transmutations of all kinds. The former is concerned with inner experiences aimed at transforming the personality or facilitating the experience of divine truths. The great split between inner alchemy and practical alchemy is only a few centuries old, for throughout most of its history alchemy held these opposites together. The alchemist of the Middle Ages did not distinguish between the religious nature of alchemy and its more practical uses and applications. Though the split is often lamented as leading to the demise of true alchemy, it may well be part of the continuing evolution of alchemy as it moves into the next millennium. The union of spirit and matter that alchemy represented is surely dead, but that does not preclude the possible emergence of a new union. The history of alchemy is not yet complete, for the tradition continues in various ways in the present day. Literary critics, psychologists, practical alchemists, and those who pursue the esoteric path still write about it and nurture the images to which it gave birth. More importantly, individuals still experience the revelations and visions that were so instrumental in the creation and development of alchemy, and understand them in terms similar to those of the ancient and medieval alchemists.

Alchemy has had a long and varied career. The alchemists of the three periods I have discussed would not have always agreed with each other, but there was much that they held in common. The goals they sought were similar. The creation of gold from inferior metals was a goal that remained constant throughout alchemy's history. To be sure, commentators still debate the nature of the gold the alchemist sought to create. Some alchemists seemed intent on the creation of actual, physical gold, while others had a more spiritual "gold" in mind. In either case, however, gold was the image for the end result of the work.

Many alchemists, especially after the time of Paracelsus (died 1541), were physicians who did not seek gold as much as a healing elixir. With this curative substance, they hoped to find the means of alleviating the suffering of their brethren. Some even hoped to find an elixir to prolong life long past its normal span, and even hinted at the possibility of physical immortality.

To create gold or a healing potion, most alchemists believed that they must first create the philosopher's stone, and that it alone had the power of effecting transmutations and healing. The stone had another capacity as well; to open its possessor to the Divine mysteries. Although there were other beneficial side effects to creating it, essentially the stone was the goal of all alchemical endeavors. With it all the other goals could be achieved; without it, they would be difficult or impossible to attain. It is fair to state that, in all their efforts and all the processes they devised, the alchemists' ultimate intention was the creation of the philosopher's stone.

The major processes by which the alchemists accomplished this task remained constant through the history of alchemy. To begin with, the alchemist had to find the right material from which to generate the stone. The nature of this material remained one of the greatest secrets of alchemy that was never revealed, possibly because there was no one answer. There are hundreds of recommendations, hints, and veiled allusions to the identity of this elusive substance that was called the *prima materia.*

Normally, alchemists would obtain a substance that they believed to contain the mysterious *prima materia* and subject it to a number of operations. The aim of these processes was to destroy the original form, and to reduce it to a preformed state. This preformed state *was* the *prima materia*. In other words, the *prima materia* was matter before it was formed, which the alchemists called "chaos" among other things. Having reduced the substance to this chaotic state, the alchemists believed they had actually "killed" the original material. Hence the process by which matter lost its original form and became reduced to chaos was known as the *mortificatio* or the *nigredo*. The alchemists described the process as having a black color and often a bad smell.

Plate 1

The fluid, chaotic state was often equaled with mercury. Thus, alchemical mercury was frequently considered the *prima materia*, though alchemists were quick to point out that the mercury they used was not ordinary mercury. Mercury contained within itself a sulfur, which if removed and separated from the mercury, would later reunite with it in such a way as to create a new form. As the sulfur and the mercury interacted, fought with each other, and then reunited, the matter underwent successive changes. If the sulfur and mercury united in a balanced way, the philosopher's stone would emerge.

Though there were many variations on the theme, the alchemical drama consisted of the death of the original substance, which resulted in its reduction to a primal state. Next the alchemist separated the *prima materia* into its component parts, sulfur and mercury. The parts were then reunited in such a way as to create a new substance—the philosopher's stone. Alchemy proceeded by separation and reunification, *solve et coagule*, a procedure that might be repeated many times.

There were a number of processes alchemists used to effect these changes. Although there were dozens of alchemical processes, there were five that occur most frequently in alchemical texts. The *nigredo* was the reduction of the substance to its primal condition and was effected by one of the other main procedures. Though the *nigredo* might occur at the start of the work, it could actually take place at any time when the alchemist destroyed the substance in question in order to transform it once again.

There was no set order to the other processes and no general agreement among the alchemists about the relationship between the processes. *Solutio* was the process of liquefaction, of turning a solid into a liquid. Often the transformation from solid to liquid demonstrated that the old form had been destroyed and reduced to chaos. The liquefaction was also seen as a reduction of matter to mercury, or of its being devoured by the mercury. *Separatio* was the means of rending apart the components of the *prima materia*, while the *coniunctio* rejoined them. Separation might be followed by union many different times during the work.

Fire was a central symbol in the alchemical lexicon. *Calcinatio*, the process of burning a substance and reducing it to ash, served as a method of purification. Fire also effected separation, splitting the ash or body of the material from the spirit, which rose to the top of the alchemical vessel as vapor. When the alchemists aimed specifically at creating a vapor, the process was called *sublimatio*. And when they wished to reunite the body with the spirit, they performed *coagulatio*, which turned liquid back to solid, or reunited the vapor with the ash.

All of these processes aimed initially at creating the desired *prima materia* and then transforming it in a variety of ways, until finally it transmuted into the philosopher's stone. Even then the alchemist might not call it quits! Through the process of *multiplicatio*, he could augment the power of his stone both qualitatively and quantitatively. Theoretically, the power with which the stone could be invested was unlimited, and the *multiplicatio* could be repeated many times.

Alchemists also associated changes of color with the successive transformation of matter. As noted earlier, the *nigredo* was associated with the color black. After a number of procedures, the material would slowly start coming back to life. As it moved from death to new growth, the alchemists often noted a green color. The return to life might also be associated with the appearance of many colors, a phase called the peacock's tail, the *caudis pavonis*. As the substance continued to grow and change, it would reach an initial resting-place, often called the first stone. At this stage, it would regain form and have the power to create silver from other metals. This stage was associated with white, and was therefore referred to as the *albedo*.

Some alchemists were content to stop the work at this point for they felt that the *albedo* denoted the formation of a powerful stone. Most, however, wished to create the second stone, with its power to transmute metals into gold. To do so, they subjected the matter that had turned white to another death, and turned it black once more. When it came back to life this time, however, it would have reached a whole new level of being. This new state of being was indicated by the color red. When the material turned gold or reddish, therefore, it had entered the final state known as the *rubedo*. Some alchemists included a state in which a yellow color might appear between the white and the red, but most described the color changes as moving from black to white to red.

The color symbolism was important in alchemy, and the alchemists carefully noted changes in the material's color. As Jack Lindsay has pointed out, change "in quality which was also a change in inner organization was linked or identified with the colour changes."[12] For the alchemists, therefore, when a substance underwent a change in color, it was simul-

---

12. Jack Lindsay, *The Origins of Alchemy in Graeco-Roman Egypt*, p. 116.

taneously undergoing a change in its inner nature. Change in color therefore symbolized a transmutation of the substance and its movement from one level of being to another.

This is only a brief review of some of the major processes and stages of the alchemical work. Much has been written about them, and those readers who are interested in learning more about the processes and their psychological meanings might want to read Edward Edinger's excellent work on alchemy and analysis, *Anatomy of the Psyche*, or M.-L. von Franz's *Alchemy*.[13]

Alchemy was a tradition that lasted for two thousand years. Despite its many changes, it retained a remarkable cohesion and continuity through the centuries. Alchemists from one period would have been able to converse intelligently with others from a century far removed without too much difficulty. Alchemy was a strange mixture of visionary states and experiences and physical work with material substances. This book focuses on the former elements. Alchemy provides a model and a map for defining inner experiences, as well as a symbolic system for their expression.

One could derive several maps from the alchemical literature, but I use one proposed by the alchemist Gerald Dorn, who wrote in the 16th century. I shall discuss this man and his work in more detail, but here I need only point out that his delineation of the alchemical *opus* emphasizes three major plateaus. Each is characterized as the creation of a union that produces the stone at differing levels of perfection. Most importantly, each has associated with it certain psychological experiences. Jung discussed the first

---

13. Edward Edinger, *Anatomy of the Psyche* (La Salle: Open Court, 1994); Marie-Louise von Franz, *Alchemy* (Toronto: Inner City Books, 1980).

two unions that produced the philosopher's stone in his monumental work, *Mysterium Coniunctionis*,[14] but he only touched on the third union. I propose to discuss the nature of the third union in some detail. In order to do so, I have had to present two controversial ideas, that of the psychoid world and the center of that world, which I call the self of the psychoid.

Each level of union in Dorn's formulation may be understood as the crystallization of a new center of the psyche, a center Jung termed the self. The first stage unites the conscious and the unconscious; the second makes this union permanent; the third unites the self already created with a center that transcends the human psyche, a center that one might call Divine. I suggest that one good way to understand the alchemical symbols and processes is in terms of Dorn's map and the nature of the center created at each step of the way. The first two centers are psychic, but the last is psychoidal, in that it creates a center that is in part transpsychic. No one, to my knowledge, has written of the third state in detail, and my discussion is controversial. Nevertheless, it provides interpretation to alchemical images and understanding of inner experiences that are new and revealing. One major theme throughout this work will therefore be the nature of the psychoid and the experience of the third level of union.

I also take the position that alchemical images symbolically portray psychological states and experiences. It would be wrong to suppose, as many do today, that these images

---

14. C. G. Jung, *Mysterium Coniunctionis*, Collected Works, vol. 14, R. F. C. Hull, trans., Bollingen Series XX (Princeton: Princeton University Press, 1963, 1970).

are merely metaphors for ordinary life events, or even for analytical experiences. They are indeed metaphors for such things, but beyond that, they are symbolic expressions of states of consciousness and felt visions that are unique in themselves. It is not incorrect to understand alchemy as a metaphor. Neither is it incorrect to approach it as a guide to actual transmutative experiences, in which the gold being created is an enlightened consciousness. I take this latter approach to alchemy and discuss the nature of the conscious and transcendent experiences alchemy describes and helps foster. To do this successfully, it is necessary to turn to Jung and to extract from his writings a model for spiritual experience that makes alchemy decipherable.

CHAPTER 1

JUNG

as a

SPIRITUAL TRADITION

I went to Zurich in 1972 to study at the C. G. Jung Institute. Though I took many classes there, my real training lay with a group of analysts then known as the "Kusnacht Mafia." This was an assemblage of individuals who had been most influenced by the teachings of Marie-Louise von Franz. A student, colleague, and friend of Dr. Jung, von Franz seemed to us to hold the key to a deeper understanding of Jung's theories. We spoke frequently of the written tradition versus the oral tradition of Jungian psychology, for there were major differences between the Jung of the Collected Works and the Jung as von Franz presented him. Von Franz spoke of a Jung who was a spiritual teacher, who knew full well that the inner work was of paramount importance. He was concerned far more with experience than with theory, and the stories of his many adventures with the unconscious were fascinating and inspiring.

It was an exciting time to be studying in Zurich. Many of the "old teachers" were still active. As students, we experienced the reality of the self first hand, and focused our efforts on living with it. We were taught to think of it as an inner figure with its own voice, one that could be heard directly in dreams, active imagination, and even in ordinary experiences. I remember Dr. von Franz explaining how she would tune in when asked a question, even one as simple as whether she would have lunch with someone. She would focus her awareness on the self and wait for the answer to come.

THE SELF

Jung's published writings are not always easy to understand, and frequently do not convey the reality of direct contact with the self. Jung does write of such experiences. For example, he stated that the self as center must become the *spiritus rector* of daily life.[1] Moreover, the experience of the self is almost impossible to practically distinguish from the experience of "what has always been referred to as 'God.'"[2] The experience of the self is from the perspective of the ego an experience of the Divine that presents it with problems and issues it would just as soon avoid. In the book Jung designed and edited for the general public, *Man and His Symbols*, von Franz presented Jung's basic notion of the encounter with the self when she wrote:

> *Some profound inner experience of the Self does occur to most people at least once in a lifetime. From the psychological standpoint, a genuinely religious attitude consists of an effort to discover the unique experience, and gradually to keep in tune with it . . . so that the Self becomes an inner partner toward whom one's attention is continually turned.*[3]

These comments occur in a paragraph in which von Franz equated the self with the philosopher's stone, an equation that Jung, himself, never failed to make.

---

1. C. G. Jung, *Mysterium Coniunctionis*, Collected Works, vol. 14, R. F. C. Hull, trans., Bollingen Series XX (Princeton: Princeton University Press, 1970), ¶ 777. From now on I'll refer to this volume as CW 14.
2. CW 14, ¶ 778.
3. M.-L. von Franz, "The Process of Individuation" in C. G. Jung, *Man and His Symbols* (Garden City: Doubleday, 1964), p. 210.

2

There were a number of factors that influenced Jung's conclusion that the stone was symbol for the self. He conceived of the self as the union of opposites and the center of the psyche. The stone was the union of opposites, and often portrayed as center. The self could be personified as an inner figure, as could the stone. The self was the repository of wisdom and so, too, was the stone. The self was the goal of all psychic life, and the end state to which the individuation process led, while the stone was the goal of all alchemical endeavors and the end to which all the alchemical processes led. Moreover, Jung thought that the self created symbols in order to make its attributes known and the stone was one such image.[4] Jung always operated under the assumption that what was said of the stone was true of the self, for in the stone the self had found a way to symbolically express itself. The comparison of the self with the stone united Jung's model with the alchemical one. He was also able to explore the spiritual ideas of the alchemist as they related to his own religious perspective.

Jung described the "religious attitude" as "careful and scrupulous observation of . . . a dynamic existence or effect not caused by an arbitrary act of will."[5] Since the self is the composite of these effects, I could describe the religious attitude as paying attention to the self, or as making it into an inner partner. The ego scrupulously observes the manifestations of the self and harmonizes itself with them. This was the tradition passed on to me in Zurich, and one I have followed for the last thirty years. This simple

---

4. For a discussion of the self and its creation of symbols, see C. G. Jung, *Aion*, Collected Works, vol. 9ii, R. F. C. Hull, trans., Bollingen Series XX (Princeton: Princeton University Press, 1968), ¶ 121 ff. Future references to this volume will be to CW 9ii.

5. C. G. Jung, *Psychology and Religion* (New Haven: Yale University Press, 1938), p. 4.

formulation conveys the heart and soul of Jung's spiritual model. Though many today would deny him any significance as a spiritual teacher, there was no doubt to those of us studying in Zurich with Marie-Louise von Franz and Arnold Mindell that Jungian work was a spiritual process. We did not confine our work with the unconscious to our analytical sessions, but made it the very fabric of our lives.

Jung was concerned with the question of how his psychology fit within the context of the Western European tradition. He found parallels to his psychic perspective in the lineage of alchemy and Gnosticism. While the question of Jung's place in history continues under debate, students of what has come to be called "esoteric spirituality" believe he belongs in that tradition. Esoteric religion includes teachers such as Jacob Boehme, Paracelsus, and in fact all of alchemy, as well as the Rosicrucian movement. In an essay on esoteric spirituality, Gerhard Wehr argued that Jung is part of the esoteric tradition. While owning that there are some difficulties with this attribution, he argued that Jung fits in this particular context for two reasons. Jung consistently referred to and quoted from older religious traditions to shed light on the workings of the unconscious. The second reason is more compelling. As Wehr points out, "The experience of depth psychology, the process of individuation that must be undergone, is itself an esoteric event which changes people to the depth of their being, extends their consciousness, and brings their personality to the maturity of the whole person."[6] The nature of the inner experiences that Jung's model creates connects it most with the earlier esoteric schools.

---

6. Gerhard Wehr, "C. G. Jung in the Context of Christian Esotericism and Cultural History" in Antoine Faivre and Jacob Needleman, eds., *Modern Esoteric Spirituality* (New York: Crossroad, 1995), p. 382.

Placing Jung within an historical context may not seem important. Today, however, more and more Jungians are redefining Jungian work and concepts with a decidedly non-spiritual emphasis. To lose touch with the deeper meanings of Jung's work, and with the traditions that helped shape him, would be tragic. Regardless of how analysts and therapists choose to apply Jungian thought to the clinical setting, originally and essentially, Jungian work was a system aimed at promoting profound transformational experience. Analytic work with individuals that does not foster such transformational experiences should only loosely be termed Jungian.

Living with the self is the key practice in Jung's spiritual model, but what is the self? Dialoguing with inner figures is a quintessential feature of the Jungian approach: the self is often experienced in this way. Personified as an inner figure, it embodies an individual's essential nature and, although often overwhelming, the self still wears a face resembling that of the conscious personality. But what is the self? Experientially, the self is an inner and subjective figure or center that feels powerful, numinous, and complete in itself. As a theoretical construct, the self has a number of attributes. It is the center of the whole personality and is thus related to what Jung calls the ego, the center of consciousness. In fact, to understand the self, one must understand something of the ego and the structure of the psyche as Jung conceived it.

The ego is easy to experience and hard to define. Experientially, it is what we refer to when we say, "I." When an individual says, "I am hungry," "I am angry," or "I am male," the "I" in those statements is the ego. The ego carries the "I-ness" of the personality. We often naively identify the whole psyche with this "I," not realizing that there are, in fact, other aspects of the psyche with which we simply cannot identify. In Jung's conceptualization, the ego is the center of consciousness and, as such, is the instrument for making experience conscious. When the ego is in touch with any psychic content, that content is conscious. When the ego is not, that content is unconscious. Not only does the ego's attention lend consciousness to a psychic content, but it can also trigger a change within that content. Part of the work of individuation is the process of the ego's making experience conscious and thereby effecting changes in the psyche.

Those parts of the psyche that are not in relationship with the ego comprise the unconscious, both personal and collective. The personal unconscious consists of complexes and other material that belongs to the individual's life experience, but which, for a variety of reasons, is not in relationship to the ego. Much of this material can and should be brought into relationship with the ego, and the process of doing so strengthens and widens consciousness. The collective unconscious, on the other hand, consists of archetypes and universal images that do not belong to any single individual, but to humankind as a whole. Archetypal structures, patterns, and images mold and shape human life, and have always done so. This material does not belong to consciousness, and while it can be brought into relationship with the ego, the ego must not identify with it or assimilate it into its own structure. Any attempt to do so can lead to inflation or even psychosis. However, the archetypes may be brought into relationship with the self, for the self as center of the psyche is capable of interacting appropriately with this collective material.

Simply put, the psyche consists of the ego that is conscious and the complexes and archetypes that are unconscious. As the ego is the center of consciousness, the self is the center of the whole personality. The self is also the archetype of wholeness, and as such, carries a sense of the complete personality. Wholeness refers to the union of the conscious and the unconscious parts of the personality and, in particular, to the union of the ego and the unconscious. We might think of this process of unifying the opposites as occurring under the aegis and following the model of the self. Jung explains this aspect as follows:

> Psychologically, the self is a union of conscious (masculine) and unconscious (feminine). It stands for the psychic totality. So formulated, it is a psychological concept. Empirically, however, the self appears spontaneously in the shape of specific symbols, and its totality is discernible above all in the mandala and its countless variants.[7]

The self is the center of the personality even before the process of individuation begins. It only points toward wholeness symbolically, for the actual union of the conscious and the unconscious is the work of a lifetime. I refer to the self prior to this union as the "latent self." As the process of joining these two parts of the psyche begins to unfold, the self moves increasingly to its own manifestation. This latter aspect I call the "manifest self." The self and its transformation from latent to manifest are the primary focus of Jung's spiritual model.

It is important to clarify just what Jung meant by spirit and spiritual, however, so that we may more easily grasp how this process unfolds. In his article "The Phenomenology of the Spirit in Fairytales," Jung wrestled with the problem of the meaning of spirit. He came to the conclusion that there were three major attributes. The first is spontaneous movement and activity. The spirit is free to do and create as it will, and is free of the control of the ego, the conscious part of the personality. The ego can experience

---

7. CW 9ii, ¶ 426.

the spirit, but not dictate to it. The second attribute of spirit is the capacity to spontaneously produce images independently, and the third attribute is the "sovereign manipulation of these images."[8] Experientially, every human being encounters the spirit in his or her dreams, for the images that populate dreams derive from the spirit. Not only the images themselves, but all that they do in the dreams are a reflection of spirit. In this sense, the ego does not make up dreams; rather, it experiences them as they unfold through the spontaneous manifestation of the spirit. Jung felt that the archetype of spirit appeared in dreams as the wise old man.

He also believed that the contents of the unconscious, including complexes and archetypes, had the capacity to manifest themselves as images. We might imagine the psyche as a chaotic place, in which every part is capable of generating its own image. With every aspect of the inner world able to personify itself as an image, the result would be a conflicting chorus of voices, each singing its own melody, with no regard for the others. This chaos is evident in severely disturbed and psychotic individuals who are unable to protect themselves from the cacophony of their inner spirits.

Balancing this disorder, however, is the self, the principle of order and harmony. I described the self earlier in its relationship to wholeness, to the potential totality of the personality. From the perspective of personified images, the self as a totality includes the whole array of images and voices that arise from the unconscious. In addition, the self is the center of the psyche, around which all the other parts orient themselves. The self brings order to the psyche, and

---

8. C. G. Jung, *The Archetypes and the Collective Unconscious*, Collected Works, vol. 9i, R. F. C. Hull, trans., Bollingen Series XX (Princeton: Princeton University Press, 1969), ¶ 393. Future references to this volume will be to CW 9i.

harmonizes all aspects of the psyche to create an orchestrated composition. Seen in this way, the self is the center of the soul around which the archetypes are grouped in their respective order. The mandala is the symbol for the self when it functions in this manner. Speaking of the mandala, Jung writes:

> [The] basic motif is the premonition of a center of personality, a kind of central point within the psyche, to which everything is related, by which everything is arranged, and which is itself a source of energy. The energy of the central point is manifested in the almost irresistible compulsion and urge to become what one is. . . . *Although the centre is represented by an innermost point, it is surrounded by a periphery containing everything that belongs to the self. . . . This totality comprises consciousness first of all, then the personal unconscious, and finally an indefinitely large segment the collective unconscious whose archetypes are common to all mankind.*[9]

Jung calls the mandala, with its emphasis on order and harmonious balance, a premonition of the center of personality, or self. It is a premonition in that the self, in its capacity as the ordering center for the whole psyche, does not exist at birth. It must be produced through a variety of psychological experiences. To distinguish between the self before and after individuation, I speak of the "latent" and the "manifest" self. The latent self is a weak center, possessing only limited power to organize psychic life. With the latent self, the complexes and archetypes vie for control of the psyche; the intra-psychic situation is chaotic and difficult. The individual by no means experiences the chaos a psychotic patient does, but the individual's sense of self is tenuous.

---

9. CW 9i, ¶ 634.

The ego may believe itself to be in a strong and controlling position, but complexes can manifest at any time, disrupting the order that the ego struggles to maintain. A successful businessman who is very much "on top of things" at work may experience uncontrollable rages at home. A career woman may weep inconsolably for no known reason. The ego's order is a charade that a complex can easily puncture. If an individual comes under the power of an archetype, the fragile sense of identity conferred by the ego may easily be swept away. Obvious examples are the experience of normal and seemingly healthy individuals who are gripped by the emotions of a mob or the ability of governments to turn sensitive individuals into killing machines by appealing to patriotism.

More damaging from the point of view of spirituality is the risk of mistaking other inner voices for that of the self. An individual who is trying to listen to the voice of the inner spirit and who wants to relate to the images created by it may be dealing with an autonomous complex or archetype, and not the self at all. Turning inward in search of the still, small voice often unleashes a torrent of uncontrollable images. These images may not be related to the process of individuation, but to archetypes or complexes that are not yet part of the mandala Jung describes.

This happens all too often, as a study of spiritual experiences proves. Consider, as only one example, the fathers of early Christianity who went into the desert to seek their God and met hordes of demons instead. In all likelihood, the demons that plagued them were images produced by constellated complexes or archetypes.

In the above quote, Jung explained how the self could orchestrate the psyche, including the collective unconscious, around the powerful center I call the manifest self. As a result of the work of individuation, the self gains the position of the dominant spiritual force within the psyche.

When images manifest, they manifest as the self, and though they cannot be controlled or even predicted, they can be trusted.

As Jung pointed out, the power and energy of the self manifests as an almost irresistible urge to be oneself. The self pushes one to the experience and expression of one's own uniqueness; to this end it must order the archetypal world. The archetypes are collective forces, and the images that they produce are universal. An individual might simply follow these images, and, thereby, have numinous experiences. Yet he or she would never create the manifest self, which is unique and individual—and the central tenet of Jung's model is that one must become one's self.

Although Jung did not conceptualize the process in this way, I imagine an ordering of the psychic chaos through the action of the self. As the self brings the archetypes into harmony, it effects the patterned order of the mandala structure with each archetype in a complementary relationship to the whole. In this process, the archetypes lose their universal and collective qualities, and actually contribute to the uniqueness that *is* the self.

In summary, for Jung, the religious attitude consists of attending to the self, of living with the self as an inner partner. Because the spirit belonging to the self manifests in dreams, visions, and active imagination, one can maintain relationship with the self by engaging those images. In its normal, latent condition, however, the self competes with complexes and archetypes, which also manifest as images. The religious attitude then consists not only of paying attention to the self, but also of working with it in such a way that it becomes powerful and dominant within the psyche. This work, the spiritual work par excellence, transforms the self from its latent to its manifest state. In so doing it transforms the whole personality, including the ego and unconscious.

The manifest self must be created; it rarely emerges

from the latent self spontaneously. In conjunction with the need to transform the self, Jung often speaks of the theme of redemption. The necessity for transformation and redemption is another correlation with esoteric religious tradition. In Gnosticism and in alchemy, as in many forms of mysticism, the individual cannot simply rely on salvation. Each must diligently work for his or her own salvation, or never attain it. Alchemy expresses this fact with the image of creating the philosopher's stone from the raw material with which the work commences. We can view the *prima materia* as the latent self from which the manifest self is created, or even as the psyche's chaotic state at the beginning of the work. Recall that one name for the *prima materia* is chaos.

Figure 1 (page 14) is one example of the way the alchemists imagined the confusion at the beginning of the work. Everything is in disorder, with no obvious connection between the disparate elements, which seem hardly formed or differentiated. Figure 2 (page 16) illustrates the order created when the alchemist has accomplished the great work. The difference between the first and the second image illustrates the effects of the transformation on the psyche!

Within each individual exists a center containing that individual's unique being. This center strives to express itself. The competing voices of the complexes and archetypes, and even that of the ego, often block its voice. By following certain processes, one empowers this center so that it eliminates competing voices and organizes the inner world around itself. The formation of the self is never fully complete, for there always remains material not yet integrated into (or harmonized by) the center. As the self becomes stronger, however, its voice and its organizing force gain dominance. At that point the ego may relax and trust, and begin in earnest the religious practice of living with the self.

Until that point is reached, though, the ego must engage in the most difficult work of transforming the inner psychic condition and empowering the self. Until then, the ego cannot relax and trust. Rather, it must work and struggle to learn to recognize the self, and to find ways of vesting it with the energy and power it requires. An essential part of Jung's psychology as a spiritual path involves using various techniques to transmute the self. It's time to examine some of these techniques.

THE TRANSCENDENT FUNCTION

In his paper on the transcendent function,[10] Jung presented a paradigm for the process by which the latent self transforms into the manifest self. This transformation is based upon the union of opposites. Indeed, one of the characteristics of the self is its ability to incorporate the duality of the opposites: good and bad, masculine and feminine, inner and outer, spiritual and material. There is no linear way of explaining the union of opposites; their union transcends reason. One image for this union is the mandala and its central point around which everything else is organized. The center point is the self. It is surrounded by all the opposites, which have found their appropriate positions in relation to the center and to each other. As Jung pointed out, however, the mandala as a whole represents the self as well, so that the self includes all the opposites. The self is not only the point at the center, but the circles and the other components that surround the center.

We experience the self as a union of opposites in a number of ways. If the manifest self is alive in the soul,

---

10. C. G. Jung, *The Structure and Dynamics of the Psyche*, Collected Works, vol. 8, R. F. C. Hull, trans., Bollingen Series XX (Princeton: Princeton University Press, 1969), ¶ 131–193. Future references will be cited as CW 8.

Figure 1. The state of chaos marks the initial state of the alchemical *prima materia* and symbolizes the chaos of the psyche before inner alchemy has begun. This is a dark, brooding state in which all contents are out of order and none are in relationship. The whole of inner alchemy consists in the transmutation from chaos to order, which is created around the center that is the self. Notice in this illustration that in the midst of the chaos there is seen a central point—an image of the latent self and a promise of future growth. (From Barent Coenders van Helpen, *Escalier des Sages,* 1689.)

14

we are able to meet every situation with the appropriate response. We are kind when kindness is appropriate, and severe when severity is required. We are not afraid of our own dark side, nor are we dominated by it, but express it in a suitable manner. We see the creative spirit in the material world, and enjoy material pleasures. In short, we are unafraid to express all sides of our personality and repress none. Our willingness to be all that we are, and to embrace all of our parts, allows us to experience ourselves as whole beings. We might think of the union of opposites proceeding in this manner as sequential; first one part of the personality expresses itself, then another.

Another experience of this union is not sequential but simultaneous. This is much more difficult to explain. Having united the opposites within itself, the self, being none of them, takes its position outside all of them. Though it still operates in the sequential manner described above, the state of consciousness associated with the self can no longer be defined in terms of the opposites. The ego, a part of the manifest self, does not experience itself in terms of masculinity or femininity, nor in terms of good and evil; its locus of identification stands outside all these attributes. Since such a state of being eludes verbal description, the most one can say is that it defies definition in normal categories. As an experience, however, it feels absolutely unique and complete unto itself. Such a self defines itself, and can only be understood as one of a kind. That it can be defined only in terms of itself does not mean it lacks relationship to others and to the outer world. Relationship is essential to life experience, and the outer world is part of the union of opposites that manifests the self. The self, though, is not defined either by relationship or the outer world, but by its own particular being and consciousness. There are distinct psychological processes that form the unique self, and the most important is the transcendent function.

Figure 2. In sharp contrast to the previous emblem, this mandala presents an ordered and harmonized universe. Directly connected to the philosopher's stone, the picture depicts a clearly demarcated center in which lives the deity, here related to Christ. Everything moves and is focused around this common center. Within the psyche, the manifest self has been created and order brought forth out of chaos. (From "Amphitheatrum Sapientiae," 1609.)

The transcendent function is the psychological mechanism that unites the opposites and helps bring the self to manifestation. As a whole, the psyche includes the conscious mind (with the ego at its center) and the unconscious. To effect a union of opposites, the contents of the unconscious must be joined with the ego so as to create a third position. Because the transcendent function "arises from the union of conscious and unconscious contents,"[11] it creates the third position. What, we may ask, is the role of the ego in this process of transformation?

Although the ego is most comfortable with consciousness, it must be willing to examine its own disposition and to entertain the possibility that it is not complete or infallible. The ego must be open to the notion that there are perspectives other than the conscious one. Most important, the ego has to acknowledge the existence of the unconscious, and that the position presented by the unconscious is worthy of consideration. This is no small requirement. Not only does popular opinion reject the possibility of the unconscious even existing, but the ego is normally terrified by the prospect of not being in control of its own psychic life. Even when the ego acknowledges the possibility of taking the unconscious into account, it often substitutes fantasy for a real encounter with the unconscious, for fantasy will simply help to maintain the ego position.

Frequently it is only within the context of analysis or therapy that the ego finds itself able to consider the position of the unconscious. In many ways the analyst carries the transcendent function for the client by paying careful attention to the messages of dreams and giving them due weight. The analyst tries to educate the client in terms of the value to be found within the unconscious. In this way,

---

11. C. G. Jung, CW 8, ¶ 131.

she encourages the client to begin paying attention to the voice within. At the same time, she must provide a feeling of safety and protection for the client as the dangerous work of engaging the unconscious commences. Outside help is often essential at the beginning of the work, and even with the best of intentions, many people will find this task impossible to accomplish on their own.

ACTIVE IMAGINATION

As the first step in engaging the transcendent function, the ego turns to the unconscious with an open and receptive attitude. Given this ego attitude, the next job is to find a way to give a voice to the unconscious entity, so that its position and information may be accessed. Earlier in this chapter I identified the spiritual aspect of the unconscious contents as the capacity to create and manipulate images.[12] Archetypes or complexes manifest as images, what Jung calls "personification."[13] Dreams provide examples of this process, but Jung warned that they are not useful in facilitating the transcendent function. During dreaming, the conscious ego is asleep and, therefore, cannot interact on an equal level with the unconscious. For the transcendent function to operate successfully, the two opposites must be differentiated and have sufficient tension between them. The ego needs to be fully awake, and aware, and capable of holding its position while interacting with the unconscious image. The image created by the unconscious and the ego interact, and in

---

12. Jung says the Holy Spirit "result[s] . . . from human reflection:" i.e., ". . . devising an image, and establishing an inner connection to and coming to terms with the outer object." (From "On the Psychology of the Concept of the Trinity," G. V. Hartman, trans., *Quadrant*, XXXVII: I, Winter, 1998.)
13. See C. G. Jung, *Analytical Psychology: Its Theory and Practice* (New York: Pantheon, 1968), pp. 80–81.

this interaction, they create the necessary tension to evoke the transcendent function. Such a scenario usually occurs in experiences that Jung called "active imagination."

During active imagination, the ego, while fully awake and functional, experiences unconscious contents or products, which may take the form of an image, a voice, a feeling, or even a physical sensation. The ego, having focused its attention on the unconscious, must give up all critical thinking and simply open to whatever the unconscious presents. In this state of receptivity, it must wait for the unconscious to manifest. Once it has seen, heard, or felt something, the ego then elaborates on the image it perceives, or on the voice it hears, and expresses it as fully as possible. For example, the ego may have a fleeting image of a waterfall. It may then paint that waterfall, or continue to imagine itself listening to the sound of the water falling, or actually take a drive to a real waterfall and sit by it for an afternoon. It must do whatever is necessary to empower the experience.

Having developed the experience sufficiently, the ego must next determine the meaning of it. This is of crucial importance, for without coming to some understanding of the meaning behind the manifestation of the unconscious, the ego will not be able to discover the position that the unconscious is taking. Simply enjoying the sound of the water, or admiring the painting one has done, is not enough. Despite current theories to the contrary, just being with the image is not sufficient; the ego must derive meaning from the experience.

The realization of meaning does not necessarily involve an intellectual operation. Continuing with our waterfall as an example, one possible way of working with the image is to explore how the symbol "waterfall" appears in mythology or fairy tales, or to read what Jung and others have written about it. There is also another, more experiential way of discovering meaning. Sitting by the inner or outer waterfall creates the feeling of timeless beauty and the sudden awareness that life is not just about business and accomplishment. Life is also about being and listening, sitting without doing. While this is an obvious truth to read, it is not an easy one to live. Sitting by the waterfall makes us suddenly aware of not paying attention to the other side of life. The "meaning" of the waterfall is slowing down, paying attention to the beauty around us, and listening to the sound of life that we almost always ignore. This meaning is not intellectual, but a feeling engendered by the experience itself. Combining the experiential meaning of the waterfall with the intellectual realization that waterfalls symbolize transformation of energy, we come to the realization that taking the time to slow down and listen to nature can be transformative. Uniting intellectual understanding with the felt experience is a powerful tool in the discovery of meaning.

The process is not yet complete. Although the ego has made room for the unconscious to manifest, and has devoted sufficient attention to the manifestation to discern its meaning, it now must respond to the message from the unconscious. It is essential that this response be genuine and that it accurately reflect the ego's understanding and feeling. For the transcendent function to work neither one of the oppositional pair can dominate or eliminate the other. At the beginning of the process, the ego has invariably repressed the voice of the unconscious. Having lifted this repression, the ego must be careful not to allow the unconscious, in turn, to silence its voice. If the ego simply surrendered its position to that of the unconscious, the transcendent function would never operate. The ego would be just as one-sided as it was previously, only now its one-sidedness would be in the opposite direction. Instead of busying itself with mundane affairs, it would give up everything to sit for hours and hours by the side of a waterfall, hoping to find enlightenment. Boredom and sterility would likely result; there is no magic answer in the messages of the unconscious, but only in the transcendent function.

When doing active imagination work, the ego faces other dangers. The power of the unconscious should not be underestimated. Unable to maintain its own position, the ego could be deluged with the unconscious material and experience a psychotic episode. Or if the ego drops its perspective and buys into the unconscious too completely, the one-sided results may cause inflation.

There is a need for the ego to know itself well, and to be able to sustain its self-image and perspective in the face of strong pressure from inner forces. The ego's task is not an easy one, for it must preserve its integrity while not being too rigid or dogmatic. Keeping its feet planted firmly on the ground, it must turn within and open the doors that unleash the wisdom, but also the danger, of the unconscious. This attitude of flexible strength is essential to withstand the tensions required for the transcendent function.

Having elaborated the image of the waterfall and experienced its meaning, the *I* must respond to the information it has received. Very often, "I" will have a negative response at first, which "I" must make so as not force myself into an unreal position. "I" may decide waterfalls are all well and good, but "I" certainly have better things to do than sit and listen to water splashing. If "I" give that response, "I" am then obligated to go back to the unconscious for its rejoinder. Having heard this new reply, "I" must respond in turn. And so it continues, with the argument moving back and forth between the two positions. The ego must not simply engage in an intellectual conversation with the unconscious, but must try to bring as much real affect to the discussion as it can. This movement back and forth constitutes the transcendent function:

> *The shuttling to and fro of arguments and affects represents the transcendent function of opposites. The confrontation of the two positions generates a tension charged with energy and creates a living, third thing—not a logical stillbirth . . . but a movement out of the suspension between opposites, a living birth that leads to a new level of being, a new situation. The transcendent function manifests itself as a quality of conjoined opposites.*[14]

The self is the union of opposites, as well as the center of the psyche. This center grows by organizing the archetypal forces around itself through the union of the ego and the unconscious. The transcendent function is the means by which these opposites become united, the process by which the manifest self is brought into being. Every time the ego contacts an image from the unconscious and engages it in meaningful dialogue, it can trigger the transcendent function. Every time it does so, no matter how small the issue involved may seem, it has strengthened and transformed the self. Out of the tension created by the opposing views of the ego and the unconscious, out of the shuttling between positions, a new, third and transcendent position is created.

Should the transcendent function create a third position, it may be experienced in two ways. The ego has much to do and knows its daily tasks are of great importance. On the other hand, the unconscious demands time to be and sit, to reflect and listen to the inner voice. Using the sequential

---

14. C. G. Jung, CW 8, ¶ 189.

model, the third position allows the ego to work for much of the week, but also to take time to be in nature or to meditate. There is a time for busy work, and a time for quiet reflection. Because of the union with the unconscious, the ego is able to determine which response is called for at a given moment. It senses when it has worked too hard, and, recognizing the value of down time, takes an hour to sit quietly. Feeling reconnected, it may return to work.

The second way the union is experienced is simultaneously. The ego is able to work when appropriate, and rest when appropriate, but the way in which it does both changes dramatically. While at work, it remains conscious of the still, small voice within, and is never so identified with its labors as to forget the inner world. The ego monitors the inner sense of the self even while at work. When the time comes to rest by the waterfall, however, it does not forget its work-life either. While it rests, insights about work may come, and the sense of competence and discipline it has in work translates to an impeccable way of being with the unconscious. It does not experience rest as an opportunity to become unconscious and forget its normal life, but as chance to pay attention to inner ideas while retaining its own clear sense of identity.

As the third position is created through the operation of the transcendent function, a new state of consciousness also comes into being. The ego's sense of itself has altered, and its consciousness rests in the newly emerged self, which has found a way to unite the experiences of relaxation and work. The great distance between these two opposites has been bridged, and the experience of the self now includes both.

It may seem that Jung suggested that one can only experience the transcendent function by entering into a conflict of some kind with the unconscious, but this is not the case. The shuttling back and forth of which he spoke can take other forms besides oppositional confrontation. There can be a joint elaboration of a topic, or the expression of fear and the reassuring response, or the request for further information. The possibilities are endless, but the nature of the interaction must be real enough to generate psychic tensions as the two positions are brought into contact.

The model of the psyche that Jung described emphasizes the ultimate importance and value of the self and reveals the means by which it can be transformed into a powerful and living center. One of those means is active imagination, the best method for directly engaging the transcendent function.

Active imagination is, of course, far more than a technique; it can become a way of life. Speaking of the deep stage in individuation in which the four functions of the psyche are balanced, Dr. von Franz wrote:

> *This is the plane on which active imagination takes control. With the inner nucleus of consciousness you stay in the middle place . . . you stay within your active imagination, so to speak, and you have the feeling that this where your life process goes on....* You keep your consciousness turned towards the events which happen on the middle plane, on the events which evolve within your active imagination.[15]

The more one individuates, the stronger the self becomes. As the self gains in strength, the ego has less difficulty focusing on it and concentrating its awareness on the middle position the self provides. The more the ego becomes con-

---

15. Marie-Louise von Franz, "The Inferior Function" in M.-L. von Franz and James Hillman, *Lectures on Jung's Typology* (Dallas: Spring Publications, 1984), p. 69. Italics are in the original. Used by permission.

scious of the self, the more it lives in the world of active imagination. Beginning as a technique, active imagination becomes a state of being. This new state of consciousness defines the role of the ego within the manifest self, but in the earlier stages of individuation, active imagination is a skill that must be studied and diligently practiced if one hopes to achieve any results.

Living in the world of active imagination does not imply that we are in an altered state of consciousness constantly, having visions day and night. It means that our attention is never far from the center, and we can access the self very easily at any moment. Moreover, the world is alive and vital, filled with magical possibilities and a numinous background that takes very little to activate. Individuals in such a state of being are present in the moment, and participate consciously in every situation. At the same time, however, the world of the unconscious is also present, and imaginal encounters close at hand.

Active imagination may take many forms. While some people may paint an image or sculpt it, others may dance the effect they are experiencing, or write it in music. In my opinion, however, the ideal form of active imagination is a dialogue or interchange between an inner figure and the ego. The inner figure actually personifies the content of the unconscious we are attempting to engage, and it does so in a form that can speak and actively exchange information with the ego. Carrying on a verbal dialogue with an inner figure takes some practice, but once achieved, it is a supreme way to exchange information and generate the tension necessary for the transcendent function. As I said, there are other ways to do active imagination. Not everyone is able to dialogue with the inner voices, but some effort almost always provides access to the verbal connection. If we combine the ability to see and feel an inner figure with the capacity to hear it, then we are in a position to do some very deep active imagination work. This is not easy to accomplish and must be practiced, much as we practice a musical instrument to achieve mastery. The more we practice, the better we become.

As mentioned, an inner figure is a personification of a particular content of the unconscious, so that dealing with that figure is also dealing with the content in question. Just as, for example, one does not dream of a father complex *per se*, but of a man in a three-piece suit who looks like one's boss, so in active imagination the inner content is not perceived directly, but in a personified image. At the same time, the inner figure is autonomous; that is, it is outside the control of the ego. The autonomy and reality of inner figures is a very difficult concept to grasp. Consequently, a principle resistance to active imagination work is the feeling that the ego has just "made it all up." Such is almost never the case, however, for the autonomy of the unconscious is usually strong enough to resist direct control on the part of the ego. The ego can misinterpret, it can identify, it can fantasize, but it has a great deal of trouble manipulating inner figures. If active imagination is done properly, the inner figure speaks with its own voice.

There is another interesting feature of the inner figure that Jung mentioned. Writing of powerful archetypal images, he noted that "instead of deriving these figures from our psychic conditions, we must derive our psychic conditions from these figures."[16] In this passage, I suspect Jung was referring to the way in which the archetypes can de-

---

16. C. G. Jung, *Alchemical Studies,* Collected Works, vol. 13, R. F. C. Hull, trans., Bollingen Series XX (Princeton: Princeton University Press, 1970), ¶ 299.

termine the psychic experiences of collective consciousness, but at the same time, this influence can be detected in the individual psyche. The inner figure autonomously appears from the unconscious, and may then shape or powerfully influence the psychic conditions of the individuals experiencing them. It is well known that dreams can influence the mood or outlook of an individual, even if the dream is not interpreted. Active imagination can also have a strong influence on one's mood and sense of well being. There are two important implications of this statement of Jung's that must be considered: the inner figure stands outside the current psychological state of the ego, and at the same time can influence that state directly.

To use a simple example, let us suppose an individual is in a father complex. He experiences fear and anxiety in dealing with authority figures in the world. If he is able to do active imagination, he may summon an inner figure who has helped him in the past. Since this inner figure is not contaminated by the ego's state of mind, it stands outside the complex and is not affected by it. Furthermore, if the inner figure is strong enough, it can, just by interacting with the ego, pull the ego out of the complex and alter its perception and sense of self. The ego is now in a position to face the outer-world challenge without being handicapped by the complex.

The inner figure that one contacts in active imagination is autonomous, able to express itself without being dominated by the ego. At the same time, it is able to exercise a powerful influence upon the ego and its own psychological state. According to Jung's definition, spirit refers to the autonomous power to create and manipulate images. Every active imagination, then, is a direct experience of the spiritual power of the psyche. There is certainly a negative side to this power, for an inner figure that embodies an archetype may actually affect the state of the ego in a destructive way. The ego must develop the means of protecting itself from such influence until the self becomes strong enough to harmonize these archetypal emanations.

PSYCHE AND PSYCHOID

One might well ask how Jung came to formulate his theories about the self and active imagination. He, himself, tells us that he came to them by observing the dreams and active imagination experiences of his clients. It is also clear from reading *Memories, Dreams, Reflections*, that his own experiences of active imagination determined a great many of his theories. He attributes the origin of many of his ideas to his inner guide, Philemon. As he stated, "All my works, all my creative activity, has come from those initial fantasies and dreams."[17] He tested these ideas in his observation of others, and in his consideration of earlier traditions. In his combination of inner experience with external study, he provides a profound method for the study of the inner world.

I have tried to follow Jung's model in my own work. I paid close attention to my own inner experiences, and to those of friends and clients, in order to strengthen my understanding of visionary work and encounters. At the same time, I have studied many other visionary traditions to enrich my perceptions with the ideas of others who devoted themselves to inner work. Through my experience, as well as that of many other individuals, I have come to postulate the existence of what I call the psychoid world.

One can experience inner figures in many ways. Active imagination connects individuals with inner figures which,

---

17. C. G. Jung, *Memories, Dreams, Reflections* (New York: Vintage Books, 1963), p. 192.

while very powerful, are clearly imaginal and derived from the psyche. These figures feel as if they were coming from within oneself. Typically one experiences them with eyes closed, and attention directed inward. These are the psychic figures that personify the forces of the unconscious. However, every so often, one may experience a figure that *feels* completely different. This figure feels as if it were coming from outside oneself, as if it existed in the external world, in the room in which one finds oneself, for example. One's eyes are open, and the felt sense is that one perceives a figure that does *not* come from within. The attention of the ego is focused outward, not inward. These are the experiences I refer to using the term "psychoid."

There are other attributes of psychoidal experiences as well. They are more likely to be coupled with synchronistic experience, and their effects are often physical as well as psychological. The quality of the experience is less "imaginal" and more "real," though the reality in which one is engaging is not that of the ordinary world.

Here is one, personal example of such experiences. I was at home sleeping when I awoke in the middle of the night. My wife was sleeping next to me, and nothing seemed out of the ordinary. Suddenly I found myself on top of a mountain, almost at the very peak. The slope was very steep, and my fear of heights made me drop to the ground and grab hold for fear I might fall at any moment. At the same time, I was fully aware of being at home in bed. I was cognizant of both realities simultaneously, and at the time it did not feel particularly strange. I was not asleep, but fully awake, and the mountain scene was completely real. I could feel the cold and smell the ground. My fear was sharp and clear. As I lay there, a hooded figure appeared directly above me and said, "Do you not trust me even here?" Encouraged by his words, I stood up and looked him in the face.

Or rather I looked him in the eyes, for within the hood there was a skeleton with bright, shining red eyes. Rather than being afraid, I was filled with a deep sense of love and of being loved. He reached out his hand and touched me on the chest, and I found myself off the mountain and in bed, but in a state of deep ecstasy that lasted five or six hours. Typical of psychoidal encounters were the reality of the mountain scene, the complete aliveness of the hooded figure, the profound impact of his touch, and the state of ecstasy.

Due to this type of experience, I began to struggle with the idea that there must be different layers of visionary occurrences. I felt that to label them all psychic experience or experiences of the unconscious lacked sufficient differentiation. Eight hundred years before Jung wrote on active imagination, the great Sufi mystic Ibn 'Arabi taught the nature of imaginal states and mentioned the encounter with inner figures. In his work, *Fusus al-Hikam*, or *The Seals of Wisdom*,[18] he wrote about different levels of imaginal experiences. He differentiates between the imaginal faculty of the ordinary human being, and that of the gnostic, arguing that the imagination of the gnostic produces real experiences and beings that exist independently of the imaginative faculty. The imagination of the ordinary person, on the other hand, creates images that have reality only within that person's imagination. In other words, in ordinary active imagination, the experience is one of the psyche

---

18. I have consulted two translations of this work: Ibn 'Arabi, Muhyi-D-Din, *The Wisdom of the Prophets*, translated from Arabic to French with notes by Titus Burckhardt, and translated from French to English by Angela Culme-Seymour (Gloustershire: Beshara Publications, 1975); and *The Seals of Wisdom* (New York: Concord Grove Press, 1983).

only, but in the psychoidal experience, the image and the encounter with it take on a reality that transcends the psyche. Moreover, Ibn 'Arabi differentiated between the experience of God as self and that of God as other. The latter experience he described as occurring in prayer, but only when the individual is able to actually hear and see God.

There may, therefore, be two types of inner figures. The first type originates in the inner, unconscious world and personifies archetypes and complexes. These figures may also embody the self with its power and wisdom. The other type derives from the psychoid world, from an imaginal world that is real unto itself, and that transcends the psychic world of human beings. Figures of the second type may incarnate from this other reality in the psyche of the human being.

Elaborating on these figures, Ibn 'Arabi wrote that the "form is related to the spiritual being just as a light that shines from a lamp into the corners of a room is related to the lamp . . . the form is not other than the spiritual being itself; on the contrary, it is identical with it, even if it is found in a thousand places, or in all places and is diverse in shape."[19] In other words, the form that a psychoidal being assumes in the psyche, the inner figure in which it manifests, is identical with the psychoidal entity. There is no difference between the spiritual being, itself, and the imaginal form in which one experiences it. Active imagination with such a figure therefore relates one to the world beyond the psyche, to the spiritual domain and reality in which the divine resides. Though it may never be possible to experience that reality in and of itself, one can experience it through the form that it assumes. Since that form is no different than

---

19. Quoted in William Chittick, *Imaginal Worlds: Ibn al-'Arabi and the Problem of Religious Diversity* (Albany: State University of New York Press, 1994), p. 94.

31

the thing itself, the imaginal encounter with the form is the encounter with the divine entity from which it originates.

I introduce the topic of the psychoid at this point to illustrate the importance of the potential that active imagination carries, not only for the formation of the self, but for the experience of realities beyond our normal scope. Moreover, understanding the psychoidal nature of some experiences of active imagination will shed light on certain alchemical symbols, and on the way in which the alchemists viewed imagination and its impact on their work. As Dr. Jung wrote, "experience itself is the important thing, not its intellectual representation or clarification, which proves meaningful and helpful only when the road to original experience is blocked."[20] My formulation is in accord with the nature of psychoidal experience, and is designed to facilitate passage to these realms for those whose road may otherwise be blocked. It is also designed to shed light on the alchemical opus, which may, with great profit, be understood as it relates to the creation of the self and to the incarnation of psychoidal forces.

THE PRACTICE OF ACTIVE IMAGINATION

Active imagination is the primary method through which the transcendent function may be brought into play, and it may open windows to other imaginal worlds as well. But of what does active imagination consist? How is it experienced? For convenience sake, I divide the process of active imagination into seven main stages. While somewhat arbitrary, these seven stages reflect the nature of a complete active imagination experience. The first stage consists of

---

20. C. G. Jung, CW 14, ¶ 777.

preparing the mind to enter the imaginal space. The conscious mind must be quieted and centered, so that the ego has the opportunity to receive the message from the unconscious. Normal discursive thought must cease, and the ego must enter into a state of expectant quiet. This state of mind can be achieved by physical movement, such as yoga, or by meditation exercises, such as counting the breath or focusing on a single point. The actual method is not important, but should be one that is comfortable to the person doing the active. The only requirement is that one quiets one's mind and enters a state of inner repose.

Once this state has been achieved, the ego invites the unconscious to communicate with it. I have discovered over the years that the best way to do this is for the ego to have a particular image in mind, or at least a particular question it wishes to address. Simply opening to the unconscious often produces a plethora of confusing and conflicting images. If, however, the ego has in mind a particular inner figure that it wishes to contact, or returns to a particular dream scene or encounter, this intentionality serves to focus the unconscious in a definite way. One may safely ignore any images that arise that do not feel related to the one in question. I call this stage of the work the period of *evocation* or *intention*. Having quieted down, the ego holds its intent firmly in mind and waits. If an individual is able to visualize inner figures with ease, at this stage of the process one may simply visualize the figure one wishes to contact. Hold that figure in the mind's eye until it moves or acts of its own accord. For those who do not visualize readily, it is only necessary to keep the intent in mind until something begins to occur.

There are only a few rules that apply to this stage of the work. Inner figures should, whenever possible, not be real people, living or dead. The personified form should emerge from the unconscious, and should be unique to the person doing the active imagination. Doing actives with the images of real people is unfair to those individuals, for they might be effected in unknown ways. Psychic attacks and invasions may occur through the imaginal realm, and one way to launch such an attack is to do active imagination. Though this is rarely meant, it may occur in any case. Hence it is better not to use a real person in the imaginal encounter, lest an inadvertent attack occur. It is best not to use the image of a dead person as well, for such use may create a dependency on the deceased. (I have seen cases where individuals who have lost loved ones have done actives with them in order to hang on to them—just when they should be mourning and letting them go.) The only occasion when active imagination with a dead individual is called for is when unresolved issues exist between the individual doing the active and the deceased. Unresolved hurt and rage at a dead parent, for example, may block psychic growth until it is dealt with and allowed to subside. Active imagination work is a good way to resolve past injuries and pain.

The third phase begins when the unconscious comes alive in some way. This is the phase of *unconscious activation* and it takes many forms. One may experience an affect, a bodily sensation, a voice, or a strange thought. In the model I am using, an inner figure would make its appearance at this point. In whatever way the unconscious appears, the ego must now respond to it. The response begins the phase of active imagination I call *interaction,* and refers to the shuttling back and forth that Jung described. Using the example of the inner figure in the phase of activation, the inner figure appears and may speak, say hello, or offer some kind of greeting. It may ask what the ego wants, or how it is doing. The ego must reply. In turn, it may ask how the inner figure is doing, and then spell out the reason it wishes to speak with it. In the interactive phase, there is a dialogue between the inner figure and the ego that should be allowed to follow whatever direction it spontaneously takes.

The interactive phase of active imagination may go on for a long time, sometimes weeks or even months. This should be coupled with a stage of the work that actually occurs outside of the active. This phase I call *reflection*. Reflection refers to the necessity on the part of the ego to think carefully about the experiences that it has had. As I discussed earlier, the ego must not give up its position, but should hold to it while it considers all that the inner figure has shown it. During this reflection, the intellect has an important role to play, for the ego must seriously think about all that it has experienced. At the same time it needs to feel deeply into the experience to evaluate it from the feeling perspective. Did what the inner figure say feel good? Did it make rational sense? By allowing a period of reflection, the ego protects itself from naively falling into an unconscious position, or simply accepting at face value what an inner figure is telling it. During this stage, the ego might choose to share its experience with an analyst, a therapist, or just a good friend, in order to get some objective feedback. When the ego has reached some conclusions, it may return to the active imagination and re-engage with the inner figure.

Interaction and reflection may continue for some time but, sooner or later, the active imagination enters into a phase I call *resolution*, when the original intent or question with which the active began is resolved in some way. For example, I may desire to understand how to cultivate my own feminine nature. I ask an inner figure of a wise woman to appear and teach me about this part of the self. She appears and begins teaching me about feelings and relationships. I resist, struggle, have questions, and we deal with each of these as they appear. I begin to understand intellectually what the feminine looks like, but I still don't "get it." Then one day, during the active, I feel in my body and in my being what relationship really means, and I have an insight that is so real it becomes part of my awareness from then on. The resolution has occurred, and the transcendent function has clicked in, forever altering my consciousness and creating a new state of the manifest self. During the interactive phase, I am likely to experience different degrees of tension and discomfort, as I unite my own position with that of the inner figure. The tension that is sometimes experienced in interacting with an inner figure can be very distressing, even physical, in its manifestation. Some people find it difficult to continue the actives when the tension reaches a level of great intensity. Yet it is important to keep going with the active, despite the discomfort, for if the tension is resolved inappropriately, the transcendent function will not occur. When the resolution occurs naturally, however, that tension is resolved in the insight that presents itself.

Finally comes *integration*, the last stage of active imagination. At the point at which the ego gains an insight, it must make a total effort to integrate that insight into its outer life. If I have gained deep understanding into the nature of relationships, for example, then I must work to bring that perceptiveness into all my relationships with the people that I know and love. If I am unable or unwilling to practice my new wisdom in the outer world, then the active has failed. Only when I am capable of living in my everyday life that which I have learned from the inner world, is an active imagination complete. The fear that some entertain that work with active imagination or the self isolates one from life and from relationships is unfounded. The inner and the outer worlds must feed each other and interconnect through the efforts of the ego, which stands with one foot in each world. The ego can turn within to experience the profound wisdom of the inner figures, and then move outside, to put that wisdom into practice. In this capacity to bridge the two worlds, the ego discovers the self and experiences the infinite diversity of its own wholeness.

Jung defined the spiritual as the autonomous creation and manipulation of images. Spiritual beings are endowed with this capacity. If they originate within the psyche, they are archetypal figures and entities, and if from beyond the psyche, they are psychoidal entities. Since active imagination is the process by which such inner figures are engaged and allowed to express themselves through the spontaneous unfolding of images, active imagination is the spiritual process par excellence. Through active imagination, the transcendent function is brought into play, and through the transcendent function, the self is transformed from its potential, latent condition, into an active living and manifested form. It is my contention, as it was Jung's, that these three aspects of inner development form the basis of alchemy. Alchemy is concerned with the self and with its creation, and its symbols depict the experience of active imagination and the transcendent function.

Initially, Jung did not realize the value of alchemy for understanding the individuation process. Actually, it took him some time to discover the power of the alchemical images and their relevance for his way of understanding self-development. Having purchased an old alchemical tract, he would occasionally glance at it, only to be turned off by its apparent meaninglessness:

> I let this book lie untouched for nearly two years. Occasionally I would look at the pictures, and each time I would think, "Good Lord, what nonsense! This stuff is impossible to understand." But it persistently intrigued me, and I made

up my mind to go into it more thoroughly. . . . I . . . soon found it provocative and exciting. . . . Finally I realized that the alchemists were talking in symbols.[21]

Jung's realization that the alchemists were communicating in symbols, and that these symbols could be interpreted, opened the door to his deciphering the secrets of the alchemical imagination. We are now in a position to begin our examination of that imaginative world and our quest to discover what it can teach us in our search to know and empower the self.

21. C. G. Jung, *Memories, Dreams, Reflections,* p. 204.

CHAPTER 2

The
ALCHEMICAL
IMAGINATION

The principle development in understanding the inner world in the last century has been the rediscovery of the imagination. No one contributed more toward this evolution than C. G. Jung. His emphasis on active imagination opened new areas of study, including the identification of inner figures and the exploration of the world of the imaginal. Imagination has a long and impressive history, playing a central role in ideas about spiritual growth, especially in the esoteric lineage, such as the magical and alchemical traditions. This is not to suggest that every alchemist accepted the concept of imagination. However, there is a very significant theory of the imaginal to be found in the writings of several alchemists. Their view of the imaginative realm has much to teach us about the theory and practice of active imagination and its role in the individuation process. The study of imagination is still in its infancy, and there are a number traditional writings that need to be examined. The amount of material dealing with the imagination in alchemical writings is impressive, and impossible to cover in this book.

In order to understand the traditional view of imagination, it is important to dispense with modern biases. Today fantasy and imagination are rarely differentiated; both are seen as unreal, and to call anything imaginary is essentially to dismiss it as invalid. A number of writers, such as Corbin, Hillman, and others, have tried in recent years to rehabilitate the notion of imagination, but little seems to have been accomplished in altering the collective perception of imagination. In a recent discussion about the nature of the imaginal, I suggested that the philosopher's stone might be understood as a product of the imagination. Participants in the discussion were outraged that I would say that the stone was *only* imaginary. To them, of course, I was saying that the stone was unreal. They had no idea that something could be of the imagination and real at the same time.

To the alchemist, the magician, the Sufi mystic, and to Jung, the imagination was anything but unreal. Imaginary events were seen as occurring in a world that, though different from the ordinary world, was just as valid and real. Imagination was seen as having a real effect on the psyche, and even on physical reality, as well as helping create direct experiences of the divine. Alchemists believed that imagination was quite real, that it was an indispensable part of the alchemical undertaking. And Jung thought that imagination was so important in the alchemical worldview he wrote that the "concept of *imaginatio* is perhaps the most important key to the understanding of the *opus.*"[1] What better place, then, to start our study of alchemy than with the imagination?

FANTASY AND IMAGINATION

Like the contemporary student of the inner world, alchemists were concerned about differentiating imagination from fantasy. They were aware that true imagination possesses a power and depth that fantasy does not possess. Jacob

---

1. C. G. Jung, *Psychology and Alchemy,* Collected Works, vol. 12, R. F. C. Hull, trans., Bollingen Series XX (Princeton: Princeton University Press, 1977), ¶ 396. Future references to this title will be cited as CW 12.

Boehme was one of those who warned against the delusions of fantasy. Although not a practicing alchemist, Boehme was a mystic who used the terminology and symbols of alchemy to express his baffling mystical visions. Born in 1575, Boehme was a Lutheran who lived through the terrible period of religious warfare that decimated Germany. Partly because the violence and hatred he witnessed disillusioned him, Boehme emphasized the struggle for redemption, and the need to experience higher inner truths. Imagination was a key concept in his mystical system; not only was it useful in the quest for the redemption of the soul, it was also the means by which God created the world. Divine Wisdom, or Sophia, the creative power of God, played a large role in his system, and She was for him a "Divine Imagination."[2] His theory of imagination was part of a very complicated system of mystical theology, and I shall not discuss it at great length, but he clearly differentiated between good and bad imagination. Bad imagination was "phantasia" which was responsible for the fall of Lucifer, and in the human being it created illusions and false desires that led one away from God. By turning toward fantasy rather than the true imagination, the soul became lost in illusion and far removed from the presence of God.[3] True imagination, on the other hand, is the embodiment of divine wisdom in the soul, and could lead to redemption and union with God.

Theophrastus Bombastus von Hohenheim, better known as Paracelsus, lived about eighty years before Jacob Boehme. He was perhaps one of the most influential of the

---

2. Jacob Boehme, *The "Key" of Jacob Boehme*, William Law, trans. (Grand Rapids: Phanes Press, 1991), p. 23.
3. For an excellent discussion of Boehme's theory of the imagination, see Hugh Urban, "Imago Magia, Virgin Mother of Eternity: Imagination and Phantasy in the Philosophy of Jacob Boehme," *Alexandria Journal*, vol. 2, 1993.

alchemists, and established the view that salt had an equivalent value with sulfur and mercury. He was, above all else, a physician, and viewed alchemy as a powerful tool in the combat against disease. He was not very interested in the creation of the stone, or in the transmutation of metals, but far more concerned with the production of elixirs and balsams that were useful in the treatment of illnesses. He was an irascible, arrogant, and inflated man who made enemies far more easily than he made friends, but his work is of great interest and value, including his treatment of imagination, which was very influential. Like Boehme, whom he influenced, he believed in the power of the imagination, but also in the dangers of fantasy:

> *Moreover, there are physicians without imagination, without faith, who are called phantastics. Phantasy is not imagination, but the frontier of folly. These work for any result, but they do not study in that school which they ought. He who is born in imagination finds out the latent forces of Nature, which the body with its mere phantasy cannot find; for imagination and phantasy differ the one from the other. Imagination exists in the perfect spirit, while phantasy exists in the body without the perfect spirit. He who imagines compels herbs to put forth their hidden nature.*[4]

Boehme and Paracelsus clearly differentiated between fantasy and imagination. Both ascribed imagination to the spirit, and saw in it a spiritual function, while fantasy belonged to the physical world, and was divorced from deeper truths. Fantasy created illusion and folly, while imagination created liberation and healing power.

---

4. Paracelsus, "Hermetic Astronomy" in A. E. Waite, ed., *The Hermetic and Alchemical Writings of "Paracelsus" the Great*, vol. 2. (Reprint: Kila, MT: Kessinger, n.d.), p. 307.

Paracelsus distinguished between fantasy and imagination by not only attributing the later to the spirit, but also by correlating it with the forces of Nature, which fantasy could not discover. The union of the imagination with nature was not unique to Paracelsus; another alchemist attributed the workings of the natural world to the "will of God and the imagination of Nature."[5] The alchemists believed that their work must follow the ways of nature in order to succeed, and they saw in nature a great teacher, but also a repository of latent powers and influences. Imagination, according to Paracelsus, was the major way one could discover the secrets of nature and unleash her latent powers. While fantasy perceived in nature only the obvious physical reality, imagination could reach below the surface to see nature's many secrets. Imagination discovered that the physical world could not be understood without the inclusion of the spirit.

Anyone who endeavors to experience the inner world through active imagination will, sooner or later, deal with the thorny issue of fantasy and delusion, especially if one teaches or works with individuals in therapy or analysis. While imagination opens the door to profound experiences of the self, and makes the formation of the self possible, fantasy leads to inflation, illusion, and stagnation. It is not always easy to tell the difference in oneself or in others, but insights from Paracelsus and Boehme offer some guidelines in this regard.

Boehme believed that the imagination was "Sophia," who is the wisdom of God and, as a feminine power, played a great role in alchemy. Dr. von Franz discussed the nature of Sophia in her analysis of *Aurora Consurgens*, an alchemical text from the early 13th century. In her study, she

---

5. Michael Sendivogius, "The New Chemical Light," in A. E. Waite, ed. *The Hermetic Museum,* vol. 2 (York Beach, ME: Samuel Weiser, reprint, 1973), p. 87.

concluded that Sophia symbolized a transpersonal power that gave "the prime impulse toward all being and all knowing in their endlessly diverse forms."[6] At the same time, Sophia was an "ordering principle" that guided and directed the steps of the alchemists. Figure 3 (page 46) is a reproduction of the wonderful emblem from Michael Maier depicting the feminine guide, either Nature or Wisdom, showing the way for the alchemist who struggles to follow Her. This emblem captures the idea that the alchemist must do his best to follow Nature's way, or follow the guidance of Wisdom. In either case, it is the imagination that allows the alchemist to discover the hidden path.

Sophia is a transpersonal force that creates endlessly, and at the same time illuminates the way to the ultimate goal. M.-L. von Franz interpreted this symbol psychologically to mean that "there exists in nature and in the collective unconscious, at least potentially, a kind of objective consciousness or mind from which the individual ego-consciousness is derived only secondarily and through which it is expanded by 'illumination.'"[7] Sophia referred to an inner Mind, a wisdom that belonged not to the ego but to the unconscious, though it could illuminate the ego from time to time. According to Boehme's formulation, the inner mind—the core of inner wisdom—is the imagination. Imagination is the spiritual function, and belongs to any spiritual agency. The archetypes have the power to manifest through images, and this is why von Franz attributes wisdom to the collective unconscious. However, though this inner knowing can be attributed to the collective unconscious, it finds its purest expression in the self. In fact, von Franz finally concluded that Wisdom is the

---

6. Marie-Louise von Franz, *Aurora Consurgens* (New York: Bollingen Foundation, 1966), p. 165.

7. Marie-Louise von Franz, *Aurora Consurgens*, p. 171.

feminine form of God. In the ecstatic final visions of *Aurora Consurgens* there is a union between Wisdom and her lover that results in a profound manifestation of God.[8] This epiphany symbolizes the emergence of the manifest self that occurs through the guidance of Sophia.

Wisdom is the imaginative power of the self, which guides the ego toward the creation of the manifest self. True imagination transcends the ego, and creates the experiences by which it can encounter the inner world. Moreover, the imaginative process serves as a pathfinder to the person struggling to find his or her way toward transformation and the encounter with the self. From a more mystical perspective, imagination is the means by which the soul experiences God and shares in the creative expression of the Divine.

Fantasy, on the other hand, never transcends the ego. While imagination contains information about the other parts of the psyche and discloses the path to be followed, fantasy is about the ego's needs, desires, and quest for aggrandizement. Caught in the mood to fantasize, I might indulge in contemplating my great success as a writer, and how the world will now seek me out, and so forth. Another person might engage in sexual fantasies that play out the ego's forbidden wishes, while still another will fantasize about a rise to political fame and fortune. In almost every case, fantasy, though it may reflect the input of both complex and archetype, centers on the ego, and not on anything transcendent. There is in fantasy no real experience of inner wisdom; it is only the playing out of one image after another that titillates, amuses, or even terrifies. Even in the case of negative fantasy, however, the ego is the star of the piece.

Suppose that an individual's self is expressing a need to play music. In an active imagination, the ego encounters the

---

8. Marie-Louise von Franz, *Aurora Consurgens*, p. 403.

Figure 3. Inner wisdom, the imaginative power of the self, leaves behind its footprints, or the symbols that it creates, which the inner alchemist follows on his or her path. Wearing the spectacles of insight, guided by the lamp of consciousness, supported by the staff of inner authority, the alchemist endeavors to follow Sophia's lead. Notice the plants and fruits symbolizing the endless creativity of Sophia. (From Michael Maier's *Atalanta Fugiens,* 1618.)

inner figure of a musician who urges him to develop the musical side of his personality. He resists because it would be too much work, and he does not have enough time; besides, he would never be any good. The inner figure counters that mastery is not required, only the effort to play. Finally the person realizes that playing music is about heartfelt expression and fun, and not about being skillful. He tentatively begins to take piano lessons, and spends a little time every day with it. This is an example of imagination, for the inner figure emerges with a distinct message from the inner world, and the ego encounters that messenger with integrity.

In a fantasy, the need to make music would lead to the ego's picturing itself playing in Carnegie Hall, or writing the great American concerto. The message from the unconscious would not be about the inner world or the manifestation of the self any longer, but about the ego's need to inflate. The illusion thus created might lead to piano lessons, but when the person realized he was not a great talent, he would soon abandon the effort.[9]

Of course, everyone engages in fantasy. There is nothing wrong in that, for fantasy can be useful. It is sometimes very helpful, for example, in understanding what the ego wants to inflate itself about. The fantasies that it spins will

---

9. Imagination teaches about the nature and needs of the self, of the world, and of the unconscious. In the imaginative experience, the ego encounters "the Other," and must find its correct position in relation to the Other. Such experiences are often disconcerting to the ego, which likes to think of itself as master of the whole psychic world. The ego finds itself in a position of being only a partner, and not even the managing partner at that. Imagination is a challenge that requires the ego to transcend its previous ideas and step into the unknown. Fantasy is endlessly repetitive and produces nothing new or creative. Boehme's belief that fantasy caused the fall of Lucifer, and the estrangement of the soul from God, makes sense on the psychological level, for fantasy, by inflating the ego, separates it from the self, and makes true imaginative work very difficult.

often reveal the places in which developmental work needs to occur. However, confusing fantasy with imagination, and confounding active imagination with ego manipulation is damaging and at times dangerous. An inability to differentiate fantasy from active imagination precludes a real relationship with the self, and perpetuates the ego's illusions that it alone is of value.

For Paracelsus, imagination belonged to the spirit, while fantasy belonged to the body. Imagination discovered the latent forces in nature, and compelled herbs to yield their power. It is no surprise that imagination was paired with the spirit, for the spirit has been defined as the capacity to create images. Imagination was able to uncover the powers of nature, because Paracelsus believed, as Boehme did, that imagination could be equated with wisdom. The wisdom of the imagination teaches the mysteries of both the soul and the outer world. By using the imaginative capacity, the alchemist could see behind the outer, physical form of the herb or metal, and detect its symbolic meaning. By so doing he came to understand its true uses and essential nature. This was an idea that was widely held in the Renaissance; each object had a hidden meaning beyond its physical appearance. If one could understand the secret essence, he or she would be able to use the substance in magical, alchemical, or healing ways. In his essay, "Concerning the Signature of Natural Things," Paracelsus wrote that the outward appearance of a person indicated his or her real nature, as, for example, "large eyes denote a greedy, voracious man, especially if they project far out of the head."[10]

---

10. Paracelsus, "Concerning the Signature of Natural Things" in A. E. Waite, ed., *The Hermetic and Alchemical Writings of Paracelsus the Great*, vol. 1 (Kila, MT: Kessinger, n.d.), p. 177. Originally published in two volumes by James Elliott, London, 1894.

To be sure, much of what Paracelsus wrote strikes us today as absurd and superstitious. But to dismiss such ideas in this way is to miss the point. The real meaning of what was called the "signature of things" is that everything in the world might be understood at both the physical and imaginative level. Paracelsus saw in nature a mystery containing a hidden world of symbols and signs. The true alchemist must be able to see underneath the surface. In this regard, fantasy involves intellectual thinking, the mind locked into appearances, that can never penetrate the hidden meaning behind the surface. Imagination, on the other hand, is the light of nature that reveals all her secrets and allows the physician to determine the correct substance to heal a particular disease. It is humbling to think that Paracelsus would most likely label all our sciences and much of our medicine as fantasy!

The theory of the imagination that Paracelsus and others were developing was a precursor to Jung's view that life is meaningful. Jung found meaning in the direct expressions of the unconscious, such as dreams and active imagination, but knew that there was significance in outer world events as well, such as in synchronicities. The alchemists also argued that there was meaning in all of outer life. Hidden within the physical appearance of things was an imaginative part that could be seen and used. While Paracelsus saw fantasy as a belief in the physical *appearance* of things, our modern culture seems to really believe in physical appearance. If one is concerned with cancer and its treatment, for example, one seeks only to find the cancer gene, or the new cancer medication, or the diet that will protect one from it, but one never wonders what the meaning of cancer in a particular person at a particular time might be. It's true that new agers and those interested in alternative therapies are interested in understanding the reason why one is ill, but usually only to find out what one did wrong to become sick in the first place. We are still missing getting to the core.

One can say that any outer "worldly" situation can provide clues about something that is meaningful. Many outer
situations point to an inner image that can be experienced
directly through active imagination. By seeking the meaning of life events, the ego escapes from the illusory world
of fantasy that only sees concrete reality and appearances.
A conflict with a boss, a car accident, a headache, a sick
pet—all of these events—may be perceived with the eyes
of the imagination. Such a perspective frees one from the
sense of being trapped in the situation, and permits one
to seek the meaning related to it. Working with meaning
opens up possibilities that were hidden before. One views
an external state of affairs as if it were a dream. Dreams
can be interpreted and understood; one does not simply
need to identify with them.

For example, I worked with a client who felt oppressed
by the machinations of her sister-in-law. No matter what
the client did, the sister-in-law misconstrued her intentions
and motivations, and presented her to the rest of the family
in the worst possible light. The client felt like a victim, and
was unable to think of any way out the dilemma. We shifted
our focus from the outer world situation to the symbols
contained in that predicament. The sister-in-law was rec-
ognizable as the archetype of the wicked stepsister, always
jealous of the heroine and causing her great trouble. Seeing the sister-in-law as the archetype led to my client's doing
an active imagination with the figure of the wicked stepsister. After a great deal of argument with this figure, my
client was able to recognize that she had been caught in a
particular pattern most of her life. She was always misunderstood and misinterpreted, even as a child. The wicked
stepsister revealed to her ways in which she invited this
process, and finally showed her ways to escape from it. The
real life sister-in-law never changed her attitude, but my

client came to see her as the embodiment of a pattern. She felt that she was then able to free herself from the pattern, no matter what the real sister-in-law did or said. Though she could not change the outer person, she was able to shift her own ways of responding, and liberated herself from the archetype that had so long dominated her life. By seeing through the eyes of the imagination, she came to recognize the hidden patterns that were controlling her life, and was able to free herself from them. In this way, we use outer life situations as imaginative expressions of hidden forces and powers, and discover the right remedy through further imaginative work.

Not only does imagination open up the hidden dimensions of the outer world; it triggers the power of herbs, to use Paracelsus's formulation. One could say that perceiving the hidden meaning of a content or outer situation activates a type of power contained in that situation. Paracelsus referred to the healing efficacy of herbs, so that understanding the true significance of an herb allowed the physician to use it to its best effect. It is very possible that seeing an outer situation with the imaginative vision elicits a transformative and healing process that directly effects the situation. Imagination not only creates insights, but transformation as well. My client's perception that the sister-in-law symbolized an archetypal pattern helped free her from this pattern, as well as from the manipulation of the outer person. Liberation from the pattern opened up new ways of expressing herself, ways that were much more in line with her inner nature. Seeing through the illusion created by fantasy triggers processes of self-expression and transformation, and allows the imaginative power to unlock new ways of being.

To summarize, fantasy deals with the ego's needs and desires, while imagination transcends the ego to provide insight into the nature of the self. Imagination is the wisdom of the self, wherein the self guides and encourages the processes of its own manifestation. The ego that follows the insights afforded by imaginative experiences is in harmony with the self and on the way to its own redemption. The ego that participates in fantasy is divorced from the self and lost in an illusory world. Fantasy creates the belief that the physical world is the only world, and this delusion precludes the ability to see into the heart and meaning of a situation in order to gain wisdom about it, and to create changes within it.

The individual undertaking active imagination, or trying to guide others in this attempt, should be able to distinguish between fantasy and a true imaginative experience. It is necessary to ask if the experience transcends ego needs, and points to something beyond. The experience should provide new information, and open the door to the meaning of whatever situation one is examining. A good active imagination leads to the unexpected and creates insight and a fresh perspective. Fantasy, on the contrary, is repetitive and concerned with the ego. It feels sterile, if enticing, and provides no new information or insight. Keeping these ideas in mind will allow an individual to embark on the dangerous, but exciting, adventure of experiencing the diverse worlds of the imagination.

ALCHEMY AND IMAGINATION

The alchemist viewed imagination as a key to revelation that was often considered an indispensable means for successfully performing alchemical work. The alchemist was unable to discover the *prima materia* without either working with a teacher, or having direct communication from the spirit world. Calid spoke for all alchemists when he wrote that "our mastery and honourable office of the secret Stone, is a secret of the secrets of God, which hee hath concealed from his people, neither would he reveale it to any, save

to those, who like sonnes have faythfully deserved it. . . ."[11]
The mystery of the stone is one of God's greatest secrets,
and only God can reveal it, and then only to those who
have shown themselves worthy. It should not be overlooked
that alchemy was a type of mystery religion, based on tradition and direct revelation. It placed a great responsibility on the individual alchemist to show that he warranted
the knowledge that he sought, for this knowledge was the
key to the secrets of immortality and divine wisdom. Revelation was necessary, and revelation was directly linked with
imagination.

There were a number of ways in which the alchemists
tried to merit divine inspiration, including living a moral life,
devoting themselves to the good of others, and refusing to
be tempted by the gold they were ostensibly trying to create. They never sought material wealth for its own sake, but
only for the good it could do. But as in all gnostic systems,
living morally and ethically were not enough to guarantee the
reception of wisdom. The alchemists had to work for their
revelation, and such work included prayer, meditation, and
contemplation. All of these forms of inner activity directly
relate to the practice of active imagination.

One alchemist declared that everyone who became involved in alchemy knew how effective prayer was, and "how
often those things which he long sought and could not find,
have been imparted to him in a moment, and as it were
infused from above, or dictated by some good Genius."[12]
In addition, he stated that the understanding of difficult

---

11. Calid, "The Secrets of Alchimie" in Stanton J. Linden, ed., *The Mirror of Alchemy* (New York: Garland, 1992), p. 28.
12. L. G. Kelly, *Basil Valentine: His Triumphant Chariot of Antimony with Annotations of Theodore Kirkringius (1678)* (New York: Garland, 1990), p. 7.

texts could only come through revelation and this "unfolding of the Riddle opens to you the mystery of all great things and shews you how available Prayer is for the attainment of things Spiritual and Eternal."[13]

Prayer formed part of the labors of the alchemist as he sought the knowledge required to bring his work to fruition. In addition, through prayer, he could invoke the spirit world, so that some good genius would dictate to him the requested information, or infuse him with divine wisdom. There is a cooperation that must occur between the alchemist and the spirit, or the enterprise fails. Paracelsus spoke of this cooperation when he wrote that when a man imagines within himself, his "imagination is united with heaven, and heaven operates with him that more is discovered than would seem possibly by merely human methods."[14] The heavenly powers and spirits cooperate with the alchemist to create more than the latter could create on his own. Prayer was the means by which the alchemist summoned the spirits to the joint effort of creating the stone.

Many alchemists depended upon the power of meditation to discover the secrets of their work, and Paracelsus clearly indicated that imagination was a part of meditation. Through imagination the alchemist experienced ways of knowing that seemed, as Paracelsus put it, to transcend "merely human methods." That these ways of knowing are related to active imagination was made clear by the definition that Ruland, a disciple of Paracelsus who wrote a lexicon of alchemy, gave to meditation:

---

13. L. G. Kelly, *Basil Valentine*, p. 7.
14. Paracelsus, "Hermetic Astronomy" in A. E. Waite, ed., *The Hermetic and Alchemical Writings of Paracelsus the Great*, vol. 2, p. 313.

The name of an Internal Talk of one person with another who is invisible, as in the invocation of the Deity, or communion with one's self, or with one's good angel.[15]

Jung was very interested in this quote. He argued that it proved that when the alchemists spoke of meditation they meant "explicitly an inner dialogue and hence a living relationship with the answering voice of the other in ourselves. . ."[16] Meditation was, at least in part, a form of dialogue active imagination, and, as many references to the Eugenius or good genius indicate, the alchemist imagined dialogues with helping spirits and good angels. These spiritual beings would reveal to them the mysteries of the *opus*.

The quest for insight about the nature of the work involved the alchemists in what we would call active imagination experiences. The alchemists were open to many kinds of visionary experiences, such as seeing spirits and images of all sorts. Raymond Lully, for example, wrote, "you can see certain fugitive spirits condensed in the air in the shape of divers monsters, beasts and men, which move like the clouds hither and thither."[17] Referring to the alchemical work and the experiences it could produce, Sendivogius, one of the most influential of later alchemists, wrote that the "eyes of the common men do not see them, but the eyes of the understanding and of the imagination perceive them with true and truest vision."[18] Imagination was the means

---

15. Martinus Rulandus, *A Lexicon of Alchemy or Alchemical Dictionary* (Kila, MT: Kessinger, n.d.), p. 226.
16. C. G. Jung, CW 12, ¶ 390.
17. C. G. Jung, CW 12, ¶ 351. Raymond Lully, from the "Compendium Artis alchemica . . ." in Manqetus, *Bibliotheca Chemica Curiosa*, 1702.
18. C. G. Jung, CW 12, ¶ 350. Sendivogius, "Novum Lumen," from *Hermetic Museum.*

by which the alchemist was able to experience higher wisdom, wisdom necessary to create the stone. The alchemist experienced the imagination in visionary states, but especially in what today is called active imagination.

If we apply the teachings of the alchemists concerning revelation to the modern *opus*, we could say that the means by which the self may be experienced and manifested could never be known by reading or intellectual studies alone. In fact, the successful achievement of the work requires revelation, which means that the spirits within must teach the individual how to proceed with his or her quest. Without cooperating with the imaginative forces, there is no way one can attain the self. This is sometimes a difficult concept for individuals to grasp, for it seems often that good intention, a willingness to learn, and careful attention to outer life situations might be enough. They are not; for without the experience of discernment which often follows direct interaction with inner figures, the self remains elusive and beyond the grasp of the ego. Individuation, defined as the production of the manifest self, is similar to the alchemical endeavor to create the stone; neither will succeed without the direct revelation from inner figures.

The alchemists mentioned three characteristics of revelation. It required effort and struggle and intense prayer, engagement with an inner figure such as a good genius, and heavenly infusion of knowledge. Paracelsus pointed out that the latter occurred when the imagination was united with heaven. In all these cases there was the implication of relationship between the alchemist and the spirits with whom he was working. Out of this relationship emerge the necessary wisdom. The alchemist, or the ego, must work very hard in its own right to understand what it must do to create growth. Without repeated effort on the part of the ego, the spirits do not manifest the essential experience. In addition to working hard, the ego must pray or invoke the spirits. Finally, the imagination must unite with heaven; that is, a real encounter with an inner figure must occur.

Let us take the case of a woman who needs to develop a sense of inner strength that will allow her to face the challenges of the outer world. She must learn to meet such challenges by trusting her own inner wisdom. If she develops this inner strength and trusts in her own ideas sufficiently, she begins to be her own person and can follow her own insights. She knows that she needs to do this work, but she has no idea of how to proceed. She goes to her analyst, who knows many techniques, and who makes many excellent suggestions, but none of them seem to help her very much. She is sincere and wishes to follow these suggestions, but nothing seems to make any difference. At some point, both the woman and her analyst must acknowledge that they simply do not know how to create such a pool of inner strength. She must seek the help of the self to accomplish this task. She continues to struggle to build up her faith in herself, and suffers from the knowledge that the requisite strength is still lacking. Now, however, she begins to pray and invoke the self by asking for dreams, or doing active imagination and asking for a guide to show her the way. Finally, after much effort, an inner figure appears who is the embodiment of strength. The inner figure comes in the form of a warrior knight, who takes her on a quest and shows her what it is like to fight monsters and defend truth to the death. After many such actives, she gains a sense of what inner strength *feels* like, and by struggling to integrate this feeling, she allows the transcendent function to work its magic. She has integrated an aspect of the knight, creating in herself a sense that she can fight for her own position, and defeat her own inner monsters of self-doubt and fear.

Whenever any transformation is sought, the individual seeking it must sooner or later acknowledge that ego knowledge is not sufficient. Only cooperation with the unconscious can create the necessary conditions that allow change to occur. In analysis, the analyst must trust the inner revelations of the client more than any technical knowledge. The imaginative encounter between the ego and the unconscious provides two essential types of knowledge: it illuminates the next phase of the work, thus pointing out the path that the ego must follow, and it provides the experiential encounter with an inner figure who actually creates the change being sought. Today the self, like the stone of centuries past, can only be created when consciousness and imagination cooperate to bring into being the obligatory processes and experiences.

Imagination is the means by which inner knowledge is acquired, and in the imaginal encounter with interior figures, one attains gnosis. The alchemists knew that imagination was the key to wisdom. One of the major roles that imagination played for the alchemists, and for us today, was the acquisition of spiritual wisdom. It was, however, not the only role it played, for it was also the source of the requisite power to transmute physical and psychic components.

The alchemists believed that imagination possessed a power beyond anything that we would conceive of today. It could not only alter the nature of physical substances, but it could also heal the body and even determine the fate of an unborn baby. Imagination could condition one's own life experiences as well, so that there was almost nothing that imagination could not accomplish. Many alchemists believed that imagination was necessary for the creation of the stone, and that the stone itself had an intimate connection with imagination. Their view of imagination and its relationship with the formation of the stone has many implications about the individuation process, and the nature of the self's association with imagination.

That there was a power in the human being to affect outer reality was declared early in the history of magic and alchemy. Dr. Jung, in his discussion of synchronicity, presented the following quote from Albertus Magnus:

> I discovered an instructive account [of magic] in Avicenna's Liber sextus naturialium, which says that a certain power to alter things indwells in the human soul and subordinates the other things to her, particularly when she is swept into a great excess of love or hate or the like.[19]

The alchemists connected this "certain power" to imagination. In his usual outspoken way Paracelsus wrote of imagination:

> It is necessary that you should know what can be accomplished by a strong imagination. It is the principle of all magical action . . . all our sufferings, all our vices are nothing else than imagination. . . . And this imagination is such that it penetrates and ascends into the superior heaven, and passes from star to star. This same heaven it overcomes and moderates. . . . So also a strong imagination is the cause of both good and evil fortune.[20]

Another wrote, "Man is the central seat of all created things. Through the force of his imagination (this being the focal point of everything), all things in the world must obey him, as before the Fall."[21] Sendivogius wrote that the

---

19. C. G. Jung, *The Structure and Dynamics of the Psyche*, Collected Works, vol. 8, R. F. C. Hull, trans., Bollingen Series XX (Princeton: Princeton University Press, 1969), ¶ 859. Future references to this title will be to CW 8.

20. A. E. Waite, ed., *The Hermetic and Alchemical Writings of Paracelsus the Great*, vol. 1, p. 122n.

21. Ali Puli, *The Center of Nature Concentrated* (Edmond, WA: The Alchemical Press, 1988), p. 21.

soul was the seat of the imagination, and that it "has absolute and independent power to do other things than those the body can grasp. But, when it so desires, it has the greatest power over the body, for otherwise our philosophy would be in vain."[22] And, finally, Henry Cornelius Agrippa wrote:

> *The philosophers, especially the Arabians, say, that man's mind, when it is most intent upon any work, through its passion, and effects, is joined with the mind of the stars, and intelligences, and being so joined is the cause that some wonderful virtue be infused into our works and things; this, as because there is in it an apprehension, and power of all things, so because all things have natural obedience to it, and of necessity an efficacy and more to that which desires them with a strong desire.*[23]

The power of imagination included the ability to alter the body and chemical reactions, to determine one's own fate and wrest control of it from the stars, and, in effect, to order and control all life. Imagination was connected with the human being's special place in the order of creation. To understand why the alchemists believed in the power of imagination, one needs to understand how they defined it. The clearest expression of this definition comes from Ruland, who defines it as the "star in man, the celestial or supercelestial body."[24] Dr. Jung found this definition most amazing and tried to uncover its implications:

---

22. Quoted in C. G. Jung, CW 12, ¶ 396. Sendivogius, "Novi luminis chemicum . . ." in Waite's *Hermetic Museum.*
23. Henry Cornelius Agrippa, *Three Books of Occult Wisdom*, Donald Tyson, ed. (St. Paul: Llewelyn Publications, 1995), p. 208.
24. Martinus Rulandus, *A Lexicon of Alchemy or Alchemical Dictionary*, p. 182.

This astounding definition throws a quite special light on the fantasy processes connected with the opus. *We have to conceive of these processes not as the immaterial phantoms we readily take fantasy-pictures to be, but as something corporeal, a "subtle body," semi-spiritual in nature. . . . The* imaginatio, *or the act of imagining, was thus a physical activity that could be fitted into the cycle of material changes, that brought these about and was brought about by them in turn. In this way the alchemist related himself not only to the unconscious but directly to the very substance which he hoped to transform through the power of imagination. The singular expression* astrum *(star) is a Paracelsian term, which in this context means something like quintessence. Imagination is therefore a concentrated extract of the life forces, both physical and psychic.*[25]

Imagination is a star within the soul of man, or a "concentrated extract of life forces" which may alter not only the inner world of the unconscious, but the outer world of physical reality as well. It should be noted that when Jung used the word fantasy in his quote, he really meant imagination, and not fantasy in the negative sense discussed earlier. This explanation was profound, and shed light on his own views of imagination. Jung did not write a great deal on this topic, and this was certainly one of his most intriguing statements concerning it.

There is an aspect of imagination that transcends the inner world of the psyche, for it has effects on the outer world, at least according to the alchemists. By placing the imagination in the subtle realm, and equating it with the subtle body, both Ruland and Jung imply that it is more than psychic; it has a physical or material dimension to it.

---

25. C. G. Jung, CW 12, ¶ 394.

That it would have such a dimension explains how it might be able to impact the physical world, but raises questions about the underlying nature of the imagination. It also raises questions about the nature of the self.

The self manifests when opposites are unified to form a new state of consciousness and being. The new center so formed is a union of opposites. Since the self includes the inner and outer dimensions of realities, it would then transcend both psychic and physical realities, and live in the world beyond both, though one that also includes both. Keeping in mind the models discussed in the last chapter, it is possible to say that a sequential union of opposites creates a self that is at one moment psychic and the next physical in its manifestations. Considered from the perspective of the simultaneous union, however, the self is both physical and psychic *at the same time.* Thus, the self belongs to neither reality completely, but to a third that unites them. It is in this sense that the manifest self does not exist in the outer world alone, or in the psychic world, but in the world of subtle bodies, wherein physical and psychic are united. Just as Ruland defined imagination as a subtle body, the self to which it belongs is also a subtle body.

Marie-Louise von Franz made a statement that the individuated person lives in the world of active imagination; that the ego does not identify with the outer world, nor the inner world, but with the imaginative world—which includes both of the others. The conscious ego that is united with the manifest self experiences life from a central position based in the imaginative worlds, and neither identifies with outer life events nor inner archetypal states. The ego's union with the self would not simply be expressed in a state of awareness, but in an ongoing creative and imaginative experience. Normal ego consciousness would be replaced by an imaginative consciousness that beheld the world through the eyes of imagination. It would see underneath the apparent solidity of ordinary reality to the meaning hidden there. It would behold the spiritual powers at play in ordinary life, and it would possess the freedom that perceiving symbolically bestows.

Imagination as the spiritual manifestation of the self has the power to affect both physical and psychic worlds because the self transcends these worlds, and yet encompasses them. The imaginative power that the alchemist described would only be potential within the latent self, but with the emergence of the manifest self, that potential would be realized.

The self has a power concentrated within it—the power of imagination. As the self emerges from its latent condition and becomes more conscious, its powers of imagination increase and multiply. Imagination as the spiritual power of the self is required in its transition from latent to manifest. This power is essential for its own transformation, and through it the self will operate on both inner and outer realities in order to promote its own development. It is important to keep in mind that the powers being discussed do not belong to the ego. Alchemy is not about the inflation of the ego through identification with such imaginative capabilities, but rather about the expression of the imaginative power of the self for its own creation. The ego is an essential part of this process, but by no means is it in a position to manipulate the great powers being discussed. If it should try, the imaginative experience would degenerate into mere fantasy, and the very powers the ego was seeking would disappear.

IMAGINATION AND THE PSYCHOID

I mentioned in the last chapter that the nature of certain inner experiences might require the differentiation between psychological inner figures and those I have called psychoidal. Some of the characteristics of the psychoidal experience include a profound impact on body and mind, and a sense that the figure came from outside the psyche. Understanding the imagination as the alchemists did makes psychoidal experiences appear more reasonable. Imagination as a subtle body is a union of the physical and the psychic, and as part of the self can create experiences that are either psychic, physical, or both. Jung has shown, however, that imagination belongs not only to the self, but to the archetypes as well. It is possible that psychoidal figures also express themselves through the power of the imagination, appearing as images and figures. The entities that give rise to such figures and experiences might well belong to the realm of subtle bodies, just as the manifest self does. In this case, though they do not belong to the human psyche, they unite in themselves characteristics that are both physical and psychic, yet neither, but some third state that we might call psychoid. Because inner figures that embody psychoidal entities come from the dimension in which the opposites of physical and psychic have been united, they have far greater power and impact, and are able to effect physical changes. The psychoid world would correspond theoretically to the world of subtle bodies, and the potent experiences they create would derive from their imaginative power. Imagination would include experiences that were purely psychic as well as those that were psychoidal.

If we consult once more the theories of the Sufis, we find corroboration for such ideas. According to Ibn 'Arabi, spirits embody themselves through the power of imagination.[26] They do this by taking on the characteristics of the

---

26. See William Chittick, *Imaginal Worlds: Ibn al-'Arabi and the Problem of Religious Diversity* (Albany: State University of New York Press, 1994).

physical world in order to express themselves. For example, a spiritual being might appear in the imagination of a person as a beautiful creature with wings. The wings, borrowed from the physical world, denote the spiritual nature of the figure, giving a suggestion of flight and freedom. A client of mine once had a dream about a magical cat, in which the cat said that it was certainly not a cat at all, but a spiritual being that could only express itself through the image of the cat. The psychoidal beings that emerge from these subtle realms possess the power of imagination. Through this power they express themselves as personified figures. They are then in a position to interact with human beings.

It is also interesting to note that the alchemists' quest for immortality often took the form of creating a subtle body. The subtle realm unites and transcends the physical and the psychic, and as the self progressively unites the opposites through active imagination experiences, it increasingly becomes part of the subtle realm. As the latent self becomes manifest, it might feel the movement into the subtle realm as a tangible sense of becoming immortal. Imagination is thus intimately connected with the creation of the immortal body that the alchemists sought.

To review briefly, the definition offered by Ruland places the imagination in the subtle or psychoid realm, at least potentially. As the star in the human psyche, the imagination would correspond to the self, or be an expression of the spiritual power of the self. This power is neither purely psychic nor physical, but a union of the two, which creates a third state that is difficult to conceptualize. As the self unites these opposites through imaginative experiences, it gains in strength and solidity. As it does so, its own powers of imagination grow, leading to new experiences of even greater impact, which in turn lead to a further strengthening of the self. The more the self grows, the more its powers of imagination help it grow. The ego, in union with the manifest self, lives in an imaginative world, a world of active imagination that is nevertheless real enough to transcend ordinary reality, though at the same time it is inclusive of this reality. The ego is not in a position to control the imaginative experience, which is aimed at the expression of the self. The powers that imagination possesses are necessary in the earlier work of creating the manifest self, and in the later work of allowing the self to express itself.

ALCHEMY AND ACTIVE IMAGINATION

Albertus Magnus indicated that the human being, especially in states of strong excitement, could influence outer events and substances. The alchemists thought this ability was essential in order to create changes within their metals. They believed that this power would manifest when the imagination of the alchemist joined with celestial forces that were symbolically depicted as heaven and the stars that inhabited it. Uniting their mind with the power of the stars, they would concentrate the celestial force within the stone they were forming, in order to imbue it with magical powers. They might also focus celestial force in a particular solution or compound in order to effect its magical transformations.

Imagine the alchemist sitting in his laboratory. He has a solution cooking in his vessel. His goal is to transmute the material in the solution into something new, a new material that has spiritual power concentrated in it. If he were able to accomplish this task, the new material would then be able to magically impact other materials, transmuting them from their current state to gold. Or he might wish to create a magical elixir, able to heal the body. In either case, the substance he tries to create must contain the power of the stars in order to be effective. The means by which he can experience the star power and focus it in his solution is imagination. How might this occur?

There are probably any number of ways the alchemist might accomplish this, but one corresponds to active imagination. Ruland defined meditation as a dialogue between the alchemist and an invisible entity. If the alchemist seeks to incarnate the power of a star in matter, he engages in a dialogue with that star, which must first manifest as a personified figure of some kind. The star could be a spiritual being, or an archetypal force that appeared as an embodied image with whom the alchemist could dialogue. In his communication with the inner figure he could ask it to teach him how to transmute his matter. Alternatively, he might request that it manifest within the material form and so bestow its power on it. Imaginative interaction with such figures would be the means of creating magical physical substances. Jung explained this process by saying, "through a dialogue with God yet more spirit will be infused into the stone, i.e. it will become still more spiritualized, volatilized or sublimated."[27] The dialogue need not be with God, for any star will do, if its spiritual essence is transferred into the stone.

As part of the processes of inner alchemy, this imaginative undertaking is very significant. The stone corresponds to the self, which is fairly undeveloped at this point. The inner alchemist wishes to give it power in order to help it grow, and will attempt to do this by constellating the power of a particular star. Symbolically, the star denotes an archetype, and relates to the theme of the *scintillae* that Jung discussed at length in *Mysterium Coniunctionis*.[28] He related the

---

27. C. G. Jung, CW 12, ¶ 390.
28. C. G. Jung, *Mysterium Coniunctionis*, Collected Works, vol. 14, R. F. C. Hull, trans., Bollingen Series XX (Princeton: Princeton University Press, 1970).

scintillae, or sparks of light seen in visions and depicted in several alchemical symbols, to split-off parts of the psyche, such as the complexes or the archetypes. The scattered sparks are symbols found in many spiritual traditions and usually associated with the doctrine of redemption. According to these beliefs, God has been scattered all over the universe in the form of sparks of light, and the mystic must discover these sparks one by one and unite them into a whole, which would rehabilitate God and restore It to Its whole state.[29] All of the tiny sparks of light, representing complexes and archetypes, are brought together into a unity. Some texts depict this process as the creation of a single radiant flame that glows with the powers of the smaller sparks. The image of the single flame would denote the self that comes into being when the fragmented aspects of the psyche are united into a whole and harmonized around a central point.

The inner alchemist is attempting to interact with an archetype, and, through this interaction, to channel its power into the latent self, creating a transmutation that generates the manifest self. She can only do this through active imagination, in which she experiences the archetype as an inner figure with whom she interacts. Her goal is to relate to this inner figure with sufficient depth to activate the transcendent function. When the transcendent function comes into play, the inner being is transformed in such a way as to become part of the self. The process by which the alchemist unites her imagination with the power of the stars is thus experienced as active imagination with the archetypes.

I once dreamed that I was standing by a magic pool. The waters of this pool had the property of reflecting one's true nature. As I looked into it, the god Mars walked by.

---

29. For a discussion on this whole theme, see CW 14, ¶ 42–50.

He was a twenty-foot giant, but I knew it was Mars. I also knew that I must seize him and make him look into that pool. If I could do so, he would see his true nature and realize that he belonged to a greater whole, and could no longer do whatever he liked, such as cause meaningless wars and wreck havoc. At the same time, however, Mars became aware that if he looked into the pool, he would lose his freedom, and so he resisted. The dream ended with me trying to catch Mars by the big toe (!) to force him to look at his reflection in the water.

The dream ushered in a long period of intense work in which I dialogued with Mars and studied war historically and mythologically. I knew if I could do enough work with him, he would be transformed, and the rage he had would no longer move autonomously within me, but would become part of the self. Mars appeared to me repeatedly as an inner figure of gigantic proportions, but very gradually he became somewhat related to me. Through our dialogues, I tried to convince him that pure aggression for its own sake was not useful to him or to me, and he, in turn, tried to convince me of the power and transformative benefits of war and conflict. When finally the transcendent function occurred, the ability to fight and be aggressive at the right moment became part of my self.

The transcendent function is not only a change in consciousness, but an energetic change as well. When the transcendent function unites two previously separated opposites, the psychic energy that belongs to each is transformed, and part of it becomes available to the self. The self thereby gains psychic energy, which allows it to express itself more readily and to become a stronger, more stable psychic component. Alchemy refers not only to the changes in consciousness that occur through active imagination, but the changes in the energetic status of figures within the psyche.

The unification of the alchemist with the stars symbolizes active imagination experiences in which archetypes are both related to and transformed. Their power is transmuted into the self. The archetypes, though the energy they possess is much reduced, do not cease to exist. They are now, however, organized around the self. Thus, the power of imagination that the alchemists described is the power to activate the transcendent function, and to transform the state of the unconscious.

There is another power of the imagination to which Paracelsus referred. He wrote that the imagination had the power to penetrate the heavens, passing from star to star, overcoming and moderating heaven. On the one hand, this description refers to the process I have just discussed, because the power to moderate the heavens by moving from star to star is that of taming the archetypes by dealing with them one by one, and organizing them around the self. Yet Paracelsus also connected this process with fate, declaring that a strong imagination is the source of one's fortune, either good or bad.

When the alchemists spoke of the stars, there was always a reference to astrology, for they believed that the stars and planets influenced the formation of metals in the center of the earth, and also affected the destiny of a human being. The imagination provided a way for people to free themselves from the dictates of fate, and to determine their own destiny.

Jung discussed this motif in relation to the symbolism of the ascent through the planetary spheres, an imaginal journey that appeared often in alchemical texts. Jung explained the ascent by discussing the role of astrology in the Middle Ages. At that time, individual planets correlated to specific temperaments; therefore the placing of the planets in an astrological chart determined the personality of an individual. The ascent through the planets "meant something like a shedding of the characterological qualities indicated by the horoscope, a retrogressive liberation from the character imprinted by the archons."[30] Jung rightly compared this quest to the ascent of the gnostic, who sought to liberate himself from all false influences and find his way back to the true God.

The idea being expressed by the alchemists is that through certain experiences and processes one can free oneself from fate, and from earlier, determinative experiences. Rather than being a product of one's environment or the times in which one was born, one is able to discard these influences in order to find the truth of one's own being. The self is self-determining, and the alchemical motif of the ascent points to the power of the self to discard unwanted influences and discover its own essential nature. Living free of external controls and the universal compulsions of the archetypes, one comes to live from one's own center and to express in the world what is true to that center.

Paracelsus appeared to be unique in that he related the ascent through the heavens to the imagination, and indicated that through imaginative experiences one can be free of the collective and archetypal influences that are untrue to one's nature. Through the process of active imagination, the individual can recognize and make conscious compelling influences previously unknown to him or her. The individual strengthens the self enough to harmonize and organize those influences in such a way that they aid rather than hinder the development of the personality. The freedom to be one's self and to make that self the center of one's life is perhaps the most important power that imagination possesses. However, there is still one attribute of the imagination that I have yet to consider: the ability to heal physical diseases.

---

30. C. G. Jung, CW 14, ¶ 308.

HEALING AND IMAGINATION

From the beginning of alchemy, practitioners were concerned with creating healing potions and ingredients, the most powerful of which was the philosopher's stone. Paracelsus wrote about the influence of imagination on disease, but it was left to one of his later students to develop this notion in a systematic and detailed fashion. Joan Baptista Van Helmont (1579–1644) played an important role in the history of science, but his major biographer, the student of alchemy and the history of science, Walter Pagel, revealed his reliance on the spiritual point of view, and especially his use of imagination in healing processes. Unfortunately, it is almost impossible to obtain any of Van Helmont's writings in English,[31] so I must rely on Pagel's explanations and quotations. Given Pagel's reputation as a scholar, and the fact that he studied Van Helmont for fifty years, this seems an acceptable risk.

I cannot, of course, detail all of Van Helmont's theories, but shall discuss his understanding of imagination only. It is important to keep in mind that Van Helmont was an alchemist and believed in the possibility of creating the philosopher's stone. His writings on imagination form part of the alchemical tradition. Influenced by Paracelsus, he was nevertheless an original and creative thinker in his own right, and did not hesitate to disagree with Paracelsus when he felt it was appropriate.

---

31. After writing this book, I came upon a work by Van Helmont translated into English. A careful reading of this work, *The Image of God in Man or Helmont's Vision of the Soul,* confirmed much of what Pagel had presented. This book was in the Ferguson Collection of the Glasgow University Library. It was translated by Walter Charelton in 1650 and published in that year in London by James Flesher.

In Van Helmont's system, the center of the individual was the *archeus*, an individual unit in which "spirit and matter had been united to become inseparable and indistinguishable in a new being. This was neither matter nor spirit, but had something of both, namely a physical and a psychoid aspect. . ."[32] Though comparisons are always somewhat dangerous and misleading, it seems that the *archeus* might be compared to the latent self. The *archeus* acted as a kind of intermediary between the seminal images that imprint upon matter and the material world itself. The *archeus* had its own imagination, by which it guided these images in the way that is required, because the *archeus* had "knowledge of what is to be done."[33] When this imagination was distorted through a type of "bad seed," the end result was disease. In such a case, the image took over from the vital spirit, and the person developed the "disease through a complicated chain of psycho-physical events in which imagination, 'magnetic attraction' of the virus, and above all fear, play a prominent part."[34] Pagel pointed out that Paracelsus greatly influenced the ideas of Van Helmont, and that for both of them, illness was "the result of a dialogue between spirits, that is, invisible powers with an astral energy far superior to anything within the reach of the merely material humours."[35] From this point of view, disease was a spiritual entity, that is, it was imaginal, and in its manifestation in the imagination it corrupted and distorted the imagination of the *archeus*. It was as if there were an unconscious

---

32. Walter Pagel, *Joan Baptista Van Helmont: Reformer of Science and Medicine* (New York: Cambridge University Press, 1982), p. 96.
33. Walter Pagel, *Joan Baptista Van Helmont*, p. 97.
34. Walter Pagel, *Joan Baptista Van Helmont*, p. 145.
35. Walter Pagel, *Joan Baptista Van Helmont*, p. 149.

active imagination going on between the image of the disease and the *archeus*, and through this dialogue the former
overcame the latter. It is not hard to compare this model
to that of an active imagination in which an archetype overcomes the self, creating if not physical disease, at least a
psychological one. Every disease might be attributable to
the imagination of the archetypes that interfere with the
development and expression of the self. The theory that
disease might have an imaginal core has been elaborated
recently by Dr. Arnold Mindell and his school of Process
Oriented Psychology, which has developed many methods
of working with body symptoms as images.[36]

Since imagination was responsible for the onset of disease, it also had a great part to play in healing. The image
was causing the disease, and another image had to be introduced that created healing, and in effect interacted with
and overcame the disease idea. This was done through a
number of methods, which included words of power and
the *arcana*.[37] There were powers that lay in certain minerals
and stones, and to be sure in the philosopher's stone. These
powers acted to create a counter-idea in the imagination of
the patient. Pagel's explanation of how this occurred broke
down at this point, and was not very clear. If we recall the
description of the way in which disease began, we may
arrive at a better formulation. Since disease occurred as a
result of a dialogue between two spirits, the addition of
a word of power, or a powerful medicine, introduced a
third idea or image into the mind of the patient. This image, related to the medicine or power of the physician,
joined in the discussion, and if strong enough, overcame

---

36. Arnold Mindell, *Dreambody* (Boston: Sigo Press, 1982).
37. Walter Pagel, *Joan Baptista Van Helmont*, p. 195.

the image of the disease, liberating the *archeus* from the poisonous effect of that image, and uniting it with the healing image.

The *archeus* was not a physical entity, nor merely a spiritual one; rather it was psychoidal in that it united the spiritual and the material in itself. This relates the *archeus* with the definition of the self as a union of opposites, and with descriptions of the imagination as a subtle body. It is interesting to note how many important concepts in alchemy relate to the psychoidal plane. The *archeus* operated more or less unconsciously, and certainly not in connection with the ego. Consciousness entered into the scene only through the intervention of the physician, who deliberately attempted to create a new image in the psyche of the patient. Disease, being spiritual in its origins, has the power to create images, and therefore can only be treated successfully in the realm of the imagination.

In addition to some of the methods elaborated by Dr. Mindell, active imagination remains a potent force in the treatment of illness. The supposition of Paracelsus and Van Helmont—that the disease creates an image—means that through active imagination the ego may interact with that image. By making the disease-image conscious and relating to it, the ego finds ways of transforming it and creating a healing experience. The goal is to find the image related to the disease and then interact with it, just as one would with an image derived from an archetype. If the disease-image comes into relationship to the self through an experience of the transcendent function, then the meaning of the disease as expressed in its image can become part of the self.

Suppose, for example, that Janet has developed a migraine headache. Alchemically, one could say that the image of the headache has corrupted the center so as to make her imagine the headache. Healing would consist in discovering a new image that could interact with the symbol of the headache to alter the situation. If Janet enters into active imagination, she might begin by asking the unconscious to produce the image of the disease. If this image were a little man with a hammer banging on her head, she would then engage the little man in a dialogue of some kind.

It is popular today to perform visualizations when dealing with disease. In this example, Janet visualizes poisonous arrows piercing the little man and killing him. Such an approach has the merit of seeking healing effects in the realm of imagination, but unfortunately does not sufficiently perceive the difference between imagination and fantasy. For the ego to simply envision killing the disease-image is simply a fantasy, for there is no interaction between the ego and the image, but only a manipulation on the part of the ego. This can work only in a limited fashion, and should not be confused with performing active imagination with the disease. In the latter case, the ego does not impose its will on the disease, but must engage with it in an objective way, hoping to create enough tension for the transcendent function to occur. In our example, Janet must engage the little man in a dialogue, ask him why he is hurting her, and listen attentively to his reasons. She must come to terms with the little man's point of view, without ever losing her own. If he says he is hurting her because Janet thinks all the time and never expresses her heart, she must take this argument into account, and consider changing her attitude. But she must also tell the little man that hurting her head is not a very good way to communicate, and he should stop it at once. And so it should go, back and forth, as in true active imagination.

Taking a disease or a symptom on the imaginal level opens up a new possibility of transformation, including seeing the disease as an expression of meaning, rather than simply as an enemy to be nuked with one modern drug or another. However, it is also significant that Van Helmont never rejected the use of medicinal drugs and potions. Certainly, his idea of what they were, and how they were made, differed greatly from a modern physician's. Nevertheless, one could easily take a pill for a headache while still performing an active imagination. One could imagine the form the medicine itself would take and welcome it into the discussion. The essential point of this alchemical view of sickness, however, is that disease is never a purely physical event, but includes the spirit as well. Healing, too, must therefore include the spiritual dimension, and this is most effectively accomplished in imaginative process.

Imagination has been shown to be a central part of the alchemical enterprise and to be a crucial element in alchemical theories. Imagination was the means by which revelations could be had, either directly or through dialogues with helping spirits of all kinds. The encounter with imaginal figures was one method used by alchemists to obtain knowledge. Furthermore, imagination possessed a great deal of power to effect change and produce transmutation. Imaginative activity could transmute substances magically and create healing potions. Imaginative power was not then simply psychic, but also included a physical dimension; in this sense imagination was psychoidal in some way.

The alchemical notion that imagination is both psychic and physical is important in that it allows for healing power to effect the body. One may further envision imagination as a power that can be transpsychic in its operations. Unfortunately imagination and the concept of the unconscious are frequently equated, which creates confusion in their definitions. Viewed alchemically, imagination belongs to the spirit. Any spiritual entity has the capacity to create images, and the source of the imaginal experience must be sought in the spirit that created it. At times that spirit is an inner archetype, and the imaginable experience refers to an intrapsychic state. Sometimes, as just noted, the image may actually derive from a physical cause such as a disease, since the illness is also a spirit. In other cases, the source of the imaginal experience is an entity that does not belong to the psyche, but as a spiritual being still has the capacity to create images. Finally, the source of the experience may be the self, and such experiences are particularly important ones.

Thinking of imagination in these terms widens our understanding of it, and allows for the possibility of encountering new types of experiences. It is too simplistic to argue that imaginal experiences derive from one of these sources alone, but rather that each makes its contribution to a particular situation. The imaginal power of the self might well interact with that of an archetype, for example. The important point is that in the understanding of the alchemical imagination, one must acknowledge that it is a very complicated and far-reaching theory. The powers of the imagination and the diversity of the imaginal experiences are still by and large unknown. Dr. Jung's contribution to the technique of active imagination is of critical importance for understanding some of the issues that the alchemists raised about the imagination. It is just as critical, however, that the imagination and its effects not be limited in our theories. Imagination is the mode of perception by which the inner world comes alive, and the method of interaction through which it may be transformed. By the same token, imagination is the means by which the body and physical illness may be perceived on a spiritual level, and likewise subjected to processes of transformation. Through imagination it is also possible to perceive the spiritual realms that transcend the psyche. In the older imaginal traditions of the Sufis and shamans, these spiritual realms were explored and mapped, but our culture remains woefully ignorant of them. Liberating the imagination from its identification with the unconscious or the inner world allows it to expand and enliven our perceptions, and opens untold realms of untapped experiences. Though it may be difficult to prove the transpsychic world theoretically, it is not so difficult to experience if we develop our imaginative sense deeply enough to allow it to take flight.

Finally, it is through imagination that the self may be encountered and transformed; all the processes of individuation are intimately associated with imagination and active imagination in particular. The alchemists, like von Franz's individuated person, lived in the worlds of active imagination, and identified neither with the psychic nor the physical, but with that strange intermediate realm where imagination takes root. It is there that they looked for that mysteriously elusive entity, the philosopher's stone. It is through the imagination that they found the path that led to transformation, a path that will form the subject of the next chapter.

CHAPTER 3

The
CREATION
of the
SELF

One of the many ways in which the imagination of the alchemists found expression was through the creation of alchemical drawings or emblems. These emblems represent the mysteries of alchemy so powerfully and concisely that their study can lead to a profound understanding of its nature. The term "emblem," emphasizes the symbolic aspects of the alchemical *opus*. The artistic side of alchemy was present almost from its beginnings: throughout the history of alchemy alchemists used emblems, diagrams, and drawings to illustrate the written texts. The production of emblems, in particular, was stimulated around the time of the Renaissance, when ancient Egypt and its language came into vogue. During the Renaissance, Europeans believed the ancient Egyptian religion to be one of the purest expressions of spiritual truth which great sages had revealed. They saw in Egyptian hieroglyphs, which they could not understand, a symbolic system depicting these mysteries. The incorporation of hieroglyphs or pseudo-hieroglyphs into emblems inspired artists and writers alike, and the belief that symbols could convey profound truths better than written discourse became more widespread.

In the early 15th century, a book titled *The Hieroglyphics of Horapollo* was rediscovered and translated into modern

European languages. This work, dating from late antiquity, purported to explain the meaning of Egyptian hieroglyphics, though it was more an encyclopedia of symbols and not at all accurate in its presentation of actual hieroglyphics. Horapollo believed that hieroglyphs were used as symbols to convey profound Egyptian ideas and mysteries. For example, the Egyptians used images of the sun and the moon to indicate eternity, or the serpent devouring its own tail to portray the universe.[1] This work had a great impact on alchemists who in turn used these symbols in their own emblems. The hieroglyphic images disclosed secret information that could not be portrayed in words. Building on an already ancient system of symbolism, the alchemists used images to reveal secrets in a direct and immediate way.

In the introduction to his translation of *The Hieroglyphics*, George Boas stated that the writings of Plotinus were responsible in large measure for originating the tradition of emblems. According to Plotinus, in the intelligible worlds, the gods see reality in beautiful images that express truth far better than any written text could. He believed that the Egyptian sages expressed their insights in pictures as well, and "each picture was a kind of understanding and wisdom and substance and given all at once . . ."[2] The gods perceived reality through the imagination, just as wise Egyptian teachers presented their knowledge in symbols. Higher reality could only be understood imaginally.

The alchemists certainly felt themselves to be working in this tradition. Thus their emblems were designed to express reality as deeply and directly as the Egyptians did

---

1. See George Boas, trans., *The Hieroglyphics of Horapollo* (Princeton: Princeton University Press, 1993).
2. George Boas, trans., *The Hieroglyphics of Horapollo*, p. 8.

in theirs. Alchemical pictures were not simply illustrations for a text, but attempts to communicate truths independently of the text. In some cases, the emblems portrayed secrets that were explained in the texts, while in others the two seemed quite independent of each other. In some cases, the text that accompanied the emblems seemed almost banal in comparison with the beauty and intricacy of the images. In any case, the emblems were a profound expression of the alchemical imagination.

Jung was always interested in symbolism, and in the nature of symbol formation. In his theory, a true symbol was never created by the ego, but emerged from the unconscious. In other words, symbols emerged from the imagination, and, as the expression of the imaginal, are closely related to the inner figures that appear in active imagination. The imagination's symbolic expression conveys the wisdom of the spirit in visual terms. The theory that the alchemists held about the nature of hieroglyphics applies to any imaginal symbolic expression, for each symbol, like a hieroglyph, would be the best possible expression of inner truth. Just as inner figures connect one to Sophia, or the imaginal wisdom of the Self, so do true symbols.

As products of the imagination, emblems expressed wisdom of an esoteric kind, but in addition, served to link one with the powers and forces needed for the alchemical work. Just as the alchemists' dialogues and prayers focused and concentrated power in the stone, so too symbols helped alchemists to channel power into their work. The idea that an image could incarnate the power that it portrayed is an ancient magical one that was certainly known to the alchemists. The great magician of the Renaissance, Henry Cornelius Agrippa, wrote, "an image rightly made of certain proper things, appropriated to any one certain angel, will presently be animated by that angel."[3] Ruland, in his *Lexicon* wrote that *imagines* are "Effigies in Wax or metal, wherein the celestial virtues operate."[4] In other words, images created properly could embody the spirit or celestial power they represented. It seems reasonable to conclude that the emblems were therefore not only intended as the communication of wisdom, but as the embodiment of energies needed by the alchemist. Meditating on an emblem thus connected the alchemist with the wisdom and the puissance of the imagination, and connected the student to a specific part of the alchemical work.

Clearly, we cannot simply study emblems from an intellectual perspective; we have to meditate on them to unearth their hidden meaning. Symbolic expressions may be interpreted in many different ways, and when we interact with them we should attempt to derive our own particular meaning. Meditation on the symbols of the alchemists will not only bring us more deeply into the alchemical tradition, we will also stand a good chance of duplicating the experiences the alchemists portrayed in our own psyche.

THE BOOK OF LAMBSPRING

There are hundreds of alchemical emblems, and most of them are quite fascinating. I present a particular series of pictures that together with their text form the *Book of Lambspring*. I have chosen this specific set of emblems not

---

3. Henry Cornelius Agrippa, *Three Books of Occult Wisdom*, Donald Tyson, ed. (St. Paul: Llewelyn Publications, 1995), p. 112.
4. Martinus Rulandus, *A Lexicon of Alchemy or Alchemical Dictionary* (Kilo, MT: Kessinger, n.d.), p. 181. Originally published in 1893; reprinted by Samuel Weiser, York Beach, ME, 1984.

only because of their intrinsic interest, but also for the fact that they actually comprise a map of the whole alchemical process. In this series, moreover, the images do not stop with the formation of the philosopher's stone, but continue to depict the deepest processes in alchemy, through which the stone becomes related to the divine world. Viewed from the perspective of alchemy as a psychological process, this set of illustrations portrays the creation of the individual self and its union with the world of the infinite. The emblems provide a descriptive map of the major steps in the production of the stone or the self.

I approach these representations as illustrative of the inner processes by which the self is generated and establishes relationship with the divine. My interpretation will focus on this aspect of the emblems, which could be interpreted in a number of different ways. I combine amplification of the major symbols that are found in the emblem with my own meditation on and inner experience of the symbols in question. My goal is to allow the imagination to express itself as clearly as possible through my comments.

In order to understand these emblems, it is important to have a context in which to view them. There are many paradigms of the alchemical *opus* and each alchemist had his own idea about the stages and processes of the work. Gerald Dorn, in the late 16th century, presented one of the most convincing and penetrating of these. Dorn was a student of Paracelsus, and a deeply religious alchemist whose work included many interesting texts. Jung discussed Dorn's writings at great length in his work on the *coniunctio*, in *Mysterium Coniunctionis*.

Dorn identified three stages of the Great Work, the first *coniunctio*, the second *coniunctio*, and the third *coniunctio*. The word *coniunctio* means "union," or "conjunction," so in Dorn there are three levels at which the opposites unite. Since the self is the union of opposites, each stage corresponds to a different level of self-formation. The first union begins when the ego discovers the reality of the unconscious and makes an effort to pay attention to it. Beginning with its own dreams, the ego attempts to gain some insight into the nature of the unconscious and to listen to its messages. Moving from dreams to active imagination, the ego begins to experience the power of the transcendent function, and through the union of the opposites that results, begins to forge a new center, the manifest self.

At the stage of the second *coniunctio*, the self progresses to such a degree that it takes on a life and reality of its own within the psyche. The self comes alive and begins to function in its own right. At the same time, the ego experiences a profound transformation and comes to realize itself as part of the manifest self. At the second level, all the work performed at the first level comes to fruition in a deep inner revolution that binds together the unconscious and the ego in an indissoluble union.

With the formation of the self, the individuation process has entered a stage that is ongoing but stable. However, Dorn, as well as the author of the *Book of Lambspring*, depicts a third level of union. In this *coniunctio*, the individual self that has been formed comes into union with a level of reality that transcends it, with the divine world that Dorn called the *unus mundus*. By this, Dorn meant the one world before spirit and matter were separated. Union with the *unus mundus* joins the individual self with the world in which matter and spirit are one. This is the psychoid world I mentioned in earlier chapters. The third level then ushers in a union between the individual self and the transcendent psychoidal world. Jung explained Dorn's idea as follows:

> *The creation of unity by a magical procedure meant the possibility of effecting a union with the world—not with the world of multiplicity as we see it but with a potential world, the eternal*

Ground of all empirical being. . . . On the basis of a self
known by meditation and produced by alchemical means, Dorn
"hoped and expected" to be united with the unus mundus.[5]

According to Dorn, the alchemist first manifests the self,
and then unites it with the original world of creation—
the world of the spirit and synchronicity. Unfortunately,
it is not at all easy to understand just what he meant by
the *unus mundus,* or what an experience of it would be like.
Fortunately, the images in the *Book of Lambspring* provide valuable information, not only about the first two stages of
the *coniunctio,* but about the third as well.

Let me summarize this overview of the process of self-
formation. The first level is a period in which the opposites are held in tension for the purpose of engaging the
transcendent function. During this phase, an individual experiences the self from time to time, but is unable to sustain the experience. The second level is an interval in which
a more profound experience of the self, the manifest self,
is achieved, one which is stable and consistent. The third
coniunctio is the process by which the manifest self comes
into relationship with a greater reality, the reality of the
psychoidal world. Though the nature of this reality is difficult to describe, the imagery in the *Book of Lambspring* presents this realm as a world of spirits and energies that exist
at a level deeper than our ordinary world.

The *Book of Lambspring* or *De Lapide Philosophico Libellus* was
written by an unknown alchemist and published several
times during the latter part of the 16th and the beginning
of the 17th centuries. While the text includes some written commentary, its most striking aspect is the collection

---

5. C. G. Jung, *Mysterium Coniunctionis,* Collected Works, vol. 14, R. F. C. Hull,
trans., Bollingen Series XX (Princeton: Princeton University Press, 1970),
¶ 760.

of beautiful and impressive emblems. I will not refer to the written text in my interpretation except where it provides useful information about the emblems.

EMBLEM ONE

The first emblem (figure 4, page 88) depicts two fish facing in opposite directions in the middle of an ocean. On one side of the ocean sits a forest, and on the other, a town and castle. In the water, one boat with some men waving is prominent, while there are several boats in the background. Notice, however, that there is no bridge connecting the two shorelines.

The image that dominates the emblem is that of the two fish. As a dream symbol, the fish points to contents within the collective unconscious. The sea, or any large body of water, symbolizes the collective unconscious. The fish, as a creature living within the sea, is like an image living within the waters of the unconscious.

The written text refers to a fish without bones, a motif often found in alchemical writings. One alchemist referred to the son of the philosophers, another term for the stone, as "a fish without bones, which swims in our philosophical sea."[6] Another connects the fish "with no spiny bones" to the original primal matter the alchemists sought to discover.[7] Jung summarized the symbolism of the fish by writing that the fish "characterizes the self, in this state, as an unconscious content."[8]

---

6. Michael Sendivogius, "Treatise on Salt" in Zbigniew Szydlo, *Water Which Does not Wet Hands: The Alchemy of Michael Sendivogius* (Warsaw: Polish Academy of Sciences, 1994), p. 254.

7. C. G. Jung, *Aion*, Collected Works, vol. 9ii, R. F. C. Hull, trans., Bollingen Series XX (Princeton: Princeton University Press, 1970), ¶ 218.

8. CW 9ii, ¶ 219.

Figure 4. Depicted here is the beginning of the work. The two fish facing in opposite directions represent the latent self split into opposites. The split existing within the psyche between the ego and the unconscious is further highlighted by the forest on the left side and the city on the right side. The forest, the world of the unconscious, and the city, the world of consciousness, are not connected in any way. The boat in the center represents the alchemist, or the ego, preparing to begin the work of inner alchemy. (From Nicolas Banaud Delphinas, "The Book of Lambspring," in *The Hermetic Museum*.)

The fish could represent any content of the unconscious, but when united with the imagery of the stone, it refers to the latent self, the self that is still unconscious and unknown. The work of creating the self would obviously begin with finding it within the unconscious, where it lies dormant and obscured. The image through which an individual experiences the self would correspond to the fish. Our image, however, depicts two fish, and it is necessary to determine why this doubling occurs. Two as a symbol, and especially doubling or twinning, usually refers to a content within the unconscious that is ready to cross over into the conscious sphere. To dream of two of anything will often mean that the image within the dream is ready to connect with the ego, and will do so, either spontaneously or through the efforts of the ego. The double fish therefore means that the process around the self is ready to commence, and that the image of the self is moving toward consciousness. The self-image might now appear in a dream, or be readily available in an active imagination.

Given the two fish in the image, the alchemist's preparations have activated an image of the self, or of the stone, which he will now be able to experience. An individual doing an active imagination might ask repeatedly for an image of the self to appear, and it is now ready to do so. Doubling not only means that the self is ready to move toward the ego, it is also a sign that the process of creating the self can begin with a fair chance of success.

The greatest dilemma in alchemy is the composition of the *prima materia*. If one cannot determine its nature, one simply cannot make the stone. If an individual is unable to make contact with the self, any effort to transform it will fail to produce significant results. The image personifying the self must make its appearance in the unconscious, and the ego must be able to connect with it. The fish must first appear within the water, and then it must be caught.

The fish in our emblem simply appear, with no discussion of the process by which they are caught. Other alchemical texts did discuss the means by which the fish without bones might be snared. According to some texts, the magnet of the wise catches the fish, and Jung explains that this symbol refers to *theoria*, or a system of thought that governs the alchemical undertaking.[9] *Theoria* means theory, and the magnet of the wise would symbolize the theory of the alchemist, which allows him to determine the nature of the self that he is seeking. This is an important idea for anyone beginning inner alchemy, and needs some explanation.

The imaginal encounter between the ego and unconscious unites conscious expectations and suppositions of the ego with the living reality of an inner figure. The ego cannot control or manipulate the imagination to produce the experience it may desire, for too much contrivance produces fantasy and eliminates unconscious participation. Instead of directly controlling the imagination, the ego brings its attitudes with it, and these guide and channel the experience. The unconscious is a vast ocean filled with many diverse kinds of fish, each one representing a content capable of personifying through the imagination. The ego's belief system acts as a magnet to attract just the right fish for that particular ego.

Suppose one begins an active imagination looking for an inner figure that embodies the self. Since all parts of the unconscious can manifest in images, it may not always be clear to the ego which figure personifies the self. It would not do to mistake a complex or an archetype for the self, for the inner figure must embody the self if the transformative

---

9. CW 9ii, ¶ 219.

work is to be performed as expected. The ego's theory of life and of spirituality, which is determined by collective influences as well as individual choices, activates an image that is most suitable for that system belief.

To give but one simple example of this, suppose an individual is fishing for the self and catches the image of a powerful man, with magical abilities and great wisdom. If the ego has the idea that the self is connected to magic and wizardry, it will not be surprised or put off by the self appearing as a Merlin character. On the other hand, if one were a devout Christian, the self would almost certainly appear as Christ, and the inner figure of Christ would personify the mysteries of the psychic center. The Merlin figure, ideal for the first individual, would not do at all for the Christian. If the individual is a Muslim, she might encounter Khidr, while a Jew might experience an image of a burning bush. In other words, the deeply held belief system of the ego working with the unconscious determines the nature of the image of the self one experiences. The expectation that one brings to the unconscious often determines the unconscious response.

Ibn 'Arabi, who believed that this fact explained religious diversity, also knew that conscious belief will determine the nature of imaginative experience. People of different faiths experience the images of their beliefs in the imagination, and for this reason all religions should be equally respected, for all derive from the imaginative encounter with God. The imaginative power of the self expresses itself in terms that are familiar and comfortable to the ego, and this allows an initial period of cooperation to occur. Later on, as this cooperation deepens, the self may challenge the ego to expand its theories.

There are certainly exceptions to this rule, for sometimes the image will compensate a narrow attitude, or push a person to revise his or her theory. Nor does the influence of *theoria* deprive the unconscious of its autonomy, for it will sometimes shock the ego with the experience it generates. Nevertheless, it is often the case that the attitude of the ego is of critical importance in creating the image encountered. Jung believed that the *theoria* used by the alchemists to catch their fish was part of a secret tradition. The presuppositions they brought to their work were not commonly revealed, but passed from teacher to student. This secret tradition, he wrote, taught nothing less than that "God himself, in his everlasting fires, may be caught like a fish in the deep sea."[10] In other words, the fish in the sea is the unredeemed God, and the theory of the alchemists allows him to seek the God that lies hidden in matter, or in the dark waters of the unconscious. The secret tradition to which Jung refers had to do with the redemption of the divine trapped in matter. From the inner perspective, there is within the human soul a divine core that is unconscious. In Jung's terms this is the self. The alchemist, versed in his theory, will catch the fish that he is seeking (the self) through his expectation of finding it. He seeks the God within in order to subject it to processes through which it will be redeemed.

The two fish therefore refer to an image of the self that is about to appear to the ego. The specific nature of the image will depend upon the conscious expectations of the person doing the work. In our text this would be the alchemist, so his expectation was that he would find an image of God trapped in matter. Since our anticipation is that the fish will embody the self, the particular image we shall encounter will be one of sufficient depth and breadth to embody all that we expect the self to be. Our expectations about the self and its nature will form the hook on which we will catch the image of the self.

---

10. CW 9ii, ¶ 222.

There are other ways that the duality of the fish may be interpreted. Jung wrote about the astrological sign of Pisces. He believed this sign had much to do with the tension of opposites and the need to find a means for their unification.[11] The two fish swimming in different directions in our image could refer to the tension between the two sides of the self, or the tension between the opposites that form the self. In addition, number symbolism in alchemy is significant. All things begin as one, that is, as a primary unity. But life itself and all of its processes actually commence with the number two, when the primary unity breaks down into its opposites. The opposites in turn, as the number three, enter into all kinds of conflicts and interactions. The fish appearing doubled signifies that the latent self has broken down into its opposites, and that the process of transformation has begun.

The text accompanying this image declares that the fish are really one, but also two, so that the fish are two aspects of the same primary unity. As developed clearly in later images, these two are opposites in tension with one other. The writer knew that, despite their apparent enmity, the two fish are both aspects of the same essential being. The self is one in its beginnings, but breaks into two when the work required for its transformation has begun. The two fish symbolize the unconscious and conscious as opposites that are inherently part of the self but must be separated for a later reunion.

The ship in the center of the water is an interesting image as well. Jung discussed the ship as the "vehicle that bears the dreamer over the sea and the depths of the unconscious. As a man-made thing it has the significance of

---

11. See "The Historical Significance of the Fish," in C. G. Jung, CW 9ii.

a system or method. . ."[12] The ego is in the ship in the center of our picture, which is its *theoria*. In addition, vessels in dreams (ships, cars, trains, and buses) often symbolize the ego, itself. The size of the vessel can reflect the strength of the ego.

I had a dream early in my work in Zurich where a boat played this role. I had done an active imagination with an inner figure that turned out to be far more powerful than I had first thought. I had to quickly end the active as I began to feel ill and overwhelmed by its force.

> *That night I dreamed I had gone fishing for bass, but had gone far out to sea in my small boat. Suddenly there was a mighty yank on my line, and I discovered to my astonishment that I had caught a whale! As I tried to reel the whale in, my boat began to rise in the air. I knew that if the whale went down, with my line attached, my boat would be pulled down with it. Suddenly an old man ran across the top of the water. He was carrying a huge pair of scissors with which he cut the line, separating me from the whale.*

My analyst's only comment was that I had better get a bigger boat before I went fishing again! The boat in the dream would symbolize the strength of my ego, but also the depth of my theoretical understanding, and my ways of dealing with life and the unconscious. If the boat is not big enough, the ego will be unable to relate safely with an inner figure. As both ego strength and theory, the boat is essential for sailing safely on the waters of the unconscious. The man in the boat in Emblem One (figure 4) would symbolize the ego securely riding above the unconscious in a

---

12. C. G. Jung, *Psychology and Alchemy*, Collected Works, vol. 12, R. F. C. Hull, trans., Bollingen Series XX (Princeton: Princeton University Press, 1977), ¶ 305. Further references will be cited as CW 12.

very well-constructed boat. The alchemist's ego is quite safe in the waters he is plying, and this bodes well for his ability to catch the self-fish he seeks.

Going back to our emblem, on one bank we see a forest, the other shows a castle or a city, and there is no bridge between the two. The forest symbolizes the untamed world of the unconscious, while the city is the scene of conscious life. The two sides of the river repeat the notion that the opposites of conscious life and the unconscious have emerged from the primary unity of the latent self, and the absence of a bridge means that they are completely unconnected at the moment. No unity between the world of consciousness and the inner imaginative world of the unconscious has yet been created. However, the ego is in a boat in the middle between the two shores. The ego is not strictly identified with the conscious side of the opposition, but is in the middle. Not only is the ego strong enough to deal with the fish, it has ended its identification with the world of consciousness. The ego has shown itself to be fluid and flexible enough to be in the middle, between the opposites, and is not totally identified with one or another.

At the beginning of the work leading to the first *coniunctio*, there is no abiding connection between the unconscious and the conscious ego. However, as I indicated in the first chapter, the ego must disengage from the conscious world in order to entertain new ideas and possibilities as they emerge from the unconscious. Though it must hold its own position, it needs to be open enough to other possibilities to allow the dialogue necessary for transformation.

My fishing dream indicated that the unconscious will often symbolize active imagination as fishing, and such may well be the case in the present emblem. The ego is strong and flexible enough to do active imagination work, and embarked on its boat, it has begun that process. It is specifically attempting to do active imagination with the image of the self, which having doubled is ready to make contact with the ego as well. Taken this way, our first emblem would indicate that active imagination has begun, and that there is a good chance that the inner figure personifying the self will emerge. Moreover, the ego is healthy enough, and has enough theoretical understanding to safely find itself between the two banks, right in the center of the psyche.

The emblem gives one the sense of great potential, there is an expectant feel about it. Not only is the work about to begin, but all is in readiness with good possibility of success. The first step toward the creation of the self has been taken, and the ego is prepared for the active imagination work to follow.

EMBLEM TWO

Presumably the fish has been caught, for the next emblem (see figure 5, page 98) describes a scene on land. We are in the forest and we can catch sight of the city in the background, but it is clearly on the other side of the water now. Emblem two describes a scene within the unconscious, where a knight is about to encounter the black beast. This beast is clearly a dragon, so it is important to begin with the amplification of the symbol of the dragon.

To mention all the references to the dragon in world symbolism is impossible. Even within alchemy there are dozens of references to the dragon as a symbol of great importance. The dragon as inner figure would be powerful and numinous indeed, and one would imagine it to be both wise and dangerous. There is an alchemical text in which the dragon speaks for itself:

> *I am the poysonous dragon, present everywhere and to bee had for nothing. My water and my fire dissolve and compound; out of my body thou shalt draw the Green and the Red lion; but if thou dost not exactly know mee thou wilt with my*

fire destroy thy five senses. A most pernicious quick poyson comes out of my nostrils, which hath been the destruction of many. . . . I am the Egg of Nature known only to the wise . . . . I am called . . . Mercury. . . . I am the old dragon that is present everywhere on the face of the earth; I am father and mother; youthful and ancient; weak and yet most strong; life and death; visible and invisible; hard and soft, descending to the earth and ascending to the heavens; most high and most low; light and heavy. . . . I am dark and bright; I spring from the earth and I come out of heaven.[13]

A most formidable beast! Notice in its description of itself that the dragon unites within its own nature all of the opposites: heaven and earth, light and dark, life and death, and so on. It is found everywhere and originates from the earth while coming forth from heaven. The dragon relates itself to *Mercurius*, and by so doing, places itself at the center of all alchemical symbolism.

Mercury is certainly one of the most significant of alchemical images, and the range of its meanings is quite wide. So diverse and profound are its ramifications that Jung wrote a long essay trying to uncover its essential meaning.[14] He wrote by way of summary:

Mercurius . . . is the arcanum, the prima materia, the "father of all metals," the primeval chaos, the earth of paradise, the "material upon which nature worked a little, but nevertheless left imperfect." He is also the ultima materia, the goal

---

13. Thomas Vaughan, "Coelum Terrae" in A. E. Waite, *The Magical Writings of Thomas Vaughan* (Kilo, MT: Kessinger, n.d.), pp. 136–137.

14. The Spirit Mercurius" in C. G. Jung, *Alchemical Studies*, The Collected Works, vol. 13, R. F. C. Hull, trans., Bollingen Series XX (Princeton: Princeton University Press, 1970). Future references will be to CW 13.

Figure 5. The war between the ego and the chaos of the unconscious takes place as the ego, and its armor of conscious values, confronts the dragon, beast of the forest, representing the unrelated and chaotic unconscious. By holding strongly to its own position and viewpoint, the ego is able to face the unconscious without being swept away, and at the same time uses the sword of transformation to stimulate change within the unconscious. (From Nicolas Banaud Delphinas, "The Book of Lambspring.")

of his own transformation, the stone, the tincture, the philo-
sophic gold, the carbuncle, the philosophic man, the second Adam
. . . the king, the light of lights . . . indeed the divinity itself
or its perfect counterpart.[15]

It would seem then that the dragon was not idly boasting, but is the secret of the work. He is both the *prima materia* and the end of the work itself. He is the magical substance out of which all creation flows, and the perfect philosophic man. More, he is the light of lights and the divinity hidden within matter. He is the union of opposites. He is the personification of the latent self, the self that lies hidden within the unconscious—dormant and undeveloped.

In the previous Emblem One, the two fish indicated the beginning of the process, and we noted that the image for the self must be found if its transformation is to proceed. The self now appears as the dragon, and carries a wealth of meaning for the alchemist. As Jung indicated, the dragon is both the beginning and the end of the work. An important dictum in alchemy was that the alchemist "need not a number of things, but one thing only, which in each and every grade of your work is changed into another nature."[16] The dragon is the material that, through successive changes and transmutations, becomes the stone. Yet at the start it is a poisonous and deadly being who must be handled with great care. The self, in its latent state, is part of the chaos of the collective unconscious, and is dangerous because it is not yet in relationship with the ego. Accordingly, it could overwhelm the ego through the sheer intensity of its manifestations.

---

15. CW 13, ¶ 282.
16. A. E. Waite, trans., *The Turba Philosophorum* (New York: Samuel Weiser, 1976), p. 41.

In the first emblem, the ego required a ship within which it could safely move into the unconscious. Having done so it activated an image of the self, but that image is wild and untamed, and carries within itself great dangers. One of the ways that the ego protects itself is to have a theory, a way of anticipating and understanding its interaction with the unconscious. Though the unconscious works through this paradigm and appears in forms that are consistent with it, there still remain real dangers in dealing with it. Without a strong center, the unconscious can erupt in chaotic forms, and any complex or archetype can manifest as easily as the latent self. Though the ego's having a particular viewpoint helps to bring order to the unconscious, it only works to a certain degree. In the first encounter with the ego, the unconscious often manifests as chaos, as a wild beast that holds great promise and danger simultaneously. The ego, representing the world of consciousness, must be prepared to deal with this imminent danger adequately, or risk failing in the work, or even worse, being overwhelmed by powers and forces it could not contain.

In order to deal with the dragon, the ego must be fully prepared and protected. For this reason it appears as a knight in full armor, with sword drawn and ready. The knight comes from the world of the city and the castle seen in the background, but has entered the deep, dark inner world in order to confront the dragon-self. There are those who underestimate the powers of the unconscious, who naively approach the imaginative worlds with the expectation that goodwill and a pleasant smile will protect them and insure experiences of light and love. There are others who believe that the imagination should be trusted above all else, and that the ego should only honor what it finds there, and never resist it or try to transform it. Both views are misguided. The ego that approaches the unconscious must be armed and ready. It must be willing to hold its position at all costs, lest it be overwhelmed. It must anticipate not light and love, but the awful tension of the transcendent function. The goal is an ecstatic one, but the way to that goal is filled with terror and struggle. The heroic attitude of the knight is a necessity. As one alchemist exclaimed: "Know also that unless you seize hold of this Nature and rule it, ye will obtain nothing."[17]

It is not the unconscious or the latent self which in themselves are dangerous, nor is it truly they which must be overcome. It is the chaos that rules at the beginning of the work that must be conquered, and this chaos is part of what the dragon represents. There needs to be order where there is none, and so the ego finds no safety in its own inner domain. One of the mercurial and chaotic aspects of active imagination is the tendency of the unconscious to create images that just won't stand still. The ego enters into an active in order to speak with a dark-haired handsome animus figure, and before two words have been exchanged, the image has transformed into a old man, and then a witch, followed by a horse that is running in a field. As this endless and chaotic shifting continues, the ego gets confused and lost. Under these circumstances, there is no real dialoguing, and no possibility of experiencing the transcendent function. Any tension that might be generated dissipates in this endless swirl of seemingly unconnected images. I have seen several cases where the randomness of images is connected with an equally haphazard influx of emotions. The ego may be taken over by one or more of these emotions and feel strange for hours or even days. Carried to an extreme, this chaos has the potential to so confuse and distract the ego that it not only forgets its

---

17. A. E. Waite, trans., *The Turba Philosophorum*, p. 96.

purpose in doing the active imagination, it can lose its connection to itself and become susceptible to possession by a complex or archetype. In order to create any real connection with an inner figure, order must be established.

The knight and his sword have several different meanings in alchemy, all of which are related to the establishment of order. The knight is the hero and represents the heroic attitude needed by the ego to deal with the dragon-chaos of the inner world. He is also the principle of order, discrimination, and unity, as is the sword that he carries. Most often, he is associated with the death of the dragon, as he is in our emblem, or the stage in alchemy known as the *mortificatio* or *putrificatio*. He slays the first matter in its primary form, in order to effect its transformation. He slays chaos by attempting to establish some kind of order within the unconscious. Edinger summarized the meaning of the sword when he wrote:

> *Swords, knives, and sharp cutting edges of all kinds belong to the symbolism of* separatio . . . *Logos is the great agent of separatio that brings consciousness and power over nature—both within and without—by its capacity to divide, name and categorize. One of its major symbols is the cutting edge that can dissect and differentiate on the one hand and can kill on the other.*[18]

The knight with his sword represents the masculine principle of Logos, the world of conscious thought and discrimination, and the ego's ability to categorize, label, evaluate, and discriminate. The cutting edge of the sword is the mind's sharpness, which separates experiences into their individual parts so that understanding may be gained. But as the ego

---

18. Edward Edinger, *Anatomy of the Psyche* (La Salle: Open Court, 1994), p. 191.

gains this understanding, it also slays the chaotic dragon, and actually sets the stage for its transmutation.

Using the example mentioned earlier, if a woman begins an active with her handsome inner masculine figure, and other figures intrude and interrupt, she must use her sword of discrimination to reject any image that does not feel related to the active she is attempting. She must reject the figure of the old man, for that brings in her father issues, and the old witch must not distract her, for that image rejects her inner lover. She must hold to her intention and purpose in order to find the image she is seeking. Having done so, she can allow it full freedom of expression without allowing the chaos of the unconscious to intrude. If she does not want to simply reject the other images, she may label them, and put them aside for later work.

As the conscious mind descends into the inner world, it brings the light of reason and discrimination, and these qualities are essential if it is to survive the descent. The sword symbolizes the ordering function of consciousness, but there is another meaning to the sword. Jung discussed the symbolism of the sword at great length, and as a result of his research, concluded that it means more than just the principle of discrimination. Referring to earlier writings of the Gnostics, Jung concluded that the "sword is very much more than an instrument which divides . . . it is the force which turns something infinitesimally small into the infinitely great. . . . What it means is the transformation of the vital spirit into the divine. The natural being becomes the divine pneuma."[19]

---

19. C. G. Jung, *Psychology and Religion: West and East,* Collected Works, vol. 11, R. F. C. Hull, trans., Bollingen Series XX (Princeton: Princeton University Press, 1969), ¶ 359.

The sword is the instrument of transformation, and symbolizes the process of change itself. Moreover, as Jung suggested, this transformation is from the purely natural human being into a divine spirit of some kind. The latent self amid all the chaos of the unconscious is human nature in its unredeemed form. However, the process of transformation that moves the latent to the manifest self transmutes human nature from its primal form into a divine essence. Human nature thus becomes divine, as the self becomes the embodiment of the divine powers in a particular human being.

The premise of my book is that Jung offered a spiritual model for the modern world, and that this model is closely related to earlier traditions such as alchemy. The main element of this model is the generation of the manifest self, which Jung described as the process of individuation. The profound implications of transforming a self are often overlooked, for it is not simply a question of being more whole, or even more unique. Manifesting a self implies the most intense inner transformation imaginable—the transformation of one's own inner nature into that of a divinity. This does not suggest that human nature be left behind, but that it finds its true depths in union with the divine. The manifestation of the self transforms the unconscious and the ego into a higher category of being. Only a thorough study of Jung's writings reveals how deeply he felt this transformation and how he envisioned it. He perceived in the movement toward individuation a progressive union of human and divine.

Seen from this perspective, the dragon symbolizes human nature in its unredeemed form. It is potential divinity, overlain with chaos and unconsciousness. This state of ignorance and discord must be slain so that a new, higher condition can be created. The dragon must die in order that the self be born. The sword then represents the principle of Logos that understands, defines, and organizes, but at the same time *is the process* of transformation itself. Through the sword and its power, the nature of the human being is transmuted into a higher, divine form.

It is the ego that carries this sword, without which there is no process of transformation. The ego is of central importance to the work, and there can be no evolution to higher levels of being and consciousness without it. The ego through its intention and will, its attention and discrimination, alters the very nature of the unconscious, ending chaos and beginning the difficult and prolonged work of self-redemption. The divine nature of the human being, hidden beneath the chaotic waters of the unconscious in the latent self, is awakened and pushed toward its own manifestation through the efforts of the ego.

The knight signifies the heroic attitude required by the ego to enter the inner world and slay the dragon of unredeemed human nature and chaos. In a very real sense, the knight is slaying himself through his efforts, for the ego will experience the death of the latent self as its own death. As the dragon dies, or is subordinated to the sword, the ego encounters the death of its own previous identity. As the alchemists knew all too well, they suffered the fate of their material. If it died, they too would experience a death, and they would endure all the torments they inflicted upon it.

I have equated the knight with the ego, but more properly the knight belongs to the principle of consciousness, as the dragon is the principle of the unconscious. The knight and the dragon are the first two opposites to emerge as the process begins. The principle of consciousness would be more than the ego; it would include theory, cultural values, collective standards of behavior, as well as a system of ethics and moral values and the like. All of these elements are represented by the symbol of the knight. The ego is the center of consciousness, and so is most clearly identified with all of its aspects, but the knight is more than the ego, just as consciousness is. In a way similar to the way in which the collective unconscious surrounds the personal unconscious, the collective consciousness surrounds the personal consciousness of an individual. Just as the collective unconscious exercises a great impact on the ego, so does the collective consciousness. Those archetypes from the collective unconscious that a particular culture has differentiated, elaborated, and made conscious form its collective consciousness. Jung called the contents of this consciousness "generally accepted truths." He also pointed out that they are in conflict with the archetypes of the collective unconscious, and between the two exists an "almost unbridgeable gulf."[20] The knight, strictly speaking, embodies the collective truths that greatly influence the ego. At this point in the work, the ego has not yet embraced its individuality, but still identifies to one degree or another with socially accepted norms and ideas. At the same time that this is a shortcoming for the ego seeking to find its own truth, it also is a strength, for it provides protection against the dissolving forces of the unconscious. A maladapted ego that has not experienced socialization and learned to share joint values has very little armor to protect itself from the power of the unconscious. Yet the ego must not totally identify with these values, as that might preclude its discovering its own ideas and beliefs.

As pointed out in the discussion of the first emblem, the ego must be flexible and able to hold a middle position, and not just take the side of the knight. The ego carries the principle of consciousness into the darkness of the

---

20. C. G. Jung, *The Structure and Dynamics of the Psyche*, Collected Works, vol. 8, R. F. C. Hull, trans., Bollingen Series XX (Princeton: Princeton University Press, 1969), ¶ 42.

unconscious and this effects transformation. But consciousness must also be seen as part of the self as it is balanced with its opposite—the unconscious.

EMBLEM THREE

The next emblem depicts a scene still within the forest. (See figure 6, page 108.) The action described is occurring within the unconscious. A deer has replaced the dragon, and a unicorn the knight. Note how the horn of the unicorn is in exactly the same position as the knight's sword in the previous emblem. The process has entered a new stage, which is symbolized by the new figures.

Though the deer seems to be a stag in the picture, the text refers to it as a deer, and it is related to the feminine world of the soul and the unconscious. The unicorn is representative of the masculine world of consciousness, and so is closely related to the knight. However, there are some paradoxes in this emblem. The feminine animal is clearly portrayed as a stag, which often symbolizes the embodiment of masculine forces. The unicorn can appear in alchemy as a symbol of the feminine because of its white color. There seems to be the suggestion that the opposites have moved closer together; the feminine animal has elements of the masculine within it, and vice versa. One could perhaps think of the yin-yang image in this context, in which some small measure of the masculine appears within the feminine symbol and the other way around. The two animals in this emblem are closer together than might first appear, and certainly they are less at war than they were in the previous picture. Some of the tension has gone into the process of unification, but the tension is not completely gone.

The philosopher's stone was known as the fugitive stag and the stag was a symbol of transformation and longevity, as it was thought to shed its antlers and therefore renew its life force so that it might live for centuries. The dragon has

Figure 6. Through the ego's efforts, an intermediate stage has been reached. The knight has been replaced by the unicorn, and the dragon is replaced by the stag/deer. Both animals represent masculine and feminine attributes indicating that the opposites, previously locked in deadly struggle, have mellowed and each has assumed aspects of the other. The ego and the unconscious have moved closer together and some of the tension within the psyche has drained away. Notice, however, the crevasse separating the two animals, indicating that the split between them is by no means resolved. (From Nicolas Banaud Delphinas, "The Book of Lambspring.")

shifted quite a bit to become the stag. It seems no longer so dark or so dangerous, and though it is by no means tame, it is much more relational than a fire-breathing poisonous dragon. There may be another way that the stag relates to the dragon, for in some myths the stag was able to reject any poison that it swallowed and so nullify its effects.[21] It is possible that the stag image in this emblem denotes the neutralization of the dragon's poison, indicating that the process has moved beyond some of its more dangerous aspects.

The fact that the unicorn has elements of masculine and feminine within it relates it to mercury, which could be either male or female. As a union of opposites, mercury symbolized the self. The unicorn, like the dragon, could easily be seen as the masculine part of the self. Its horn has replaced the sword of the knight, which also indicates a lessening of tension between the conscious mind and the unconscious. The one horn may also represent one-pointedness, a reference to the focus and organizing force of consciousness. The horn is also a reference to the quest for unity that pulls together the opposites as the self is coming into form.

All in all, this emblem indicates an intermediate point in the work. The opposites that were locked in deadly struggle have mellowed, and each has already begun to take on aspects of the other, pointing toward their eventual unification. There is a crevasse in the ground separating the two however, which indicates that although they have moved closer together, they are still separated. Some of the tension has been released, and much of the dangers of the process avoided. Reaching this stage in the process of individuation would indicate that the ego and the unconscious have become more related and less at war. There is

---

21. For a discussion of the stag, see C. G. Jung, CW 14, ¶ 188.

a cross-fertilization occurring, in which the ego is beginning to integrate the messages of the unconscious, while the unconscious, itself, has been altered by the introduction of the light of consciousness. Active imagination done at this point would be less difficult and chaotic; the image one seeks would be more accessible and stable, and less likely to disappear or alter quickly. There is also a growing sense of bonding and partnership between the ego and the self, and though it may not have reached the point of real friendship, the ego views the unconscious with less concern and more regard. In doing the actives, the ego feels more at home and at ease, and eager to experience inner contact. Though inconclusive in itself, the emblem indicates that progress is being made.

EMBLEM FOUR

The opposites have come even closer together in the next emblem (see figure 7, page 112). Notice that the crevasse in the ground has disappeared, and the two animals are standing close to each other. Moreover, though still male and female, they belong to the same species, suggesting the possibility of mating. Mating is a well-known symbol of the *coniunctio*, and it looks possible now, for appearing here for the first time is an indication that union is not far away. At the same time, these are lions, and therefore an element of wildness and ferocity has returned to the symbols. Some of the fierceness of the dragon has reappeared, but not in a chaotic or poisonous way. Rather, both animals share some of this ferocity, and their wildness indicates the depths at which transformation is occurring, while also demonstrating that the process is instinctual and outside the control of the ego.

The lion can symbolize the stone, and often is presented in texts as the equivalent of the dragon. The lion may be very dangerous and can represent devouring acidic power. In such a case, instead of being slain, the lion often has its paws cut off. The lion can refer to wild desires and to the wildness and chaos of the unconscious, but as a solar animal, it points to the masculine principle of the sun. In short, the lion has elements of both the chaotic world of the unconscious and the ordered world of consciousness. The mixture of the two elements hinted at in the previous emblem has evolved in this one, so that the same animal represents both elements. They are not at war any longer, but have come into potential union. They have each taken on the characteristics of the other to a large degree.

At this point in the work the ego and the unconscious have both dramatically changed. The ego and the principle of consciousness it represents have gotten closer to the inner world of instinct and freedom. The ego has left behind a great many of its previous rules and laws, and moved closer to the spontaneous capacity to follow inner feelings and hunches. It has abandoned many of its previous positions to take into account the advice of inner figures of all kinds, and in its new freedom, has become more wild, and less domesticated. It has added some of the unpredictability of the unconscious, and moved closer to its own inner nature. At the same time, the unconscious has moved closer to the world of consciousness by casting off its chaos and confusion, and by allowing a certain level of harmony and order to affect it. It appears related to the ego and the world of consciousness now; the dangers of the beginning of the work are only a memory. Its wildness and ferocity are now ordered by its relationship with the ego; the two are cooperating and entering into new depths of relationship. When the ego does active imagination and enters the world of the unconscious, it now feels as if it is going to meet its lover, while the figures from the unconscious are eager to help it solve its problems and find ways of going still deeper within. The first *coniunctio* in which the ego and the unconscious

Figure 7. The process has continued and the opposites are now even closer together. Notice that the crevasse in the ground has disappeared and the two animals, male and female of the same species, are standing close together. There is the real possibility of relationship in this depiction and even of mating, which would symbolize union between the opposites. Such a union is now quite close. The emblem portrays the ego and the unconscious almost as twins now capable of forging the first *coniunctio*. (From Nicolas Banaud Delphinas, "The Book of Lambspring.")

become parts of the same whole being is about to occur. The first manifestation of the self is at hand.

EMBLEM FIVE

With the appearance of the next emblem (figure 8, page 114), it might well appear that a step backward has been taken. We see tension and enmity, and the two animals—a wolf and a dog—seem to be at each other's throats. In fact, the text presented with this emblem speaks of fury and jealousy, and indicates that the two animals kill each other in their rage. Though things look bad, this is the normal course of events in alchemy. The *coniunctio* is very frequently associated with death, and the death of the two partners is often required for the true mingling of their essences. In *The Chemical Wedding of Christian Rosenkreutz*, for example, the young king and queen were beheaded at their wedding and their blood mixed together. When they are brought back to life they have been transmuted into marvelous beings.

Nicholas Flammel described a scene similar to the one in our emblem when he wrote that the Coruscene dog and the Armenian bitch were to be put in the sepulcher (the alchemical vessel):

> *These two . . . do bite one another cruelly, and by their great poison and furious rage they never leave one another from the moment that they have seized on one another . . . till both of them by their slavering venom and mortal hurts be all of a gore-blood, over all the parts of their bodies, and finally, killing one another, be stewed in their proper venom, which after their death changeth them into living and* permanent water.[22]

---

22. Nicholas Flammel, *Alchemical Hieroglyphics* (Berkeley Heights, CA: Heptangle Books, n.d.), p. 45.

Figure 8. The two animals are now a dog and a wolf locked in fero-
cious battle. In fact, they kill each other in their rage. Though it might
appear that a disastrous regression from the last picture has taken place,
actually union demands the death of the old form, and is never without violence. Yet bloody as it is, the *coniunctio* has taken place. Notice
in the background two unmistakable indications of union. A bridge
has been built connecting the two banks of the river, and where once
there was only forest there are now city buildings. A transformation
of the unconscious has taken place, but at the cost of the death of
previous ego identification and of the self's latent condition. (From
Nicolas Banaud Delphinas, "The Book of Lambspring.")

The *coniunctio* is not a very gentle thing, but correlated with death, violence, dismemberment, and gore. The reader might well wonder if indeed we have arrived at the conjunction so long sought after, or if in fact there has been a regression of some kind. At times alchemists will place their chapters and emblems in the wrong order just to fool the uninitiated. Could that be the case with this emblem? Unfortunately, it is not. Not only does the symbolism of the *coniunctio* often present itself violently, there are images in this emblem that show that the first union has occurred.

The image in the background of the emblem takes us back to the first picture in which there was a body of water. On the right bank was a castle and a city, and on the left the forest. Note the change in this picture; the city has crossed over to the left bank that now has several man-made structures on it. More importantly, there is now a bridge connecting the two banks. The boats have all but disappeared, as they are no longer needed now that there is a bridge. Bridges are symbols of connection, and the appearance of the bridge in this emblem announces that the first *coniunctio* has been achieved. The worlds of the unconscious and consciousness are now joined; they are bridged by the union that has occurred and are much more interrelated. Moreover, the left side of the unconscious has been transformed and now has structures of consciousness within it. These structures, and the bridge connecting the banks, point to the formation of the manifest self, for the whole psyche now is unified.

Why, then, do so much blood and gore characterize such a happy development? The alchemical enterprise is, like most spiritual journeys, based on the theme of death and rebirth. There is no growth without a previous death, or, as the alchemists liked to put it, there can be no generation without putrefaction. In the individuation process, that truth also prevails. For the ego to enter into a true partnership and union with the unconscious, it must die to its previous state of being and consciousness. No matter how much it desires this union, and no matter how prepared it has become, the experience of union is a jolt and brings first death before new life. I remember joking with friends years ago that whenever a big change occurred within my psychic life something awful in the world would happen. It was predictable and always ushered in unpleasant feelings and situations. My first experience of union was instantly followed by kidney stones and the hell that only they can create. The death that the ego must undergo is a very real experience and most unpleasant. There can be no passage from one state of being to another without dying.

Moreover the unconscious passes through a death as well. The wolf and the dog kill each other. The latent self has already faced death at the hands of the knight, when its pernicious and dangerous characteristics were altered. Had death occurred for the knight instead, that would have meant that the ego had been overwhelmed and no *coniunctio* would have occurred. The first death must be dealt to the chaos of the unconscious self, but the second death alters it yet again. This second death seems to me to denote the self's coming into consciousness. I suspect that entering the world of the ego is very much a death for the self, and much of the imagery around lost paradise points to this fact. Entering into relationship with the ego means that the self leaves its unconscious paradise behind in order to come into the "real world." This union of course occurs within the imaginal realm, but the ego brings with it all the cares and needs related to ordinary life, and for the self to come to terms with these things is a major transformation. The buildings that appear on the left bank in this emblem could signify that the world of ordinary life is now part of the unconscious. I recall Dr. von Franz speaking of the need for the unconscious to learn about the ego and discover what limitation and restriction are all about; this learning process would be its death experience.

The two animals in the image that must die are the dog and the wolf. Nicholas Flammel in the quote mentioned earlier refers to the Corascene dog, which is a well-known alchemical symbol. In fact, Jung discussed this image at great length in *Mysterium Coniunctionis*. He believed that all the references to the Corascene dog and its union with another animal, wolf, or dog, derive from the *Liber Secretorum* of Calid. The original passage is worth quoting:

> *Hermes said, My son, take a Corascene dog and an Armenian bitch, join them together, and they will beget a dog of celestial hue, and if ever he is thirsty, give him sea water to drink: for he will guard your friend, and he will guard you from your enemy, and he will help you wherever you may be, always being with you, in this world and in the next.*[23]

Jung wrote extensively on the meaning of the dog of celestial hue and finally concluded that this dog is the same as the self, "At once bright as day and dark as night, a perfect *coincidentia oppositorum* expressing the divine nature of the self."[24]

The dog is a domesticated animal and "man's best friend." This aspect of the dog is conveyed by the nature of the puppy that is celestial, for in that image the self is presented in the form of a guardian spirit that will protect and guide one, not only in life but in the world after life as well. The self born of the first *coniunctio* is friend to the ego and a guardian spirit of sorts. However, as Jung pointed out, there is still a certain ambivalence about the self, for it contains within it the wolf as well. The wolf is

---

23. C. G. Jung, CW 14, ¶ 174.
24. C. G. Jung, CW 14, ¶ 176.

a slightly more tame form of the lion, but it still represents something of the wildness of the unconscious and its powers and effects. Thus, though the dog is companion and protector, it has much of the wolf about it as well. The self may never be bent to the will of the ego, nor ever truly tamed. It offers friendship as a free and equal partner, never as a servant. If the ego is able to return that offer in kind, the *coniunctio* can take place.

This emblem as a whole is a very nice expression of the transcendent function. The attitude of the ego must die, as must the position of the unconscious, in order that a third unifying position develops. The transcendent function itself would be imaged in the bridge that unifies the two positions, yielding the new binding experience.

The ego that has reached this level in the work will have the nasty surprise of meeting its own death. If it is fluid and open enough to allow that experience to occur unhindered, it will quickly move to the next stage. The unconscious is now not only more accessible, it has transmuted and become part of the manifest self. I have written previously that the ego is part of the manifest self and this is accurate. Experientially, however, the ego does not feel lost in a greater whole, but rather as if an inner friend has been created, a friend with whom it can share its life. The inner friend is guide and protector, and will teach the ego what it needs to know, and provide it with all that it requires. The friend is not a magical familiar who does whatever the ego may require, but a guiding companion that creates the experiences that both it and the ego need to continue to grow. Within the psyche, where heretofore there had been two divergent forces, there are now two friends, united on the same path and having the same goals.

The first *coniunctio* thus creates a major transformation within the psyche, yielding two major components united with each other. However, the first *coniunctio* is a transitory experience, for the self is not yet strong enough to manifest all the time. It is still relatively weak compared to the other forces within the unconscious, and so it appears and then disappears. This is unfortunately a most frustrating experience for most people. Having tasted the reality of union with the self, it is most disheartening and even agonizing to lose it. Faced with this great loss, most people believe that they have done something terribly wrong to make the self go away again, and will often put intense pressure on themselves to be "perfect" enough to have the self remain with them. Each time the self disappears, they scrutinize their life and behavior to locate their mistake, for they are sure they must have committed one. The only mistake lies in the scrutinizing itself, for it throws the ego into one or more complexes, or triggers a phase of self-criticism and recrimination; all of which, naturally, make it harder than ever to experience the self.

In order to navigate this phase of the work one must bear in mind that the self cannot remain in contact with the ego for long. It manifests in an experience that the ego will enjoy, and then it will disappear to the ego's horror. The ego must accept this pain and expect the periodic disappearance of its friend. This may sound easy to those who have not had the experience, but it is an ordeal at best. Nevertheless, it is part of the process and any overreaction on the part of the ego makes things much worse. The first *coniunctio* therefore moves gradually to the second, with periodic manifestations of the self followed by shorter or longer periods in which it is absent.

EMBLEM 6

The dragon reappears in the next emblem (figure 9, page 120). Recall that the alchemists always viewed their work as being about one substance, one matter: the *prima materia* that becomes the stone. The dragon is this *prima materia* and,

Figure 9. Though the first *coniunctio* has taken place, the self is not strong enough to remain in relationship with the ego for very long. There are periods of relationship followed by periods in which the self disappears within the unconscious once more. In this emblem, the dragon reappears as the *uroboros*. The self is fully absorbed with its inner transformation and purification and its gaze is directed at itself. It is busy with its own development so that it may move from the first to the second *coniunctio*. At times like these, the ego cannot participate in the processes that are unfolding but must wait patiently for its partner to reappear. (From Nicolas Banaud Delphinas, "The Book of Lambspring.")

as such, is the self. In its first appearance, it was the latent self, with all its chaos that the knight of conscious discrimination had to slay. It now reappears as the self that has already experienced the transformations we have been discussing. The emblem takes us back into the forest, and the crevasse in the ground that had disappeared is once more in place. This emblem illustrates the process that is occurring within the self when it has disappeared from the ego's world and is no longer consciously felt. The ego experiences its loss, as the self is busy in a process deep within the unconscious.

I mentioned that the self is unable to maintain its own manifestation at first, for it lacks the requisite strength and durability. Having experienced the first *coniunctio*, it immediately sets in motion those processes by which it can create the second, more permanent, manifestation. In order to do this, it separates from the ego and becomes completely centered upon itself.

The dragon appears, biting its own tail, and this is the well-known symbol of the *uroboros*. The *uroboros* has a variety of meanings, and is a widespread motif in alchemy. In early Greek alchemy it represented the unity of all life as it manifests in time. It was thus eternal movement and development.[25] At the same time, it could symbolize a guardian at the gate who had to be destroyed if the alchemists were to gain the arcane medicine they sought. Jung thought that *uroboros* meant "nothing other than the *deus absconditus*, the god hidden in matter."[26]

The uroboric image in this emblem does not refer to the initial state, nor is it cosmic in its implications. The text

---

25. For a full discussion see Jack Lindsay, *The Origins of Alchemy in Graeco-Roman Egypt* (New York: Barnes and Noble, 1970).
26. C. G. Jung, CW 13, ¶ 138.

informs us that the dragon is eating its own tail and devouring its own poison. The symbol indicates that the self is fully absorbed with its inner transformation and purification, and that its gaze is directed at itself. There are certain processes that can occur within the psyche that the ego is not involved in directly, and this is one such process. I have seen this in clients' dreams when an inner image, most often related to the self, is busy with tasks in which the dream ego cannot participate. I recall one dream in which the dreamer went down into his basement and discovered workmen busily redoing his furnace and plumbing. He was told that there was nothing he could do, and that the plumbing would be fixed when the pope was on his throne. In the events going on in the dream, the self is attempting to repair a serious inner problem, and the ego is not directly involved. As the alchemists knew quite well, only the self can create itself. At this point in the work, the ego has done all it could. It must deal with the pain of the absence of its friend, but other than that, it can only wait for this self-process to run its course and reach its own conclusion.

EMBLEM SEVEN

The process continues with the next emblem (figure 10, page 124). Once more there appear two living creatures, but they are not animals; this time they are birds. This emblem is quite complex, and has several different symbols worth discussing. First of all, the scene is in the forest, but higher up than previously, on a hill or small mountain. The birds are in the tree; one is trying to fly away without success, and the other sitting in the nest. A snail sits beneath the tree, and in the distance there is a house or a castle.

Any time alchemical imagery takes one to the heights, on a mountain, or hill, or soaring in the air with birds, one is dealing with the process known as the *sublimatio*. Sublimation separates the spirit from the body, and allows the spirit to fly into the spiritual realm. While the spirit remains aloft, the body is purified and readied for the eventual return of the spirit. The spirit in alchemy is separated only for a short time; the body and spirit must be reunited for the process to be complete. The symbols portray a union of opposites as one bird sits in the nest and the other is trying to fly away. The written commentary makes it clear that a state of union exists between the two birds; a state the author calls matrimony. Though the process is continuing, the first level of union has by no means been lost. It still binds the two partners together in a marriage, albeit there is clearly tension between them.

The conjunction between the bird that flies and the one that does not is similar to the winged and wingless dragon, and in alchemy is called the uniting of the fixed and the volatile. The first *coniunctio* has been accomplished, but the problem remains that the self is volatile, for it cannot stay in conscious connection with the ego for very long. Despite the best efforts of the ego to pay attention, the self comes and goes with frustrating inconstancy. The old tendency within the latent self to sink below the waters of the collective unconscious where chaos reigns has been tempered, but not fully resolved. A process must occur to fix the self in place, so that it functions as a new center without interruption, and may be easily accessed by the ego.

The reason that the self remains volatile so long is not completely clear, but the fixing of the self requires a further transformation of the psyche. When this is fully accomplished, the process has reached the second conjunction. This is symbolized in the emblem by the bird on the left that cannot fly away any longer, and is now in permanent connection with its mate.

The image of the bird is used to portray the issue of uniting the fixed and the volatile, and to indicate the need to hold the self in place long enough for a new union to

Figure 10. In order to move from the first to the second *coniunctio*, the self must be "fixed" so that it does not lose connection with the ego. Notice that in this emblem two animals have returned as two birds. One is in the nest, or alchemical vessel, and the other is trying to fly away but is tied fast to the nest. The text says:

> *The one that is below holds the one that is above,*
> *And will not let it get away from the nest,*
> *As a husband in a house with his wife*
> *Bound together in closest bonds of wedlock.*

Through the marriage of the first *coniunctio* and the processes that follow, the self is bound fast to the ego and fixation has occurred. (Illustration and quote from Nicolas Banaud Delphinas, "The Book of Lambspring," in *The Hermetic Museum,* p. 288.)

occur. The bird as a symbol in alchemy generally relates to soul and spirit, and can also be seen as a mediator between earth and heaven. As the elevation onto high ground indicates a movement into the spiritual realm, or a process of sublimation, the two birds also symbolize the union of the soul and spirit. This union reflects Dorn's characterization of the first *coniunctio*, which he also referred to as the *unio mentalis*, or the mental union. He warned that the first union "does not make a man wise," for this level of union is still transitory and ungrounded. The process of fixation attempts to redress this difficulty.

Jung wrote that fixation in Chinese alchemy was related to circulation. Through the process of circulation all the different parts of the psyche become ordered around a common center.[27] In a later essay he further explained the role of fixation in Western alchemy:

> The "fixation" refers alchemically to the lapis but psychologically to the consolidation of feeling. The distillate must be fixed and held fast, must become a firm conviction and a permanent content.[28]

The union of the two birds in marriage is the symbolic portrayal of the mental union. One bird joined or fixed to the other suggests that the consistent experience of the first union makes the self more permanent and more alive in the ego's awareness. Jung indicated that the process included feeling, conviction, and the establishment of the self as a permanent content.

The ego must work on feeling the self and on paying attention to the feelings generated in interactions with it. By closely monitoring these feelings, the ego contributes

---

27. C. G. Jung, CW 13, ¶ 37–38.
28. C. G. Jung, CW 13, ¶ 222.

what it can to the process of fixation. I do not equate "feeling" in this sense with emotion. Instead, I mean the felt experience of the presence and manifestation of the self. During the first conjunction, the ego has engaged with the unconscious often enough in active imagination that the self has come into being. Now the attention of the ego shifts to the self and the feelings that its presence generates. If it can feel the self, then it is in conscious union with it, and if it cannot, then it has lost the conscious connection. The felt perception of the presence and communication of the self provides a measure of one's actual union with it.

The feelings that the self generates at this stage are very clear and marked; they are different than those produced by any other part of the psyche. Such feelings include an inner sense of solidity, an experience of being centered, a more or less ecstatic sensation of being loved and of loving in return, and a penetrating awareness of inner partnership. Such feelings are unique to the experience of the self. When the ego begins to have them, it knows it is well on the way to union. As mentioned earlier, however, these feelings come and go in the first stage of union. The ego must be open to them as much as possible when they do occur. By focusing its awareness on them, and responding to them in some way, the ego helps to strengthen the felt sense of the self that is part of the fixation process.

In addition, the ego must hold to the conviction that it is in union with the self, and to act in that fashion even when it cannot feel the self's presence. The frustration arising at the self's disappearance can be tempered by the ego's knowing that, although the feelings have gone, the union has not. It must trust the self to reappear when it can, and, rather than focus on its absence, should focus on the realization that union, once attained, cannot disappear. I counsel people going through this difficult part of the process to act as if they could feel the self, to talk with it, and to look for answers despite the sense of its being gone. The ego's firm conviction that the self is present and, though not felt, still in union with it, acts as *theoria* does to bring about the desired experience. A strong trust and a confident patience also contribute to the process of fixation.

Finally, in the most pronounced shift that one encounters in this process, the self ceases to be temporary and becomes a permanent content. One no longer has to struggle to feel it, for with just a modicum of attention, it is present and alive in one's awareness. Dialogue is easy to initiate, feelings are clear and intense, and the partnership is alive and well. When fixation reaches this level, the first union passes to the second. In Dorn's terms, the spirit and soul, now unified, are reunited with the body; they become grounded and fixed in a permanent form.

The nest in the emblem symbolizes the vessel in which the alchemist's creative processes occur. Within the vessel of the psyche something is being hatched. It is the union of the two birds, the ego and the self, and is a new level of being, which the self experiences as it moves to the second level of union. However, as always in alchemy, this new birth of the fixed and permanent self only occurs after another death experience.

EMBLEM EIGHT

In the next emblem (figure 11 on page 128), the two birds are devouring each other. In fact, once more the two opposites slay each other in preparation for a new birth. As should be clear by now, there is never a movement to a new stage of individuation without the death of the previous one. Nothing new is gained without the sacrifice of the old. The change from the first *coniunctio* to the second is no exception, and the death experience at this level of the work is very disconcerting and unpleasant. Indeed, so daunting is the prospect of having to sacrifice what has

Figure 11. In this emblem the two birds devour each other. Just as the creation of the first *coniunctio* engendered death and violence, so does the movement from the first to the second. All that had been won must now be sacrificed, so that a new relationship emerges. From the beginning of the work to the creation of the second *coniunctio* all union is followed by death, which is then followed by more permanent union. The two birds bound in wedlock now destroy each other so that both partners are transformed in rebirth, and a new, permanent union is created. (From Nicolas Banaud Delphinas, "The Book of Lambspring.")

been gained, some individuals will stop their growth at this point rather than lose what they have already achieved.

The experience of the first level is an intense and meaningful experience. People who have attained this level are aware of the presence of the self in their lives, and use that awareness to cultivate a vital and engaging way of life. I recall the case of one man whose life was completely altered by his interaction with the unconscious that gave rise to temporary, but profound, experiences of the self. He gave up a bad marriage, quit a job he no longer liked, and began teaching that he loved. He also developed a creative gift he did not know he had, and was thoroughly enjoying his life. At this point, he stopped analysis to cultivate all that he had gained in the outer world. About a year after stopping analysis, he returned with some disturbing dreams about death and the end of the world. In fact, the self was pushing toward the next level. I tried to assure him that, though such a development would certainly create new changes in his life, it would be even better than the life he was living. But he could not accept such statements, and finally, refusing any further work, he terminated analysis once again.

Such cases are not rare. Sometimes the individual can get away with the refusal to take the next step, and sometimes the pressure from the self is so great that he or she has no choice but to take it. The point is that because so much has already been gained, its sacrifice is almost overwhelming. Yet without such a sacrifice, one never reaches the next level.

The self, too, undergoes a death experience. Although I cannot fathom how it might experience such an event, its apparent death is even more distressing to the ego. This stage of the work might well correspond to the second dark night of the soul, about which St. John of the Cross wrote. He described the torment of a very advanced soul, when God suddenly seems to disappear. Keep in mind that the self, or God, is a felt presence and not just a concept for someone at this level who tastes the self, knows it person-ally, and feels it in their consciousness with a great deal of joy. For all that to be taken away is almost more than one can bear. The tension and *mortificatio* occasioned by the on-going evolution to the second *coniunctio* is thus a very dif-ficult and taxing experience.

Notice, too, that the boat has returned to its middle position in the water. Throughout the difficulties caused by the evolution toward a new union, the ego must still strive to retain its central position, and stay firmly rooted in the belief system from which it operates. Whatever anguish is created by the death experience is lessened by the knowledge that it is meaningful and part of one's engagement in the overall process. Having a map with which to chart the chop-py and dangerous waters not only gives one a way to sur-vive them, but some hope that the trials will not last forever.

EMBLEM NINE

The next emblem (figure 12, page 132) illustrates the break-through to the second *coniunctio*. The king sits on his throne holding an orb with the cross above, a symbol of author-ity and harmony. There are seven steps leading to the throne, the seven stages of the alchemical enterprise. The king sits with his feet on the body of the dragon, a sure sign of his mastery over chaos and capacity to effect or-der. There is a single fish to his left, and this image takes us back to the first emblem. The fish being present in this scene demonstrates that the king began as the fish, and that the process is complete from beginning to end. The king is referred to in the text as the king of the forest, and the dragon was originally called the beast in the forest. Keep-ing in mind that alchemical work deals with only one sub-stance throughout all of its changes, the king would be the fish that became the dragon, and then, through the tran-scendent function, was transformed into the king.

The background scene is now filled with houses, and the city surrounds the water, with its predominately placed bridge. There is still a boat in the water, but now it is surrounded by the signs of human development all around it. The forest has become part of the city, and the self has grown to include the entire unconscious.

The king is a common alchemical symbol. In general, he is the image of the philosopher's stone at various stages of the work. Every aspect of the king's appearance marks him as extraordinary. He is exalted on his throne, raised above the plane of ordinary people. His orb denotes that he rules the whole world, and his crown suggests the rays of the sun and his enlightenment. In the context of our series of emblems, the king embodies the philosopher's stone that emerges from the processes depicted in the pictures. A parallel meaning for the king is found in the words of Henry Khunrath:

> *When at last . . . the ash-colour, the whitening, and the yellowing are over, you will see the Philosophical Stone, our King and Lord of Lords, come forth from the couch and throne of his glassy sepulchre onto the stage of this world, in his glorified body, regenerated and more than perfect, shining like a carbuncle, and crying out, "Behold, I make all things new."*[29]

Khunrath's religious ecstasy is worthy of note. He describes creating the stone, a spiritual experience of profound intensity. The manifest self has now fully emerged, and has been established in the psyche as a permanent content and state of being. The impermanence of the previous union with the self has been replaced by a fixed and unmoving connection that may be accessed at any time.

---

29. Quoted in C. G. Jung, CW 14, ¶ 355. (From *Amphitheatrum sapientiae*, Hanau, Germany, 1609.)

Figure 12. At last, the inner alchemist has attained the second *coniunctio*. The king sits on his throne holding an orb with the cross above, a symbol of authority and harmony. He has his feet on the body of the dragon, a sure sign of his mastery over chaos. The king is the symbol of the philosopher's stone and the manifest self. Notice that the background is filled with houses, and a large bridge has returned, while the forest has become part of the city. The self has grown to include the whole unconscious and, because the ego is part of the manifest self, includes the world of consciousness as well. This emblem is a masterly portrayal of the goal of inner alchemy: the self, whole and triumphant. (From Nicolas Banaud Delphinas, "The Book of Lambspring.")

It is not an easy task to put into words the nature of such an accomplishment. It is not, however, an ideal state which one can aim for but never realize, for the experience of the permanent establishment of the self in the psyche is obtainable, though only after the most arduous work. There are many ways in which this development might be described, but there are at least three that should be mentioned.

Dorn called the second *coniunctio* the bodily union, and this reference is very significant. To move from the mental union to the bodily union indicates that integration has occurred; that is, what had previously been only an idea has become a living reality. The idea of uniting the opposites has become a fact of one's life. One does not have to struggle to achieve balance, or find a way to pull together the opposites any longer, for they are balanced and exist harmoniously, regulated by the manifest self that has come into being. The union of opposites has become an established fact in the self, and the ego now only has to stay in relationship with the self in order to stay balanced.

Take the case of a man who has attempted to remain in touch with his own feminine nature in order to express feelings and honor relationships. His ego may have to pay close attention at first to any feelings that arise spontaneously and find a way to give voice to them. In fact, the ego may not even have been aware of the feelings at first, and would have had to struggle to make them conscious. All of this required a great deal of conscious effort, active imagination work, and risk-taking in the outer world. But if the self is embodied, masculine and feminine are part of it. The ego does not have to hunt for feelings, or devise ways of expressing them; it must only stay in touch with the self. At the appropriate moment, the self will move into the feminine mode, and the ego will become aware of this fact, and allow the more feminine expression to manifest. This may sound idealized, and to be sure, complexes may always reappear to block the process described, but in essence it is an accurate description. Because the self is whole and contains all things within it, and since it is fully awake and active in the psyche, the ego must simply stay aware of it, and give voice to the inner movement that it detects. There is no need for struggle or intense effort. The ego and the self act as two partners in the experience of life. Symbolically, the description of the *tao* and of being in the *tao*, as portrayed in Chinese philosophy, would come close to this psychic experience.

Secondly, the self is the repository of knowledge, and the ego in relationship to the manifest self is connected to this knowledge. But the wisdom of the self is not intellectual knowledge, but a felt wisdom, in which the essence of things, of situations, and of people is directly accessed. The ego living with the self that is embodied does not have to think or wonder or question; it can feel the essence of things and what it needs in the moment. The ego feels when it is right to express feelings, and withdraws when it is right to be withdrawn; it feels when it must be active and when to remain passive; it feels when to go forward and when to stay behind. All that it requires comes to it as an experience of knowing, and this knowledge is beyond question. In such a condition, correct and incorrect have no meaning, for one feels what must be done and does it. The word "feeling" does not quite capture the nature of the experience I am discussing, but it is the closest word in English. By feeling the self and its messages, the ego remains in union with the new psychic center that has come into being.

There is a third way to understand this stage of the work. Within the realm of imagination, all is experienced through images and the interaction with them. The first emblem indicated that the content of the self was about to manifest, but needed an appropriate image with which to do so. The king who has emerged in this emblem may be seen as the symbol for the self that has become fixed and firm. The "body" in bodily union may be understood as referring to the image that personifies the self. With the establishment of this stage of the union, the image of the self has become permanent.

In the chapter on imagination, I pointed out that the image of an entity or inner figure is the same as that thing, not merely a symbol, so that the image of the self *is* the self. Within the imaginative realm, therefore, the self that has been created *is* an inner figure of great wisdom and power. All that has been accomplished in the alchemical work is embodied in that image. The ego thus finds it possible to experience union with the manifest self as an ongoing active imagination with the inner figure that has now appeared.

During the work with the opposites and active imagination, the inner figure of the self has undergone successive transformations. It has had to include within itself these diverse opposites, and as a result has become more powerful. With the attainment of this stage of the work, the figure has become fixed. The inner figure is now operative constantly within the imagination, and unlike other inner figures that remain present for only a certain period of time, this figure never changes or fades away.

Because this image is so strong, the ego finds it very easy to contact. The figure is available at a moment's notice, and this availability makes Marie-Louise von Franz's idea that the individuated person lives in the world of active imagination easier to grasp. The inner figure of the self is present to the ego day or night, in meditation or in engagement with outer world activities. The union between them is so fixed that dialogues are ongoing throughout the day, and the individual finds himself living in this union.

An inner figure can impact the psyche in very powerful ways. Even when the ego is in a complex, that figure stands outside the complex, and has the power to influence the mental state of the ego, as well as the condition of the psyche as a whole. The self also has this power, multiplied greatly. The self can penetrate and alter the current state of the ego. If the ego has encountered a complex, or an outer world situation that is depressing, it can turn to the self to have its mood lifted, and to gain information about how to handle the situation. Its partner is always present to impact it with a felt sense, with information, or just with its healing presence.

The manifest self is thus the culmination of the individuation process, integrating all the efforts that went into that process. It communicates with a direct and clear wisdom which the ego experiences as a certainty of knowing, and it personifies itself as an inner figure with which the ego lives in an inner marriage. The bliss of this marriage, and the ecstasy of union with the self, colors the life of the individual experiencing it. Such an individual engages with life from the center. However, the work is not yet over. Both Dorn and the author of *The Book of Lambspring* indicate that further transformation is possible. Hard as it is to imagine that further potential exists for growth and spiritual development, there is yet the third *coniunctio* to achieve.

EMBLEM TEN

With the next emblem (figure 13, page 138), the movement toward the third *coniunctio* commences. The animal symbolism returns with the image of the salamander in the fire, which has been placed there by a human figure. This figure may be a reference to Vulcan, the god of fire, or may be the alchemist, himself, performing the work on the stone.

According to mythology, the salamander is a creature that thrives in the fire and makes its home there. Jung pointed out that the salamander was almost the equivalent to the fire.[30] However, it is also true that the salamander denoted the fixed aspect of the self that was stronger than fire. As one alchemist wrote, "Our stone is an astral fire, which sympathizes with the natural fire, which as a true salamander receives its nativity, is nourished and grows in the elementary fire."[31] The salamander symbolized the manifest self in its fixity; the self or the stone was strong enough at this stage of the work to enter the fire without changing.

The goal at this point of the work is not another death, or the destruction of that which has been won, because permanence was achieved in the second union. Since the process, no matter how intense it gets, can no longer destroy the self, the salamander is a fitting symbol for the self at this stage. Fire is perhaps the most important symbol in alchemy, and remains one of the central mysteries of the alchemists. There are many types of fire, and many meanings that fire can have. From the Jungian perspective, fire has been interpreted to mean intense passion, or desires that must be frustrated to fuel the process of transformation.[32] Though this interpretation may be accurate for one type of fire, and for one stage of the work, it is not accurate in regard to fire at this particular stage. Since the self has already been created, the frustration of desire no longer has any meaning. The ego acts from the place of union with the self and not from any desire to feed its own narcissistic needs, or to move toward self-aggrandizement. Fire at this stage of the work must be seen in a different light.

---

30. C. G. Jung, CW 13, ¶ 177.
31. *The Lives of the Alchemystical Philosphers* (London: John M. Watkins, 1955), p. 216.
32. See Edward Edinger, *Anatomy of the Psyche.*

Figure 13. With this emblem the movement toward the third *coniunctio* begins. The alchemist, or perhaps the god Vulcan, symbolizing the power of fire, has placed a salamander in the fire. The salamander is a creature that thrives in a fire which never destroys it. It thus symbolizes the fixed and permanent manifest self that does not die as it moves toward the next level of union, for it has achieved permanency and immortality. Yet it is not stagnant, but thrives in the fires of inner processes as it draws closer to union with the divine. (From Nicolas Banaud Delphinas, "The Book of Lambspring.")

The symbolism of fire is so complex that a simplistic interpretation does not suffice. However, there is one major motive that is most relevant to our emblem. Fire is often seen as a spiritual force of hidden or occult power. Eirenaeus Philalethes, in "Introitus apertus," calls fire the "secret infernal fire, the wonder of the world, the system of higher powers in the lower."[33] *Mercurius* is often equated with the fire, and as such, he is called the "fire in which God himself burns in divine love."[34] In other words, fire is a spiritual principle that acts in such a way as to create transformation. It fuels the process, and need not be created by the frustration of desire or in any other conscious act, for it emerges from within the spiritual world itself. It is certainly related to the symbolism of the self, and might be thought of as the inner power of the self to create its own transmutation.

The salamander is the manifest self that can survive any process, no matter how intense, and the fire is the manifestation of its own drive to transform. At this stage of the work, the fire does not just belong to the manifest self, however. The references to the fire of God and to the higher powers being hidden in the lower, suggest that the process is being fueled, not only by the self, but also by the divinity that exists beyond the self. The process by which the third *coniunctio* comes into being aims at a new union of opposites—the union of the human and the divine. As Dorn explained it, this level of union binds the individual to the *unus mundus*, the world of pure spirit and divine unity. The motivating force for this merger comes not only from the

---

33. C. G. Jung, CW 13, ¶ 257. (From "Introitus apertus," in *The Hermetic Museum*, p. 654.)
34. C. G. Jung, CW 13, ¶ 257. (From Barcius, "Gloria Mundi," in *The Hermetic Museum*, p. 246.)

individual self, but from God itself, as the two entities are pulled together in the highest of all marriages. The fire is the spiritual force creating a final transformation in the self, through which the divine is incarnated in the human psyche.

EMBLEM ELEVEN

The first effect of the fire becomes clear as we move to the next emblem (figure 14, page 142). There are now three human figures where previously there had only been the king. The young man is the prince, son of the king, and is related to the motif of the *filius*. The *filius*, or son, is used often by the alchemists to refer to the stone, as when they term it the *filius philosophorum*, or speak of the son of the sun, and so forth. The *filius* is often discussed in ecstatic and spiritual terms. One alchemist wrote:

> *This is the* filius solis, *child of the sun, who with his singular power works miracles and great wonders, and can expell all sicknesses in human and metallic bodies. With glorified body, flesh and blood, he purifies all that is corporeal. The immortal Adam, highly endowed. . . .*[35]

I have identified the king as an inner figure personifying and embodying the self. The process that has led to the second *coniunctio* can be seen as the progressive transformation of this inner figure that incarnated more and more of the self. The self, in turn, has gained in strength through the unification of the opposites. The prince may also be looked upon as an imaginal figure, which could be interpreted in several ways. The interpretation that strikes me as most compelling is that the son of the self is the personifica-

---

35. Figulus, *A Golden and Blessed Casket of Nature's Marvels* (Kila, MT: Kessinger, n.d.), p. 333.

tion of the divinity that seeks the third *coniunctio*. Every emblem that follows will be best understood as relating to the establishment of the third level of union, which unites the individual self with the hidden divine world that stands behind our ordinary world. I have already indicated that figures may personify spiritual entities who do not originate within the psyche, but originate in the world of nonordinary reality that I have termed the psychoid.

The son of the self is an image personifying a psychoidal entity that is closely related to the self. The self, ready to unite with the *unus mundus* (or the psychoid world), experiences an image that personifies a being of the psychoid with whom it can unite. There is a psychoid figure that is closely related to the self, which I have termed the ally.[36] The ally is so affiliated to the self is that one of my colleagues in Denver who has been studying this subject for years considers the ally the self of the psychoid realm.

The notion of the psychoid postulates that there is a realm of spiritual forces and powers that does not belong to the psyche. According to the Sufis, there is a human world and a world of pure spirit, and an intermediate world of the imagination in which those two worlds can interact. They do so through the personification of spiritual beings in the imagination, which appear as imaginal figures. The psychoid world is not a world of pure spirit, but a realm in which the physical and the spiritual are united. The psychoid imagination experiences entities that are not purely psychic, but that have their own semi-physical reality. In this sense, the psychoid is a realm of subtle bodies.

---

36. Jeffrey Raff, "The Ally" in Donald Sandner and Steven Wong, eds. *The Sacred Heritage* (New York: Routledge, 1997), pp. 111–121.

Figure 14. There are now three human figures in this emblem. The king is joined by his "son" and a wisdom figure who represents the transcendent function and the power of transformation. The son of the king is the inner figure personifying the ally, or the individual manifestation of the Divinity. The son wishes to unite with his father, who holds his hand, while both are guided by the wise old man who, with his wings, represents spirit and its wisdom. The son is at once joined to the king, and to the world of spirit. The ally unites with the manifest self, but remains linked to the wisdom of God, which may be likened to the Holy Spirit or Sophia. (From Nicolas Banaud Delphinas, "The Book of Lambspring.")

The relationship between the self and God is often debated. Jung felt that the figure of the self was indistinguishable from the inner God image,[37] which is true, as far as it goes. If, however, we are formulating the idea that there is a divine being outside the psyche, the self must be differentiated from this being. Yet it seems that divinity and the self are very closely related. Taking the idea of the *filius* as an image of the self of the psychoid means that the divinity personified in this figure occupies a central position in the psychoid world, and is capable of development and its own individuation, just as the self is. Moreover, it seems that the self of the psychoid needs union with the human self in order to effect its own transformation.

C. G. Jung mentions that Dorn believed that the ultimate development of the self requires its union with the spiritual world, a world that exists outside the individual self.[38] The means by which this is effected in the world of imagination is through interaction with and relationship to an imaginal figure that embodies and personifies the center of that divine world—the *filius* or the ally. The alchemists saw in the *filius* a divine entity of some kind. Some alchemical texts relate the *filius* to the figure of Christ, so much so that Jung wrote that the "light or *filius philosophorum* was openly named the greatest and most victorious of all lights, and set alongside Christ as the Savior and Preserver of the world!"[39] For a great many of the alchemists, the *filius* was an embodiment of the divine.

In my view, the key to the union at the third level is through the imaginative experience of the *filius*. Like all spiritual entities, the ally personifies itself as an imaginal

---

37. C. G. Jung, CW 9ii, ¶ 320.
38. C. G. Jung, CW 14, ¶ 759–760. From Dorn's *Theatrum Chemicum*.
39. C. G. Jung, CW 13, ¶ 163.

figure. Unlike the other inner figures, this psychoidal figure feels as if it were independent of the psyche, and acts to bring the psyche into relationship with that which transcends the psyche. The ally figure is the personification of the self of the psychoid, whose relationship with the self is indicated by its being the son of the king.

The relationship between these two figures is complex and largely unexplored. At the third level, when the human and the divine are to be wed, the symbolism does not portray the union of opposites, though it does portray a conjunction. It is possible that the personal self and the self of the psychoid are not in opposition, but are actually very closely related; in fact, they are presented as father and son. There are other traditions in which these two figures are depicted as twins, such as in the Manichaen system. In this system, the search for one's divine twin is the goal of mystic life, and union with one's twin is the means to spiritual fulfillment. In the system of Ibn 'Arabi, God has an infinite number of names, all of which are living entities that can personify themselves as imaginal figures. The goal of the mystic is to determine his or her own name and unite with it, and through that particular name to unite with, and embody, all the other names of God. These models are very, very close to the one being presented in this series of emblems, and one that is found in other alchemical symbols as well.

To review briefly, there is the normal human world of ordinary reality and there is the divine world that transcends reality as we know it. Between these worlds is the world of imagination, in which spirits and the divinity Itself may personify themselves as imaginal figures. Since relating to the image is the same as relating to the entity itself, it is through imaginative experiences that the divinity may be known and transformed. There are two aspects of imaginal experience. The first relates to inner figures and occurs when some part of the unconscious personifies itself. The other relates to psychoidal figures and is the imaginal encounter with beings that have their own objective reality outside of the psyche. Within the first imaginative world, the self appears as a figure embodying the union of opposites within the psyche, as well as *being* the center of the psyche. The image of divinity, as it appears in the second imaginative realm, is closely related to the image of the self, and the two work together to effect a third level of union that joins the human being with God Itself.

In our emblem, the king is the manifest self, while his son is the personification of the center of the psychoid world. But a third figure appears at this time. The old, winged being forms a trinity with the other two figures, which together form a completion. The king is the manifest self as it appears within the human being, the son is the self of the psychoid, the center of the divine world, also personified in the imagination. The old man is the personification and embodiment of the transcendent function, the process that joins the other two together.

Jung studied the imagery surrounding the old man in the article mentioned in the first chapter, "The Phenomenology of the Spirit in Fairytales."[40] In this article, he pointed out that the old man (as an inner figure) acts as a guide on the path, bestowing wisdom as required, and is intimately connected with transformation. He is so connected with transformation that Jung suggested he was the personification of the transcendent function.

In the alchemical imagination, the old man parallels the Christian symbol of the Holy Spirit on the one hand, and on the other hand *Mercurius*, the psychopomp and agent of transformation. This figure is winged, which means that he

---

40. C. G. Jung, CW 8.

is of a spiritual nature. On all counts, he seems to symbolize the process that gives rise to the third *coniunctio* and that subsequently maintains it. If we think back to the discussion about the nature of the fire and its close association with *Mercurius*, it seems reasonable to suppose that the old man and fire are one. Hence, the old man personifies the motive power and means of effecting the third union. *Mercurius* is, in fact, described in just this way many times in alchemical literature. As mentioned earlier, this motive power seems to derive in equal measure from the manifest self and the divinity desiring its own transformation.

Because all three of these powers are personified as inner figures, the ego can have a relationship with all of them, and participates in the processes that effect the third union. It is a challenge to dialogue with a fire, but not at all hard to do so with a wise old man who can help one understand the nature of the processes unfolding. It is difficult to envision oneself in union with the divine world of the *unus mundus*, whose wonders and nature may transcend one's ability to comprehend. Yet, one can dialogue with and relate to an imaginal figure that personifies that world. The ally, or the self of the psychoid, personifies itself as figures that invariably are loving and lovable, and who speak of partnership and transformation. In the fifteen years I have taught ally meditation groups, the inner figures that embody the ally have always been interested in relationship and union, never in dominance or power. That they appear in the imagination in such a way makes them easy to relate to and often hides the fact that the world they come from is very alien indeed.

The psychoid self, the manifest self, and the wise old man are all figures that one can relate to in active imagination. Having set the stage for the next process, the author of the *Book of Lambspring* now goes on to depict the nature of that process.

EMBLEM TWELVE

At this point, the old man has begun to act as the guide that he is (see figure 15, page 148). He has removed the *filius* away from the world of his father to the very top of a mountain, which is another instance of *sublimatio*. This process carries the young son into the spiritual realm in order to get a higher perspective on life, but at the same time to perform a spiritual task.

The planets and the stars were discussed in the chapter on imagination. In alchemy, the stars represent celestial forces whose energies can be channeled into the stone, imbuing it with magical power. Ascending to the stars to acquire their power is one of the activities of the *filius*. Dorn described the process being depicted in this emblem as follows:

> *In the end it will come to pass that this earthy, spagyric foetus clothes itself with heavenly nature by its ascent, and then by its descent visibly puts on the nature of the centre of the earth, but nonetheless the nature of the heavenly centre which it acquired by the ascent is secretly preserved.*[41]

In other words, the being that ascends on high returns to Earth invested with the powers of the center of both worlds. Not only does it acquire qualities from the center of the psyche, the self, but from the center of the heavenly world, the psychoid realm. Jung commented that the spagyric birth Dorn mentioned is "nothing other than the *filius philosophorum.*"[42] Another alchemist wrote that "our philosophical son . . . ascending to heaven and descending thence to earth . . . [acquires] all power and might both

---

41. C. G. Jung, CW 13, ¶ 187 (From Dorn, *Theatrum Chemicum* I, "Physica genesis.")
42. CW 13, ¶ 187.

Figure 15. The wisdom guide takes the ally away from the manifest self to effect its further development in this emblem. Just as the self before the second *coniunctio* disappears for a time to work on its own transformation, the ally before the third union also disappears to empower itself with the powers of the stars. But while the dragon disappeared into the forest, the ally ascends to the highest mountain and then descends, thereby acquiring all the power of heaven and earth. The *filius* as the personification of the center of the psychoid integrates and harmonizes psychoidal forces just as the manifest self harmonizes and integrates the archetypes. When the son returns to Earth, he comes as the incarnation of the Divine. (From Nicolas Banaud Delphinas, "The Book of Lambspring.")

in heaven and earth."[43] The *filius* embodies the center of the psychoid. Thus it has the power to ascend to that realm and integrate its energies and powers.

The stars represent psychoidal energies that are normally not available to the mundane world. The alchemists were concerned with finding a way to bring those powers into the stone, and to animate it with them. Since the *filius* is an imaginal figure embodying a psychoidal being, it has the capacity to engage with other such figures, which likewise embody aspects of the psychoidal. Through active imagination experiences, in which the ego accompanies the son in exchanges and dialogues with other inner figures, the energies personified by the son may be infused into the psyche. There are also ways that an individual may experience entities from the psychoid which are not images *per se*; for example, when one has an experience of formless energy, but these energies may also be joined with the *filius* through active imagination work. Thus, alchemy at this level becomes an imaginative engagement with figures that transcend the psyche. Through interaction with them, an individual discovers ways to embody them within the psyche, creating a further transformation within the self and uniting it to the transpsychic realm. The key to performing this work safely is the ally. Julius Evola, who wrote on hermeticism from the perspective of inner alchemy and esoteric tradition, wrote that at a certain stage the body undergoes a process that allows it to receive "greater nonhuman powers so that it can itself undergo a rebirth."[44] The body, or incarnated human being, becomes a vessel for psychoidal energies through the imaginal encounter with psychoidal powers.

---

43. Figulus, *A Golden and Blessed Casket of Nature's Marvels*, p. 252.
44. Julius Evola, *The Hermetic Tradition*, E. E. Rehmus, trans. (Rochester, VT: Inner Traditions, 1995), p. 76.

Many years ago, I had the following dream:

I was outside viewing the night sky, which was filled with thousands of stars. As I watched them, I realized to my horror that the stars were disappearing one by one. Then a voice that I knew to be the voice of God said to me, "Now is the time for these stars and even for I, Myself, to disappear. But in our stead I give this sword." As the stars continued to disappear, I found myself holding a heavy and beautiful sword, on which was engraved all the stars. I knew that the powers of God and of stars were contained within this sword.

Though at that time I knew nothing of the alchemical process I have been discussing, the dream is a very close approximation of it. It is essential to remember that images such as the one I described relate to actual experiences that one can have, and are not simply theoretical depictions of some unconscious process. Some time later, I awoke in the middle of the night and saw that my room was filled with stars. I was frightened and slowed my breathing to calm down. As my breathing became regular, the stars began to vibrate in harmony with it, and one by one they disappeared and entered into my psyche. I could feel myself being filled with them, as my center took them in. When I realized that I could not stand any more, the remaining stars simply disappeared.

Visionary or active imagination experiences like these correspond to the sublimation of the *filius*. The ego travels with the *filius* to the top of the mountain and learns the secrets of the stars, at the same time helping the *filius* to put on their power. This process of incarnating celestial powers is central to the alchemical imagination, and is spoken of in the most widespread of all alchemical texts, *The Emerald Tablet*. This text is certainly quite old, probably dating back to Hellenistic times. In part, it reads:

It ascends from the earth to heaven, and descends again to earth, thus you will possess the glory of the whole world, and all obscurity will fly away.[45]

The ascent to the celestial world, and the putting on of the starry virtues, is described in this emblem. The *filius*, as a personification of the center of the psychoid, integrates and harmonizes psychoidal forces—"stellar virtues"—in the same way that the manifest self has been able to integrate and harmonize the archetypes. The mandala has expanded, now including these transpsychic forces. The image of the son provides the means by which the individual safely encounters extraordinary energies, and the means by which he or she will bring them into the ordinary world. Imagination, of course, is the vehicle by which this process unfolds.

EMBLEM THIRTEEN

The next emblem (figure 16, page 152) depicts the somewhat horrific ingestion of the son by the father. Though disturbing, this devouring is part of the process, as indicated by the figure of the wise old man, looking on and seemingly giving his benediction to the king. We find the theme of the child being consumed by the parent in many alchemical sources. Symbolically, ingestion signifies integration. Since the son has ascended to the stars and assumed their power, the father now wishes to acquire those powers for himself by devouring the son. The image of the *filius* has been able to acquire psychoidal energies through imaginal encounters with other psychoidal figures or forces. The manifest self now takes into itself the experiences of the the *filius*. The goal behind this process is the union of the individual manifest self with the celestial, psychoidal world of the *unus*

---

45. *The Emerald Tablet.* Alchemy Website (Database Online), p. 1.

Figure 16. The father eats his son while the guide looks on with apparent approval. Though the image is disturbing, symbolically it denotes the process of integration by which the manifest self takes into itself the ally and its newly acquired powers. The psyche, through its center, attempts to incarnate the psychoidal self, the ally. (From Nicolas Banaud Delphinas, "The Book of Lambspring.")

mundus. The son has acted as center of the psychoidal world and gathered within and around himself the powers of that world. Now he reconnects with the self, which attempts to integrate him into itself, and thereby into the psyche. However, and this is very important, the effort to integrate the psychoid into the psyche only works to a limited degree.

EMBLEM FOURTEEN

In the next emblem (figure 17, page 154), we find the king sick and sweating profusely. Notice in the background, however, that there is a celestial influx coming through the window. The psychoidal powers continue to enter the king through the influence of the son whom he has eaten. Sweating symbolizes a process of purification intrinsic to the alchemical process. Ingesting the son adds power to the self that it cannot contain; it must be purified of it or suffer an inflation. The manifest self may unite with the psychoidal self, but it may not assimilate it. In fact, the father gives birth—sweats out—the son once again, because the father cannot contain him for long. However, there is the implication that both he and the father have been transformed in the process.

The psychoidal forces are extremely powerful, and introducing them into the psyche, or into the physical world, may have dramatic effects. Because of their powerful nature, their introduction in the individual may be extremely dangerous. I have experienced and seen others experience terrible physical and psychological consequences because they touched such forces. I myself was gripped by insomnia for weeks after "ingesting" energy of such great power that I could not bring it into harmony with the rest of myself. Out of control, it raged through me until, finally, I could regulate it through active imagination. If an inner figure intimately connected with the self can take on this energy, the consequences of introducing it into the psyche are less dire. The

Figure 17. The efforts of the psyche to integrate the psychoid can only work to a certain degree. The king, having ingested the son, becomes quite ill. Notice in the background that celestial influx still streams through the window. The psychoidal powers continue to enter the king through the son whom he has eaten. But union between the self and the ally can never safely become a complete merger; rather the two partners must remain separate while in deepest union. For this reason, the king cannot devour the son without dire consequences. (From Nicolas Banaud Delphinas, "The Book of Lambspring.")

emblem clearly indicates that the self cannot integrate them entirely, either. It takes them in only to sweat them out in the form of the original image of the *filius*. Having experienced the psychoid through the image of the son, the king is now able to integrate some of those experiences that change him in a positive manner. The energies that he cannot retain he returns to the *filius*, which now comes alive in the psyche as the embodiment of the divinity.

The first image created in the form of the son was the personification of the center of the psychoid. Like the latent self at the beginning of the first stage, this image was weak and undeveloped. Through its sublimation it is strengthened and transformed, and has become the manifest self of the psychoid, a living center able to harmonize forces beyond the psychic world. More importantly, its gift to the king is the knowledge of these forces, and a direct conscious experience of the divine truths. The king has learned about the world beyond his own domain, of which the son has become the living personification.

The *filius* dies and is reborn through this process. The symbolism of rebirth is one familiar to us from our previous study of alchemy. The *filius*, like the original substance, moves on to the higher level only by first dying to its original state. In addition, the theme of rebirth marks the son as a heroic and divine figure. His passage through death brings the *filius* into closer relationship with the image of Christ, who likewise first died before being reborn into the higher world. But in this case, the *filius* dies to be reborn in the lower world, the world of the psyche. If a human being attempted to integrate the powers of the psychoid directly into the psyche, without an intermediate figure, the dangers are that of inflation or overwhelm. But if the ally, which previously existed in the psychoid, dies to its original form and is reborn within the psyche, union between the human and the psychoid world is safely effected. The ally does not lose its independence and remains in essence psychoidal, but it resides within the human soul.

EMBLEM FIFTEEN

Not only have father and son been transformed in his respective way, but also they have now entered into union with each other (see figure 18, page 158). The final emblem graphically depicts this union. Both king and prince now share the throne that the father had previously occupied. The self of the psychoid has become a ruling force—in union with the manifest self—within the individual psyche in which these experiences have occurred. Notice that in this union two individual images are left intact—the human self is nor absorbed into the divinity, and the divine self is not assimilated into the human self. Each remains alive and separate, fully autonomous, and yet deeply united. In this third coniunctio, the whole that is created includes the separate two parts, without the transmutation of the two into a third entity that replaces them.

Note that the guide remains as well, with one arm around father and son. He stands at the center, as the force that continuously serves to unite the two partners. The guide symbolizes the awareness that directs all processes that follow this third union. He symbolizes a deep wisdom, related to Sophia, that operates outside the control of either father or son. In fact, both father and son follow wisdom's guidance. In the union with the ally, the self does not choose how to act or what direction to follow in its life, but neither does the ally. Rather, they both follow the lead of the winged guide whose knowing and direction come spontaneously and unpredictably. Such guidance corresponds to what Jung termed. absolute knowledge, whose operations remain a deep mystery.

It is in the world of imagination, and the experiences created there by the transcendent function, that the two partners continue to share and unite. The king learns about the world beyond the psyche, and the son learns how to incarnate in the human soul. God and man are united, with neither partner losing any of their separate identity to the other. Having achieved the third *coniunctio*, the human and the divine lovers experience life, and each other, through ever new and more profound experiences. The resulting trinity connects the human self with the *unus mundus* in the personified form of the prince, and the guide that joins them leads them to ever-deeper experiences of self-knowledge.

It is hard enough to describe the experiences that accompany the first two levels of union; with the third that task is almost impossible. It is a fact that few people will ever have such experiences, and yet they do occur. Part of the map of those who work with the souls of individuals should include every possible experience, though only those who actually have them will be able to guide others in their quest.

I will not endeavor further to paint a picture of this state of being called the third *coniunctio*. I will only say that the imaginal experiences that once connected the individual with the inner world of the psyche can now connect one to other worlds and other realities. Such experiences are safe and transformative, because the self has unified the two centers of psyche and psychoid. These two worlds are now harmonized. The imagination that has its roots in the world in which body and spirit are one has been expanded and empowered to include experiences not normally encountered. All of these deep experiences are tinged with the love between parent and child, a deep and abiding union that embraces the ego in its loving arms. Though ever-new experiences unfold, these are less significant than the fact that the father-son union grows as well; with every new experience this unified center transmutes in ways that are ineffable. In his attempt to portray something of the third union Jung wrote:

Figure 18. This image depicts the attainment of the third *coniunctio*. Both the self and the ally are transformed. The king has lost his highly exalted position and the nature of his throne has changed, being less elevated. He is still the king but now shares his position with the son and the guide. The manifest self is no longer alone in its own psychic center, for the ally is now present. The ally has imparted much of its power and essence to the manifest self but is not fully contained within the psyche, remaining psychoidal in its nature and preserving its autonomy. The guide, as the wisdom of the imagination, sits between ally and self and unites them. The three figures each remain distinct and yet altogether portray the third level of the *coniunctio* in which the self and the ally are in harmony and deepest union and both are guided by the spontaneous movement of the imagination. (From Nicolas Banaud Delphinas, "The Book of Lambspring.")

*Not unnaturally, we are at a loss to see how a psychic expe-
rience of this kind—for such it evidently was—can be formulated as a rational concept. Undoubtedly it was meant as
the essence of perfection and universality, and, as such, it characterized an experience of similar proportions. We could compare
this only with the ineffable mystery of the* unio mystica,
or tao, *or the content of* samadhi, *or the experience of* satori
in Zen, *which would bring us to the realm of the ineffable
and of extreme subjectivity where all the criteria of reason
fail.*[46]

It is probably not possible to expand more on this description. In the comparisons Jung made, he illustrated plainly
that the achievement of the third *coniunctio* is comparable to
the highest state of any spiritual tradition. The alchemist
fortunate enough to create and experience the third union
attained his own enlightenment as well, and achieved the
miraculous incarnation of the divine in his soul. The alchemists realized that if the third *coniunctio* were attained, they
had reached an ineffable quality of being. They tried in their
own way to express this state. One wrote that the *filius* gives
"to man an enduring health, Gold, silver and precious
stones, a strength and a beautiful secure youth, he destroys
anger, sadness, poverty and all weaknesses. Oh three times
happy is he who has received such a grace from our lord."[47]
Having reached the third and final union, there is simply
nothing that an individual lacks, and no joy that is denied
him. Whatever life may bring such an individual, he or she
rests secure in the bonds of sacred marriage.

---

46. C. G. Jung, CW 14, ¶ 771.

47. Michael Sendivogius, "Treatise on Salt" in Zbigniew Szydlo, *Water Which
Does not Wet Hands: The Alchemy of Michael Sendivogius* (Warsaw: Polish Academy of Sciences, 1994), p. 248.

CHAPTER 4

The PROCESSES *of* INNER ALCHEMY

In the last chapter we discussed the path which led to the formation of the self. Not only did the alchemists imagine the path and its goal, they formulated a series of processes by which they might achieve their objective. A large percentage of alchemical texts dealt with the operations of transmuting the *prima materia* into the philosopher's stone. From the perspective of inner alchemy, these operations describe imaginative experiences that lead to the formation of the self. Each represents an inner transformative experience that affects the ego as well as the unconscious. Studying them psychologically provides us with an understanding of the individuation process and the work of active imagination it requires.

The alchemists' perception of these processes differed from what one might expect. They did not believe that they were in control of the operations, or responsible for making them work. They were responsible for maintaining a proper fire, which stimulated the substances into their own natural and organic transformation. The processes they sought to engender were autonomous, and took place in the material they had chosen as their *prima materia*. Having once selected the appropriate *prima materia*, an alchemist placed it in a vessel and sealed it hermetically. The next important requirement was the application of the right amount of external heat through the fire they used. The use of fire was a sensitive issue, since the external heat had to be precisely the correct temperature to initiate the inner processes. Too much heat would ruin the work, while too little would not promote the necessary processes. Once begun, the alchemical processes followed one another in the correct sequence, without any intervention on the part of the alchemist. Much of the alchemist's time was spent patiently waiting for signs indicating the process was unfolding as it should.

Patient waiting is often necessary for imaginal processes as well. Of course, an individual's desire for transformation and the experience of the self is necessary, too. That desire, coupled with attention and effort, provides the external heat necessary for change to take place. Beyond these factors, however, there is no way for an individual to control or "make" a process unfold. One cannot will the self to manifest. Working in the imaginal realm requires a willingness to follow, avoiding the temptation to control the processes. One must simply trust that the self knows what it needs to manifest. The inner alchemical processes emerge from the self and may not be directed by the ego.

THE CHEMICAL WEDDING

The alchemists expressed their imaginative insights in descriptive texts and in symbolic material of all kinds. Aside from emblems such as those in the last chapter, they made use of a variety of other figurative styles, such as dreams, visions, and parables. One striking alchemical parable is *The Chemical Wedding of Christian Rosenkreutz*. Since this allegory forms a whole book, it will not be possible for me to discuss it all. Toward the end of the book, however, there is a sequence of operations performed on the king and queen to effect their death, rebirth, and transmutation, and we will explore that here.

The Chemical Wedding was written in 1605, apparently by a 19-year-old clergyman named J. V. Andreae, though it was not published until 1616. It is hard to imagine that an adolescent produced this work, for it is a rich and insightful symbolic presentation of inner alchemy. While there is controversy about who actually wrote the book, if Andreae did, he was precocious in his alchemical understanding.

Frances Yates, whose book, *The Rosicrucian Enlightenment,* while somewhat dated, remains a classic in the area, maintains that Andreae was certainly the author of *The Chemical Wedding.*[1] She reports several details of his life and maintains that his constant concern was the reformation of religion. The Rosicrucian movement itself was primarily concerned with this goal but it was also connected with alchemy. In fact, it served, through the writings of such men as Andreae, to create a new form of alchemy that Yates called "Rosicrucian alchemy."[2] In it, alchemy united with cabalistic themes and magic. Rosicrucianism profoundly effected the evolution of alchemy, and one of the three pillars of early rosicrucianism was *The Chemical Wedding.* In order to fully understand this text, therefore, something must be said of the Rosicrucians.

The movement began with the publication of the so-called *Fama* (1614) in Germany. This was a period of intense religious hatred and intolerance, with governments of Catholic countries persecuting Protestants and vice versa. The *Manifesto* announces the existence of a secret order of sages who work for the benefit of humankind, regardless of religious creed. These sages are masters of magic and alchemy, but devote themselves completely to the good of

---

1. Frances A.Yates, *The Rosicrucian Enlightenment* (London: Routledge, 1986), p. 30.
2. Frances A. Yates, *The Rosicrucian Enlightenment,* p. 198.

all. The *Manifesto* invites others who wish to become part of the secret society to apply, though only the best and most talented would be accepted. All throughout Europe many brilliant scholars made application.

Though there were certainly secret societies before the publication of the *Fama*, they spread rapidly afterward. Though many governments viewed the Rosicrucians with grave suspicion, Rudolf II and his court at Prague accepted them with open arms. Indeed, Rudolf's personal physician, Michael Maier, added much to the theoretical and alchemical development of Rosicrucianism. It is often forgotten today that Prague was the center of alchemical writing and study under the beneficent eye of Rudolf, and such masters as John Dee traveled to live at his court. Despite years of Communist repression, there are literary and artistic treasures related to alchemy still in existence in Prague.[3] Though I shall not discuss the political references in *The Chemical Wedding*, but shall consider it only from the alchemical perspective, the reader should bear in mind that it emerged from a period of intense agitation for political and religious reform and some interpreters may approach its profundity of images from this perspective. Though the hope of the early Rosicrucians were dashed in the horrors of the Thirty Years War, their influences remained to shape both alchemy and secret societies for centuries in both east and west Europe.

In many ways, *The Chemical Wedding* is one of the richest of alchemical allegories. One could easily write a book about

---

3. See the wonderful book *Magnum Opus*, published to commemorate an international conference and exhibit on alchemy, magic, astrology, the cabbala, and secret societies in the Czech lands. Containing many Czech images and writings never published before, it is an amazing display that the beginning and advanced students of alchemy will find delightful. It was published in 1997 by Trigon Press in Prague.

its symbols and their interpretation. I cannot hope to do justice to this work, but will confine myself to discussing images that relate to the processes of alchemy. In order to maintain a sense of cohesion, I will tell the story of Christian but will not discuss all the symbols of the story. I will mention many interesting symbols that I will be unable to discuss without complicating this chapter beyond reason.

Andreae's book tells the story of Christian Rosenkreutz, an old man at the time the action occurs. He receives a mysterious invitation to the king's wedding and, after much misgiving, sets off to find the right path to the king's castle. He arrives, after many adventures, experiences a grueling initiation, and is elected to take part in the wedding.

The allegory concerns itself with the wedding of the king and the queen, familiar symbolic figures in alchemy. In the discussion of the *Book of Lambspring*, I mentioned that the king is a symbol of the self, but so complicated is this image that Jung devotes an entire chapter, "Rex and Regina," in *Mysterium Coniunctionis* to the symbolism of the king and his spouse.

The image of the king is related to that of gold, and both symbolize the redeemed and purified life-spirit. In alchemy, there were two types of gold—living and dead. The living gold was analogous to the philosopher's stone, and was "easily personified as a divine being or a superior person like a king, who in olden times was considered to be God incarnate."[4] In other words, the king was one personification of the stone or the self.

At the beginning of the work, the old or sick king corresponded to the latent self, and requires redemption and

---

4. C. G. Jung, *Mysterium Coniunctionis*, Collected Works, vol. 14, R. F. C. Hull, trans., Bollingen Series XX (Princeton: Princeton University Press, 1970), ¶ 354. Future references to this work will be cited as CW 14.

transformation. As the masculine side of the self, however, the king was also related to the principle of consciousness and, therefore, to the ego. Jung said that the king, at times, represented ego consciousness. We could perhaps better understand the king as personifying consciousness, and the self in its more masculine manifestations. The king, then, could either represent the self as the union of all opposites, including the feminine, or one aspect of the self, as it relates to consciousness. As more the embodiment of the masculine side of the self, the king is accompanied by a queen, who then reflects the contrasexual or feminine side of the self, or the world of the unconscious.

The image of the wedding symbolizes the union of ego and the unconscious; in other words, the creation of the manifest self. More accurately, however, the alchemist embodies the ego, while the king represents consciousness itself. Since the primary characteristics of consciousness are self-awareness and a sense of identity, the king personifies the self's sense of identity and awareness.

The latent self lies buried beneath the chaos of the unconscious. It is not self aware, or perhaps only so to a limited degree. Part of the work of redemption is facilitating the self's knowledge of itself. Prior to redemption, the self's knowledge of itself comes through the ego. When the king marries the queen, though, the ego's capacity for self-awareness and identity is joined to the unconscious. The resulting manifest self then possesses its own self-consciousness. So as not to confuse the king with the ego in the story, we will think of Christian as the ego and the king as the masculine, conscious side of the self.

The queen personifies the unconscious, and therefore represents the inner world with its wonders and diversity. Though many times a silent partner in the alchemists' writings, she is nevertheless indispensable in the creation of the *lapis*, or stone. The goal of the work is to unite the opposites represented by the union of masculine and feminine, and in particular to unite consciousness with the unconscious. Through this union, the manifest self emerges.

After our discussion of the different stages of the *coniunctio* in the last chapter, it should come as no surprise that the wedding of the king and the queen was only the beginning of the process. The young king and the young queen who were to wed were rather a disappointment for Christian, who found them rather plain and ugly. This plainness indicated the young couple's need for transformation and redemption. In other alchemical works, the king is often sick or dying, and his need for healing is quite apparent. In *The Chemical Wedding*, the king is not ill, only rather drab. At the end of the book, when the transmutation has occurred, the king and queen have become numinously beautiful, indicating the depth of the change that occurred. At the wedding itself, after the presentation of a play that portrayed in miniature the whole process about to unfold, the young king and queen, along with two other royal couples, presented themselves to an executioner who promptly cut off their heads. As Christian wryly noted, this seemed a very bloody wedding indeed.[5] The wedding takes place on the fourth day of the parable, which is where we shall pick up the tale.

The beheading was the first step in the alchemical process of redemption, and represented the *mortificatio* and *putrefactio* that generally followed the *coniunctio.* Every union is followed by death in alchemy, until the last and final state is achieved. Alchemy used the motifs of head and beheading in various ways. Zosimos, an early alchemist, connected the head with the omega element, by which he meant the arcane substance, or the mysterious nature of the stone. In

5. Joscelyn Godwin, trans., *The Chemical Wedding of Christian Rosenkreutz* (Grand Rapids: Phanes Press, 1991), p. 70.

the symbolism of the head, Jung saw an allusion to the head of Osiris in Egyptian mythology, and the cycle of death and resurrection.[6] Beheading, removing the head from its body, means separating the mysterious substance that leads to rebirth and transformation into its fundamental opposites. Moreover, since the head has to do with consciousness, beheading stands for the separation of consciousness from the body, and is the first step leading to the conjunction that Dorn termed the *unio mentalis*, or mental union. Beheading or *putrefactio* initiates the work and also represents the separation of the animating conscious principle from the *prima materia*.

Putrefactio "is the change and death of all things, and the destruction of the first essence of all natural objects, from whence there issues forth for us regeneration and new birth ten thousand times better than before."[7] At whatever stage of the work putrefaction occurs, it denotes the death of an original substance and the onset of a transformation process. Figure 19 (page 168) is a good example of the symbolic portrayal of putrefaction. The skeleton, Death, oversees the process, and is the dominant influence at this stage. On the other side of the coffin is a figure, probably Vulcan, indicating that fire plays a role, but does not control the process. The king and the queen in the coffin represent the pair of opposites, just as in our parable. The emblem that preceded this one in the original series showed the same king and queen in bed together, consummating the *coniunctio*. True

---

6. C. G. Jung, *Psychology and Religion: West and East*, Collected Works, vol. 11, R. F. C. Hull, trans., Bollingen Series XX (Princeton: Princeton University Press, 1969), ¶ 367–368. Future citations as CW 11.
7. Paracelsus, "Concerning the Nature of Things" in A. E. Waite, ed., *The Hermetic and Alchemical Writings of Paracelsus the Great* (Kila, MT: Kessinger Company, n.d.), p. 120.

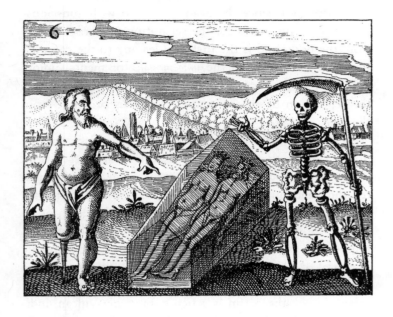

Figure 19. The king and the queen are in the coffin, symbol of the alchemical vessel and the *mortificatio.* All union is followed by death, which rules this stage of the work. While the figure on the left, probably representing the power of fire to transform, is part of the process, he shares his task with death. Only when the opposites die to their previous forms can a true union be created. (From J. D. Mylius, *Philosophia reformata,* Frankfurt, 1622.)

union, though, occurs in death, when the two partners lose their former state and join together in a new one.

As I indicated in the last chapter, both the ego and the unconscious must forego their previous states of being to come together in the first *coniunctio*. Both experience this sacrifice of the old ways of being as a death. The sacrifice of the king may be understood as the ego's sacrifice of its identification with consciousness. To achieve the first level of union with the unconscious, the ego must surrender its sense of being master of the psyche. No longer can it do what it wishes without regard for other voices in the unconscious. No longer can it reject imagination or the still small voice within.

With most people, there is little chance they will simply change their attitude and pay attention to the unconscious. Even with the best of intentions, most individuals cannot relinquish the ego's delusion of mastery and control. Loss of control is one of the most terrifying things for people to face. Realizing that the ego does not control its inner or outer world is too much for them to handle consciously. The ego can only come to accept the loss of control by experiencing it, which it does in the *putrefactio*. When the ego feels devoid of energy, of will, and of the ability to move forward in its own life, it knows loss of control. It experiences directly that the only way to live meaningfully is to give up the illusion of control and turn within. Having abdicated its prideful role as the sun ruling the heavens, it descends into the underworld and finds the vulnerability and openness required for real union with the unconscious. Death is the great teacher, and through the experience of death, the ego comes face-to-face with the self.

There is another way in which the death of the king may be understood. In active imagination, the ego must not only encounter an inner figure, it must in some fashion experience the consciousness of that inner figure. One of the most startling aspects of active imagination is the perception of an inner figure as a personality, as a being with its own consciousness. This consciousness and its corresponding self-awareness are limited in the unconscious. As the ego attends to the inner figure, that figure's self-awareness grows. It is as if the ego were transferring the power of consciousness to the inner figure in the course of their dialogues or exchanges.

In this sense, the king dies to its previous identification with the ego and its world, and unites with the forces within the unconscious. Recall the emblems from the last chapter depicting the building of houses in the previously undeveloped forest. This symbolizes exactly the movement of consciousness into the unconscious. On the other hand, the queen dies, too. As the unconscious—personified by the queen—becomes conscious and self-aware, it dies to *its* previous state and leaves the chaos that characterized it earlier. As the queen dies to her previous state, she enters into union with the king. The king brings to this union consciousness and self-awareness. The queen, who is also beheaded, sacrifices her essential feature. I believe that the central feature of the unconscious is its capacity to create images, its imaginative power. The queen is the feminine side of the self and represents the world of imagination. It is this very attribute that she brings into the marriage. The unconscious gains consciousness, and consciousness gains imaginative power.

In the ritual beheading, the alchemist sought the essential and mysterious arcane substance, the *prima materia*, represented by the figure that loses it head. In the case of the king, that substance is the principle of the consciousness. For the queen, it is the animating, spiritual force that produces images—the imagination itself. In the union of self-awareness and imaginative power, the alchemist sought to realize an essential part of the self's mystery. If the work succeeds, the self not only discovers who and what it is; it learns how to channel the imaginative power in the processes of its own manifestation.

The king and the queen die, ushering in the *putrefactio*. As they are beheaded, their blood is caught for later use. However, at this point, a very somber Christian retires for the night, saddened by the deaths he has witnessed. Before he and the other alchemists invited to the wedding leave, the Virgin who has been overseeing them admonishes them that "the life of these now rest in your hands; and if you follow me, you will see this death give life to many."[8] The Virgin is another common alchemical symbol, and in this context is most likely a reference to Sophia. She represents the feminine wisdom of God, which, for Jacob Boehme, was the source of all revelation and guidance.[9] The promise of transformation is part of the *putrefactio* from the beginning, as long as one is willing and able to follow the inner voice of wisdom that guides the work.

As Christian goes to bed that night, he glances out his window and sees seven ships, each carrying a corpse of the beheaded royal couples. The spirits of the young king and queen, whose marriage was being celebrated, those of the other kings and queens, and the soul of the executioner, who was killed as well, made seven spirits in all. These spirits hover in the form of flames above the boats carrying the corpses.

I mentioned that a ship or boat represented the ego's ability to safely sail the waters of the unconscious. There is another meaning for ship. Ships and death are often related. Almost every culture has its image of the ship of

---

8. *The Chemical Wedding*, p. 70.
9. See for example, Jacob Boehme, *The Three Principles of the Divine Essence* (Reprint: Chicago: Yoga Publication Society, n.d.).

death. Perhaps the earliest such image was in Egypt, where the boat is the vessel in which the souls of the dead travel in search of rebirth. According to some, the first boat was the coffin.[10] Placing the bodies of the dead in a boat is a symbol of setting out after death in search of renewal and rebirth. In this context, the boat signifies a crossing into another world, a journey into the land of the dead in search of renewal. The body of water symbolizes the unconscious or inner world, and the world of the imaginal.

The flame has a long history as an image for the soul. It was an image clearly related to fire, and symbolized the interior spark, the animating principle that brings the body to life and makes of it an individual being. The flame/spirit above the boat indicates that a *separatio* has occurred. As we saw, beheading symbolizes separation, just as did the sword in the *Book of Lambspring*. The spirit is separated from the body, in order that both may transform in preparation for eventual reunion.

The separation of the body from the spirit occurs in the first *coniunctio*, which, for Dorn, allowed the spirit to escape the domination of the body. Jung understands the separation of the body from the spirit to mean that the ego has moved into a closer relationship with the unconscious. The imagery of separation also indicates that the ego must remain somewhat separate from the unconscious. If the ego identifies with the feelings, images, and drives that emerge from the unconscious, it is unfree and incapable of working with them. In order to do active imagination work, the ego has to separate from the unconscious images sufficiently to be able to relate to them without

---

10. Jean Chevalier and Alain Gheerbrant, *The Penguin Dictionary of Symbols*, John Buchanan-Brown, trans. (New York: Penguin Books, 1996), p. 107.

being overwhelmed. If, for example, I suffer from a depression and cannot figure out why I am feeling so low, I can do an active imagination to determine the meaning of the state I am in. To do so, I must enter the mercurial waters of the imagination, and encounter a personification of the depression. If I am to successfully personify, I must not identify with that which I am personifying. If I simply feel depressed, angry, or sad, I cannot distance myself enough to personify the effect. Active imagination requires a certain detachment, and this detachment is an expression of the *unio mentalis*. It is in some ways an unreal state that I temporarily enter, but one that is necessary if I am to make conscious the forces within the unconscious. To enter the imagination, I need enough detachment to separate from the feelings and forces I will meet in that realm.

The separation of the spirit from the body has other possible interpretations. Representing the best of the esoteric tradition and its understanding of alchemy, Julius Evola wrote that *separatio* refers to visionary experiences. He feels that consciousness enters a trance state and separates from the body as a means of experiencing the non-corporeal.[11] The separation of the spirit, then, is an actual visionary state in which the ego moves into nonphysical realities. When I spoke of the third conjunction earlier, I mentioned that when the *filius* ascends the mountain to assume spiritual powers, the ego would accompany it in an experience of the psychoid realm. The separation of the spirit from the body is an analogous experience, for the soul can move out of the body and into the spiritual realm before reaching the third level. That is the situation here. The soul detaches as the

---

11. Julius Evola, *The Hermetic Tradition: Symbols and Teachings of the Royal Art* (Rochester, VT: Inner Traditions, 1995), p. 112.

process begins to move from the first *coniunctio* to the second. However one understands such a separation process, it indicates movement from the ordinary into the imaginal— the realm in which the alchemical work can proceed.

DAY FIVE

The theme of movement into the water is repeated in the story. The next day Christian and the other alchemists get into boats themselves, and cross the water to the tower where the coffins had been taken the night before. However, all the alchemists, save Christian, believe they are accompanying the coffins on their journey. None realize that the bodies had been taken to the tower the night before. This theme is repeated over and over again as the alchemists begin their work. Christian sees the real situation, but the others do not know what is actually occurring. The meaning of this motif becomes clear later in the book, when it becomes apparent that most of the alchemists believed that the physical work they are performing is the real alchemy. Christian, on the other hand, sees the deeper truth—that the work takes place on a nonphysical level. He symbolizes the visionary alchemists whose perceptions enable them to perform the real work. Those who can not differentiate the physical from the nonphysical succumb to illusion. Although the alchemists embark on the imaginal seas, only Christian really knows what is happening.

On their way to the tower, the travelers encounter sirens, sea-nymphs and sea goddesses. These inner, feminine figures sing a beautiful song about love and its power to reunite the separated king and queen to the alchemists:

So God will grant
That as from us homage and love
have sundered them with mighty power,

So may we too, through flame of love
With joy unite them once again.[12]

The nymphs proclaim the power of love to effect the
coniunctio. Though commentaries on alchemy often overlook
this power, it plays a central role in the formation of the
self. The love between the ego and the self—especially the
self as an inner figure—is a primary motivating force in
the *coniunctio* process. Without that love, the hardships and
difficulties one encounters on the path are insurmountable.
More than any particular procedure, it is the love between
the two partners that makes the *coniunctio* possible. The
nymphs represent feminine wisdom. They know that love,
above all else, is essential for the work. Methods and operations are incidental to that which love sets in motion.

Because alchemical symbolism links the nymphs with
the fish-woman, Melusina, they also have to do with imagination. Both Paracelsus and Dorn refer to her. She could
be either a negative figure, seductive and invasive, or she
could be a teacher of the greatest profundity. Dorn calls
her a "vision appearing in the mind."[13] Good or bad,
Melusina symbolizes the visionary power of the imagination. The nymphs in the parable represent those inner figures of the imagination that teach the secrets of the work.
In this case, they reveal the power and necessity of relationship and love. The processes of alchemy depend upon

---

12. *The Chemical Wedding,* p. 79.
13. From Dorn's work, *Theatrum Chemicum,* in C. G. Jung, *Alchemical Studies,*
Collected Works, vol. 13, R. F. C. Hull, trans., Bollingen Series XX
(Princeton: Princeton University Press, 1970), ¶ 180. Future references
to this title will be to CW 13.

the interaction with inner figures that can show the way, and willingness on the part of the ego to relate deeply with the self, and to honor the love that can grow between them. That the nymphs are directly related to the imagination reinforces the notion of water as the imaginative realm.

Christian and the others are now ferried to the tower that is called the Olympus tower. Here the symbolism is not subtle. In Greek mythology, Olympus was the home of the gods. Thus, crossing the water to the tower alerts the reader to a crossing between worlds, to movement to a higher world of gods and spirits. It is in this world that the alchemist does his work.

Like a hill or mountain, the tower suggests sublimation. Through the imagination, the alchemist connects with a higher reality, and by ascending to this higher reality he imbues his other work with the necessary power and depth. As a process, sublimation necessitates the ability to work with the imagination. The visionary state allows one to experience the spiritual realities that alchemy seeks to transform. Sublimation produces an encounter with spiritual powers, which are later incarnated in the philosopher's stone. As one alchemist puts it, the stone "rises from earth to heaven and again descends to earth, by conquering the upper and lower forces."[14] All of these forces became part of the union being forged, and the stone then has the spiritual powers necessary for its own creation and operation. Psychologically, sublimation occurs in those imaginal experiences in which archetypal forces are encountered and tamed. They are subsequently united with the self. Just as the stone conquers

---

14. Patricia Tahil, trans., *The Alchemical Engravings of Mylius* (Edinburgh: Magnum Opus Hermetic Sourceworks, 1984), p. 75.

the upper and lower forces, the self tames the unruly archetypes and makes of them one unified whole.

Upon arriving at the tower, their guide requires Christian and the others to engage in various forms of physical alchemy. In his words, they had to "grind and wash herbs, gemstones, and what not, extracting the sap and essence, then put it in little bottles and hand them over to be preserved. Our Virgin [the guide and teacher] was so industrious and organizing, she knew how to keep each one fully employed."[15] Christian has crossed into the imaginative world where spirit lives, and where the danger of inflation, or of losing one's bearings, always lurks. His guide wisely insures his involvement with tasks of mundane alchemical work, with grindings and extractions and such. Though increasingly apparent that the real work Christian will perform has little to do with such operations, they are important their own way. They serve to ground one in the ordinary world, while the inner work moves forward.

Much of alchemy—as well as many magical practices—is governed by the theory of correspondences. According to the theory of correspondences, anything that happens on one plane of reality produces a corresponding effect on another level of reality. A metal—iron, for example—in the physical world "corresponds" to a specific planet—Mars, in this case—and all of its powers in the celestial world. More significantly, the same planet might correspond to an angel or archangel in the heavenly world. Following the magical doctrines of the Middle Ages, if I identified a substance that corresponded to a planet and a spiritual being, manipulating that substance would cause a corresponding change in the planetary and spiritual worlds.

---

15. *The Chemical Wedding*, p. 80.

All worlds are parallel and congruent. Performing an operation on the physical level will have an impact on the spiritual level. Figure 20 (page 180) is an emblem from the alchemical work, *Mutus Liber*, a book made up solely of emblems.[16] In the picture presented here, the two alchemists, one male and one female, pray for success and guidance. Earlier emblems showed them busily at work with their own solutions and extractions. In this one, though, they appeal to the world above, where Mercurius stands on the sun and the moon while the stone forms. Notice that Mercurius stands in an oval shaped container in the upper world, which perfectly matches the vessel in the furnace below. The processes occurring in the furnace below are reflected in the processes of the heavens above, and vice versa. The alchemists knew that whatever they transformed in the physical world would be correspondingly transformed in the spiritual world.

Christian's visionary insight tells him that doing the physical work without perceiving its spiritual aspect does not suffice. Yet, the physical work is also part of the process. From the point of view of inner alchemy, physical operations would symbolize the effort that the ego must expend to understand imaginative experiences and integrate them in its life. For example, sometimes a dream or vision needs enactment in the ordinary world. I heard of a case in which a client, a very powerful and wealthy businessman, dreamed of a teddy bear. His analyst insisted that he buy the toy bear, care for it, clothe it, and actually carry it around with him in his daily life. By doing so, the client came to experience

---

16. Altus, *Mutus Liber* (La Rochelle, 1677). This book can be found today in Adam McLean's *A Commentary on the Mutus Liber*, published by Phanes Press, Grand Rapids, MI, 1991.

the meaning of the teddy bear, which had to do with his being less self-important, more playful. Working with the symbol at the concrete level can thus be very revealing. At other times, one must guarantee that the outer world is in order before starting deeper work. In Zurich, at the beginning of my analysis, I had the following dream:

I was in a rocket ship ready for launching. The countdown had begun and I eagerly awaiting takeoff. When the count reached "three," alarms went off everywhere! I had to get out of the ship and deal with a problem on the land.

In my analysis it became apparent that I had to deal with my physical world and its surroundings before I could go further with my inner work. I had to put my finances in order, change my living space, and work with a relationship issue. I had much "washing and grinding" to do. Although I was annoyed by what seemed to me like an unnecessary delay, I realized later that the details I attended to were all part of the inner process and had an impact on it. Taking the time to deal with concrete situations deepens inner work.

Extracting meaning from inner experiences and applying their lessons to outer life also corresponds to the physical side of the work. One cannot remain in visionary states all the time, and it is essential that the individual give physical expression to such experiences. To translate the power from the inner world into a new way of life in the outer world—into finding a new job or a different relationship—might take years. It might require additional education, or perhaps developing the ability to express feelings. Much of the work involved takes place outside the imaginal realm, yet without it, imaginal experiences would be sterile indeed.

Having entered the inner world of the tower, the alchemists' first task is to ground their experiences and integrate the meaning they hold. Inner alchemy requires a

Figure 20. While their "matter" cooks in the alchemical stove, the two alchemists, male and female, pray for the success of their operations. Notice that the woman reaches upward to the higher realm where the real alchemical work is proceeding. Mercurius, standing on the sun and the moon, is in the center of the egg-like object, which is the same shape as the center of the stove down below. The angels and the birds, representing spiritual forces, support the work. As the alchemists liked to say, "As above, so below." For any transformation to occur in the physical world, there must be a transformation in the spiritual world. The two worlds correspond and whatever occurs in one influences the other. (Plate 8 in *Mutus Liber,* Grand Rapids, MI: Phanes Press, 1991.)

balance between imaginal visionary experiences and outer world application. Yet, following the theory of correspondences, outer application directly affects inner experiences. I may become so involved in everyday living for weeks, or even months, that I cannot return to the imaginative realm. When I do return, I discover that the inner figures have altered profoundly as a result of what I have been doing in the outer world. Inner and outer worlds are much more connected than we usually realize, and work in the one feeds the work in the other.

After completing the physical tasks, Christian retires for the night. Once more, though everyone else falls asleep, he stays awake. As a result, he beholds even more miraculous sights. Looking at the sky, he first notes a conjunction of planets such as would not occur again for a long time. Alchemists were very interested in astrology and noting the position and interaction of the planets. Both beginning the work, as well as performing the processes involved, depended on astrologically correct timing for the influences of the planets to aid in the process. That Christian notes this conjunction indicates that the time is right for the union of the king and the queen, and that the planetary influences favored its consummation.

Timing is an essential factor in inner alchemy as well. I have noticed repeatedly in analytical work that a client will hear something clearly only when the time is right. I may continually point out something with no results. Then the client comes to a session and informs me that she or he has discovered a great truth that is exactly what I had been trying to help them perceive all along. Timing is a great mystery, for it cannot be controlled by the ego. At a certain moment, an experience that would have been impossible a week before unfolds with no difficul. The alchemists warned that all haste was of the devil; rushing violates the gradual evolution that accords with time. As the Chinese philosophers well knew, to be in accord with the time makes the difference between success and failure.

No matter how eager we may be for a particular inner experience, no matter how much we have prepared for it, we simply cannot make it happen. When the time is right, the experience takes place, and if the time is not right, it will never happen. Impatience and undue effort simply foul up the process, and can create such frustration for our ego that it gives up in disgust. When people present themselves to me for inner work, I ask myself three questions. How hungry are they for imaginal experiences? How protected are they? How patient are they? Without hunger, they will not make the effort required for the work. Without inner protection, the confrontation with the unconscious is too dangerous to undertake. And, without patience, they will not allow the process to evolve in its own time. Whatever process they undertake must be performed at the right moment if it is to have any impact at all.

Christian next observes that the flamespirits of the dead have reached the very top of the tower. As they do so, the wind picks up and Christian becomes so terrified that he rushes off to sleep. Going to sleep in the face of terror is not always a good idea, but it is a method Christian used throughout the book. The flames and the accompanying wind point out the readiness of spiritual energies—the spirits of the dead—to engage in the work. Though the interaction with the spirits, especially of the psychoid, may terrify the individual, such meetings are necessary to achieve the second and third *coniunctios.* If the terror becomes too great, one can always follow Christian's example and take a nap!

DAY SIX

In the morning the work begins anew. This is the sixth day of the allegory and the busiest day, with one process following another in rapid succession. Although the variety of processes and symbols presented in this chapter make it quite significant, they make it equally difficult to interpret. The day begins with the alchemists discussing among themselves the meaning of all they have so far witnessed, though there is no consensus or clear understanding. At this point, an old gentleman comes in to give them further instructions. This is the wise old man who can guide them through the difficult processes ahead. The wise old man often appears in dreams and actives when the ego gets bewildered or stuck.

The alchemists' lack of understanding elicits the appearance of the old man, who brings with him the wisdom that they need to continue. He first tells them that they must choose from among a rope, a ladder, or wings. Though they want to choose freely, he tells them the objects would be assigned by lottery. Each chooses a ticket with the name of one of the objects on it. Christian receives a twelve-runged ladder, which annoys him greatly for he will have to carry it with him. The alchemists soon discover that they are expected to climb through a hole to the next floor of the tower to carry out the next process. Those with wings fly up easily, those with ladders climb without difficulty, and those with ropes have a hard time making the ascent. This ascent symbolizes a further sublimation, a need to experience more deeply the spiritual nature of the work.

Psychologically, people with a rope have a lot of difficulty with inner experience, and have to work hard to go deeper into the inner world. These people might never have direct experiences with psychoidal figures or with visionary states. They might have to painstakingly climb to new levels of perception with willpower and small encouraging experiences. Nevertheless, they can arrive at the next level.

I have great respect for people with ropes. Though they struggle, and it is sometimes painful to watch the slow progress they make, they keep at it until the desired experiences occur. I have worked with clients who had no real imaginative talent and never seemed to make inner contact at all. Yet if they persevered, sooner or later a major experience would take place—even if only briefly—and transformations would follow. In some cases, after years of disappointment, these people have experiences, which open them to the imaginal world. After such experiences, this world, which has for so long eluded them, becomes accessible.

Those with wings are the true visionaries. They easily fly up to the next level as if there were no problem at all, and move from one stage to the next almost without effort. Their progress is quick and impressive, but often they fail in the important work of integrating their visions. Since they have not had to struggle to understand, or to change themselves to progress, their experiences often remain misunderstood and unintegrated. Christian, who serves as the model for the ideal alchemists, is not one of these visionaries. He must also struggle, carrying the ladder around with him. The ladder connects the upper and the lower realms, and while the top reaches above, the bottom remains rooted below. The twelve rungs probably allude to the twelve stages of the work outlined by alchemists such as George Ripley. Though carrying the ladder with him is a challenge, it allows Christian to ascend while staying grounded below. An individual with a ladder has a talent for visionary experience, but such experiences do not unhinge him. He also has the ability to stay related to the outer world and to join inner and outer realities.

One can use any of the three objects, but each represents a different way of doing the work. There is no choice about this either; fate declares who has what capacities in the work. In the long run, all three approaches are effective, but the process will differ according to means used in its accomplishment. A teacher or therapist who guides people in inner alchemy does well to keep in mind that each person performs the work his or her way, with its own peculiar merits and faults. Proper guidance requires that one supports the approach that is natural for each given individual.

Arriving at the higher level, the alchemists discover a vast room with six chambers. They are sent to these chambers to pray for the lives of the king and queen. (In the chapter on imagination, I mentioned prayer as one of the ways that alchemists invoked inner guides and spiritual help.) Through their prayer, the alchemists in the story set the stage for the imaginal operations to come. They do not have long to wait, for a strange object is soon brought into the center of the room.

While the other alchemists believe this object to be a still, Christian, using his deeper perception, realizes that the apparatus contains the corpses of the kings and queens. Through a complicated process, the corpses dissolve completely in hot water coming from a fountain. This process is the *solutio*, through which the physical body, from which the spirit has been extracted, is reduced to liquid. The fountain is the mercurial source, and the water falling on the corpses is a symbol for mercury or its sulphur, which has the power to dissolve all physical bodies.

According to the *Splendor Solis*, the "first thing proper to the Art of Alchemy is Solution. For the law of Nature requires that the body be turned into a water, into a quicksilver. . . . The quicksilver releases the sulfur which is joined and present with it."[17] Sulfur has a number of meanings, but

---

17. Salomon Trismosin, *Splendor Solis* (Grand Rapids: Phanes Press, 1991), p. 58.

its essential role is to shape the fluid mercurial liquid. Sulfur is hot, masculine and formative, so that when it is united with mercury it creates a new form, which is generally the philosopher's stone. *Solutio* has one other major function, for, as Edward Kelly wrote, "Solution is the action of any body, which, by certain laws of innate sympathy, assimilates anything of a lower class to its own essence."[18]

The union of any solid body with mercury symbolizes the performance of active imagination on any topic that has been previously fixed in a certain form. A solid body denotes an idea or attitude that is firm and shaped in a definite way. The ego, for example, might believe that the meaning of life is to make money. It knows this for a fact, and acts accordingly in the outer world. It is motivated by the need to make money and by little else. The attitude about money is a "solid substance." As such, it cannot be transformed; it can only be altered if it is added to mercury—to the imaginal realm. If the ego is willing to admit it might not be totally correct, and asks an inner figure about the meaning of life, the body has been reduced to the liquid mercury. Being softened up in this way, there is the possibility that the attitude may be altered to accommodate the point of view of the self. According to some alchemists, a body dissolved in mercury ceases to be physical and actually becomes a spirit.[19] This would mean that the attitude has become personified as an inner figure, and it has taken on a form to which one can relate. In this example, the belief that life is only about material gain could be personified in the figure of a greedy businessman. Once

---

18. Edward Kelly, *The Alchemical Writings of Edward Kelly*, A. E. Waite, trans. (New York: Samuel Weiser, 1976), p. 49.
19. See for example, *The Alchemical Writings of Edward Kelly.*

it is personified, the ego may relate to such an attitude, and through interaction with it, effect a change.

Adding the body to the mercury triggers the sulfur. In alchemy, there are two types of sulfur—an inner and an outer. The outer sulfur is negative, and creates barriers that prevent natural development, or the creation of the stone. Outer sulfur symbolizes influences that are not part of the self, which shape that individual into something he is truly not. Outer sulfur might be societal influences for example, or parental pressures that force one to act in ways one would not naturally do. In alchemical processes, the outer sulfur must be completely eliminated.

The sulfur triggered by uniting the body with mercury is actually the inner sulfur. Inner sulfur symbolizes the power of the self to manifest, and so the "form" that inner sulfur creates is the manifest self. When the ego enters the imaginal world, it activates the inner sulfur, or the power of the self to create imaginal experiences that help it to come into being. By moving into the imaginal world, and asking the question about the meaning of life, the ego allows the self to present its answer. Through the power of the sulfur, the self appears in an active imagination as an inner figure that teaches the ego what the self believes the meaning of life to be. Through its interaction with this inner figure, the ego can discover a purpose for its life that is much more congruent with its inner nature. Living a life that expresses one's true self is rich and rewarding.

At the same time, according to Kelly, *solutio* operates in such a way as to assimilate a content of lower value to one of higher value. In alchemy, higher value means closer to gold, so that if two metallic substances are mixed in a solution, the one closer to gold will transform the one further from gold into itself. In this way, an originally inferior metal may be worked up the metallic scale until it reaches gold itself.

This means that if two attitudes or ideas are joined in the imagination through dialogue, the one closer to the self will assimilate the other one. This idea provides a very interesting perspective on active imagination. It does not matter if the ego or the inner figure is closer to the self, for whichever one is closer will transform the other. If I become aware that I have a complex that is affecting my ability to live freely, the first step in transforming that complex is to personify it in the imagination as a figure of some kind. If I can do so, and then engage in actives with it, eventually it will be transformed into a form closer to the self. Through the *solutio*, this transformation will occur spontaneously. The ego must hold its spot and not be tricked by the complex figure; in time that figure will transmute. Alternatively, if the ego has an attitude that is not congruent with the self, and is willing to engage in a dialogue with a figure that holds a position closer to the self, the ego's attitude will be transformed.

Active imagination, therefore, acts to unite two opposite positions, and will transform a position distant from the self into one that is closer to the self. The *solutio* works only if the ego enters into active imagination work. Its willingness to do so loosens previously rigid positions, and sets in motion a process that will move either the ego or the inner figure closer to the self. Through this process, the ego invites the self to personify, and as the ego engages with that figure, it is shifted closer to the self through the natural imaginative process.

An interesting emblem illustrating the *solutio* is shown in figure 21 on page 190. The fiery man is reducing some matter to liquid in the egg-like vessel, while the lion sulfur is devouring the sun. The imagery of the solution relates to the putrefaction, and in fact is often seen as leading to it. The sun in this image would symbolize a fixed conscious position, which is devoured by the inner sulfur when that attitude is dissolved in mercury. A woman figure looks on, perhaps embodying mercury, or the work of nature. As the body is dissolved, the previous attitude is destroyed by the fiery power of sulfur so that it may shape a new one closer to the self.

In the parable, the bodies of the kings and queens are thoroughly mixed in the solution. All six of these royal figures represent pairs of opposites, which are reduced to a common solution and so made ready for further transformation. When the solution is later turned back into bodies, only the young king and queen emerge. All the others have become part of them. All the opposites have been united through the *solutio*. All the fixed attitudes and beliefs have been reduced to fluid possibility, waiting for the next process by which the self may emerge.

DAY SIX CONTINUED

The Virgin subsequently brings into the room a round, golden sphere into which the alchemists pour the solution. After a short break, the sphere is placed in a room on a yet higher level, so Christian must make use of his ladder once more. As he enters the room, he notes that there is nothing else in it but the sphere, windows, and mirrors. A mirror is placed between every two windows, and as the sun rises, the mirrors create the optical effect of filling the room with many suns. This also serves to heat up the sphere, and when it is sufficiently hot, the process stops.

Entranced by the vision of the many suns, Christian states that "in this mirroring I beheld the most wonderful thing that Nature ever brought to light: for everywhere there were suns, but the sphere in the center shone even brighter, so that like the sun we could not bear to look at it for a moment."[20]

---

20. *The Chemical Wedding*, p. 86.

Figure 21. The man of fire reduces matter to liquid form in the egg-like vessel, while the lion sulfur is devouring the sun. Mother Nature looks on, governing the natural processes by which alchemy works. The sun in this image symbolizes a fixed conscious position, which is devoured by the inner sulfur in preparation for mixture within the mercurial waters of the imagination from which the sulfur derives. (From J. D. Mylius, *Philosophia reformata*, Frankfurt, 1622.)

The sphere was an important symbol in alchemy, and, like the circle, "represented the unending perfection of the unified spiritual realm and God."[21] The alchemical vessel was constructed on geometrical principles to illustrate the squaring of the circle, for as Dorn wrote, "our vessel . . . should be made according to the geometrical proportion and measure, and by a kind of squaring of the circle."[22] The squaring of the circle is a profound image for the union of heaven and earth, and indicates the bringing into the physical world that of the pure spiritual world of perfection. Squaring the circle indicates that the self has been formed from the union of heaven and earth, and that the inner center is now filled with the emanations of the higher realm. This type of image points to both the second and third *coniunctios*. To create the vessel in the image of the goal helped the alchemists to actually reach it.

The golden sphere represents the vessel, and symbolizes the union of heaven and earth. The sphere already contains the solution in which all the bodies have been dissolved, so that it contains the physical element. The mirroring process then adds the spiritual energies of the sun to heat the physical solution.

Mirrors are among the most intriguing symbols I have encountered in dreamwork. Dreams with mirrors are often about self-knowledge and processes focused on the self. An individual who dreams of looking into a mirror and seeing herself often experiences a big surprise. I have been told of dreams in which women look in the mirror and discover

---

21. Lyndy Abraham, *Marvel and Alchemy* (Brookfield, England: Scholar Press, 1990), p. 44.
22. Quoted in C. G. Jung, CW 13, p. 86 n. 107 (from *Theatrum Chemicum* I Strasbourg, 1659).

that they have beards, and men see that they have lost all their hair or aged. I have also had a client who dreamed that he met an old man who told him that if he looked in the mirror he would finally discover who he really was. He looked, only to be blinded by the radiant light he beheld. These types of dreams indicate that mirrors symbolize the experience of self-awakening, as the ego receives information about its deeper nature.

The mirror in alchemy is related to both wisdom and mercury. According to the alchemist Sendivogius, there is a "magic mirror, in which the three parts of the wisdom of the whole world may be seen and known at a glance; and this mirror clearly exhibits the creation of the world, the influences of the celestial virtues on earthly things and the way in which Nature composes substances. . . ."[23] Mercury is named "nothing but a mirror in which may be perceived the three divisions of the wisdom of the world."[24]

Jung related the mirror to the self, and its ability to reflect on the one hand the subjective consciousness of the ego, and on the other, the objective nature of the transcendental center of the psyche.[25] Lyndy Abraham, in a wonderful study of alchemy and the poet Marvel, summarized the symbolism of the mirror by relating it to the stone, and its power to "create such a crystal surface within that all the mysteries of the creation were visible."[26]

The mirror refers to a function of the mind, which accesses the mysteries of life; since the mirror is closely tied up with the image of mercury, one can argue that the mirror

---

23. Michael Sendivogius, *The New Chemical Light*, Alchemy Website (Database Online), p. 95.
24. Quoted in Lyndy Abraham, *Marvel and Alchemy*, p. 203.
25. C. G. Jung, CW 11, ¶ 427.
26. Lyndy Abraham, *Marvel and Alchemy*, p. 203.

symbolizes the imaginative power of the mind. If the sphere is taken as the vessel in which the opposites are united, it is a self image. The process depicted in this scene is the concentration of energy and power onto the self in such a way as to inaugurate a transformation within it that leads to the creation of a newly vitalized center.

The sun is widely used in alchemy as an image for active, transformative power. As von Franz wrote, "The sun in general is an image of the Godhead . . . the sun was often spoken of as the principle of spiritual elevation. It is therefore that which makes things perfect; it exalts them to the heights. . ."[27] There is an interesting reference to an artificial sun in the writings of John Dee, a magician, philosopher, and occultist who had a great influence on the Rosicrucian movement in its initial stages. As one writer summed up this reference, "successful alchemical work, for Dee, produces an artificial sun in the 'third phase' through the efforts of a soul separated from its body by the art of controlling fire."[28] It is very interesting that Dee links the artificial sun, which is related to the stone, to the *solutio*. It may well be that Andreae derived some of his imagery in this chapter from Dee's work.

The sun is the source of all vitality and energy, and stimulates the formation and transformation of all things on earth. The mirrors that reflect and create a multitude of suns are focusing incredible power on the sphere to impart the animating, vital force of the sun to the stone, or the center.

---

27. Marie-Louise von Franz, *Alchemy* (Toronto: Inner City Books, 1980), pp. 149–150.
28. Tanya Luhrmann, "An Interpretation of the Fama Fraternitatis" in Adam McLean, ed., *A Compendium on the Rosicrucian Vault* (Edinburgh: Hermetic Research Series, 1985), p. 90.

Christian as an inner alchemist is engaged in an imaginative encounter with an archetypal or psychoidal power, whereby the energy of that entity is concentrated into the self, creating the necessary "heat" for it to perform its transformative work. Jung writes that in the *Liber Platonis Quartorum* "the solar sulfur is still a ministering spirit or familiar who can be conjured up by magical invocations to help with the work."[29] The power of the sun may be experienced as an inner figure that bestows its blessings on the center being created within.

The multiplication of the suns in this scene may refer to the many centers of light and power in the unconscious, namely, the archetypes. It may also refer to the many spirits within the psychoid that may be enlisted to help in the work of manifesting the self. In any case, one of the most significant processes in inner alchemy is active imagination work with the personifications of archetypal or psychoidal powers, whose wisdom and energy are required to trigger the manifestation of the self. This process could unfold in the imaginative world in a number of ways, but there are two that are most common.

The easiest way to perform this process is to imagine having an interaction with an inner figure who, after days of dialogue and preparation, agrees to concentrate its energy on the self, either imagined as a center within, or as a personified figure. In the imaginal world, there is a new focus of energy that stimulates the self into activity. Keeping in mind that the imagination is not fantasy, and that processes such as these are very real and numinous experiences, such an active imagination can be transformative in the extreme. In fact, they are crucial to any real manifestation of the self.

---

29. C. G. Jung, CW 14, ¶ 112.

The other form such experiences may take is a direct encounter with energies that are not personified. I suspect such energies are most often psychoidal, but if the ego is able to enter into an imaginative state, usually associated with altered states of consciousness and ecstasy, it can perceive pools of living energy. If the ego is able to stand the tension of feeling these energies long enough, it can begin to direct and channel them into the center. In the imaginal realm, the center is much like the sphere in our story; it is a container in which such energies may be stored, so that they feed the inner alchemical processes.

The alchemists now allow the sphere to cool for a bit and then open it to discover within a large white egg. The alchemists are delighted by their success and, as Christian put it, "we stood around this egg with as much joy as if we had laid it ourselves!"[30] The egg is a symbol of the whole cosmos and of the *prima materia*. It can refer to the vessel itself, as the container in which new life is being fostered. The early Greek alchemists termed the egg the "mystery of the art," and saw it as not only containing the four elements out of which all life is formed, but also the mysterious fifth element, which formed the center of the egg. It is from this fifth element in the center that the chicken or bird emerges.[31]

The influx of power from the sun has stimulated the generation of the egg within the sphere. It has impregnated the egg as well, for very shortly after the appearance of the

---

30. *Chemical Wedding*, p. 87.
31. A. E. Waite, trans., *The Turba Philosophorum* (New York: Samuel Weiser, 1976), p. 12.

egg, a magical bird emerges. The bird comes from the fifth element, or the quintessence of the egg, and so is the personification of it. The quintessence was a magical essence, which embodied all the power of the *prima materia* and was the stuff of which the stone was formed. It is a symbol of the self, and the bird that emerges from the egg is the first personification of the self. The center, empowered and fertilized through the imaginative experiences of the inner alchemists, gives birth to itself in its first manifestation. We might think of the bird as an inner figure that is born at this stage of the work to reflect the emergence of the self. All that one says about the self and its transformation at this point might also refer to the inner figure that personifies the self. Since alchemy reflects itself in active imagination experiences, the inner alchemist often works with the self as inner figure. I mentioned in the last chapter about how important it is to discover the figure that embodies the self, so that one may do active imagination work with it. Since the sacrifice of the king and queen meant that loss of the figure that one originally used, the bird would mark the emergence of a new figure that mirrors the self as it exists in this stage of the work.

The bird is the embodiment of the first *coniunctio*, and as such, is the first return of the king and queen. It grows at a miraculous rate of speed, reminding one of the magical child in dreams and fairytales, who grows from infancy to adulthood in no time at all. The self is manifesting in the first form, but as it emerges, it is black and very dangerous. The bird does not mean any harm, but simply bites and scratches wildly, so that if the alchemists had not first tied it up, it would have inadvertently hurt them. The theme of the wild and dangerous nature of the self as it first appears was noted in the last chapter. Relationship between the ego and the self tames the wildness of the self as it first emerges. As the alchemists pay attention to the bird, it becomes more and more sedate, and less and less dangerous. The more one works with the self, the more related the self becomes.

The next process involves feeding the bird, and the alchemists give it the blood of the beheaded kings and queens for its nourishment. In his commentary on *The Chemical Wedding*, Adam McLean, a well-known scholar and interpreter of alchemy, wrote:

> *In alchemical terms, this blood is the highest development of substance on the earthly realm. To alchemists, the blood of any being is its highest material vehicle. Blood is the closest form that substance can attain to a spiritual state. So by feeding the process, on the arc of its descent into matter, with . . . blood, the operators are bringing to the process the highest and most subtle substance as a vehicle into which the spiritual essence of the King and Queen can reincarnate.*[32]

In other words, the blood is the subtle essence of the king and the queen, which purifies the material body of the bird, and helps prepare it for the infusion of the souls of the king and queen that occurs in the final stages of the *coniunctio*. There are many references to blood, making it a very complex symbol. Dorn spoke of blood as a redeeming substance, belonging to the stone and the world redeemer:

> *At the final operation, by virtue of the power of this most noble fiery mystery, a dark red liquid, like blood, sweats out drop by drop from their material and their vessel. And for this reason they have prophesied that in the last days a most pure man, through whom the world will be freed, will come*

---

32. Joscelyn Godwin, trans., *The Chemical Wedding of Christian Rosenkreutz*, p. 147.

to earth and will sweat bloody drops of a rosy or red hue,
whereby the world will be redeemed from its Fall.[33]

The blood is a magical substance that has the power to redeem and transform. It is related to the stone, itself, and thereby to the self, and symbolizes its healing power. This power creates processes of transformation, which leads to a higher state of being. In *The Chemical Wedding*, the alchemists feed blood to the transforming material at several different times, and later the blood of the bird, itself, is fed to the next image that has emerged. Each time, however, the blood derives from an earlier self-image, as in this scene it comes from the king and queen. The blood symbolizes nourishment for the self and its own transformative power, so that it may move to the next level of development. Each new appearance of the self derives energy and power from the essence of its previous state. The king and queen must be killed to initiate the movement to the new state of manifestation of the self, but their blood, or essence, feeds the self as it moves toward its new condition. The bird, in turn, is slain so that its blood may feed the self at its next stage. The self is always one and the same in essence, though it appears differently at different stages of development. The essence of it, the blood, remains the same throughout its many manifestations. The unique center of each human being is always itself, though it undergoes continuous transformation.

The ego alchemist has been working with the unconscious through active imagination. In this way he has created an initial relationship between the conscious and the unconscious, but this has led to death of both, as they have

---

33. Dorn, "Conqeries Paracelsicae Chemicae," in *Theatrum Chemicum*, I. Quoted in C. G. Jung, CW 13, ¶ 381.

had to sacrifice their own independent position. The death of the king and the queen has finally resulted in the birth of an inner image that unites them. The transcendent function has created the first inner figure, which embodies in itself conscious and unconscious, and the bird symbolizes this inner figure. The blood is the purifying substance, as well as the transformative power of the self. At the same time, it derives from the original opposites, and being fed to the bird means that the bird takes into itself the vitality of both the conscious and unconscious parts of the personality. With the emergence of the bird, an inner figure has appeared that in itself embodies the pairs of opposites. Its first appearance, however, is wild and unrelated. As the ego continues to interact with it, it not only takes on the energy of the king and queen, it also comes into relationship with the ego.

The bird is generally a symbol of soul or spirit, and in this context would indicate that the self is still in a spiritual and nonmaterial form. As the birth of the bird indicates that the first *coniunctio* has been reached, it remains in a volatile and unstable state. Recall from the last chapter that the first *coniunctio* does not last for long, but comes and goes until the second *coniunctio* is reached. The need to move to a more permanent state of the self is symbolized by having to fix the volatile, so that the self does not disappear, but remains in contact with the ego. We would expect the next process to concern fixation, and such is, in fact, the case.

Christian and his friends now put the bird in a bath of a liquid that is so white it looks like milk. It is cool at first, and the bird has a good time frolicking in the bath. However, the liquid is gradually heated and the bird wants to escape. The alchemists put a lid on top of it, forcing the bird to stay in the liquid. All of its feathers having fallen off, its skin appears as smooth as a human being's, while the dissolving feathers turn the liquid blue. They let the bird out of the bath at this point, but it has become wild again, so they put a leash on its neck. A fire is built under the liquid, so that it evaporates until a blue stone is all that is left. This stone is ground up, and the resulting powder is used to paint the bird blue, which, as Christian noted, makes it appear quite strange.

The alchemists are busy in this part of the tale, and the processes they engage in include the *solutio* once more, but also the *coagulatio*, symbolized in the act of painting the bird. The *coagulatio* refers to a creative process by which spirit is turned into a body. The alchemists related coagulation to the creative act of God in the making of the world, as when one alchemist declared, "God hath created all things by his word, having said unto them: Be, and they were made with the four other elements, earth, water, air and fire, which he coagulated."[34] Through this process, the spirit is made into a body, and that which has ascended into the spiritual realm is fixed once more in the world.

This process occurs within inner alchemy in at least three ways. The ego by this time has related to—and interacted with—an inner figure for quite some time. It has learned much from this figure, and at this point it must embody what it has learned. It must start living and applying to its outer life all that the figure has taught it, and this turns what has been only an idea into an actual life experience. By doing so, the ego grounds the inner work in outer life, which normally allows the process to move into its next stage.

At the same time, the self is undergoing a transformation. It is being fixed, symbolized by the loss of the bird's feathers and the application of a leash to its neck. The

---

34. A. E. Waite, trans., *The Turba Philosophorum*, p. 21.

movement from the latent to the manifest self requires that the self become more and more permanently part of the conscious awareness of the ego. This suggests that a major inner transformation must occur, one in which the inner center has become strong enough to remain fixed. Moreover, the leash symbolizes the creation of a relationship between the ego and the self, for the leash is the cord that binds the two together.

Finally, the images which the self uses to personify itself may change with great rapidity. In order to make the relationship between the ego and the inner figure more fixed and permanent, the inner figure objectifying the self needs to become fixed as well. Rather than using many figures to give itself form, the self now uses only one. Though this figure, too, is soon to die, at this stage it fixes the self in one form, making it easier for the ego to relate to it.

The poor bird is not yet done with the process, however. The alchemists now move to the next floor, the sixth. There they find an altar with a number of objects on it. The bird is placed before it, and immediately drinks from a fountain. Then it pecks at a white snake, whose blood is collected by the alchemists in a golden beaker. The alchemists next force the bird to drink the blood of the snake, which it resists furiously. The snake is dipped into the fountain, and comes back to life. Waiting for the clock to strike three, the alchemists chop off the bird's head. Its body is burned to ashes, and its blood is collected. Thus the bird repeats, in its death, the process that the king and queen underwent in theirs.

The bird pecking the snake refers to the union of the fixed and the volatile. The snake belongs to the earth as the bird belongs to the sky. Their union is the joining of two opposites with the result of fixing the bird to the earth. The snake also symbolizes resurrection; it is able to shed its skin and apparently come back to life. The blood is the essence of the thing, so that forcing the bird to drink the snake's blood transfers this power for resurrection to the bird, while at the same time predicting its impending death. Waiting for the clock to strike three symbolizes again that the time must be right if these processes are to work correctly. It is likely also a reference to the alchemically important number 3. For example, there are three principles in alchemy—salt, mercury, and sulphur. Moreover, John Dee associated the production of the artificial sun to the third stage of the work, so that the third hour might refer to the third aspect of the work that led to the emergence of the bird.

At just the right moment the bird is sacrificed. Any progress in this work is always coupled with a sacrifice of the previous accomplishments. The blue bird symbolized the successful completion of the first *coniunctio*, for the image had become quite strong and fixed. The self was well on its way to the second *coniunctio*, at which point it would become permanent in its manifestations. However, as Christian says, the death of the bird "touched us to the heart, yet we could not imagine that a mere bird would help us much, so we let it be."[35] The self, as it appeared in the first *coniunctio*, must be sacrificed so that the second *coniunctio* might be reached. The bird is not complete enough in itself to satisfy the need of the self to manifest.

This is a very painful process, and not one as easily gotten through as Christian implies. Very often, one has worked with an inner figure that embodies the self as it exists in the first stage. The sacrifice of the first union sometimes requires the sacrifice of the inner figure with which one has been working, as a new figure emerges that more completely embodies the next level of union. The

---

35. *The Chemical Wedding*, p. 90.

period lasting from the first to the second conjunctions may extend for years, and the relationship between an inner figure and the ego that lasts for this long is intimate and deeply emotional. To sacrifice that figure, and the union one has created with it, is agonizing. At this stage in the work, when I perceived the death of the inner figure I had lived with for so long, I felt as if all the magic and wonder had vanished from my life. I did not immediately perceive that the essence of that figure would soon reappear in another form at a new level of experience, and so its loss seemed irreparable and overwhelming. I actually watched it die in an imaginative experience, and felt myself dying with it as well. Only days later did I begin to feel its consciousness return in a new form.

The union resulting in the first experience of the self is followed by another *mortificatio*. The marriage of the king and queen indicated that the ego and the unconscious were interacting, and that first period of interaction led to the death of both conscious and unconscious positions. The bird had unified them once more in the first *coniunctio*, but that union, too, is now sacrificed. The alchemists are now well on their way to the second *coniunctio*, which will bring the king and the queen back to life in a higher, more exalted state.

The alchemists are now ready to move into the seventh and final room. However, before they do, the Virgin announces that Christian and three others have disappointed her, and will not be allowed to participate in the work. This proves to be a ruse, for Christian and the other three soon discover that they have been chosen to perform the real work, while the rest of the alchemists are given meaningless tasks to keep them occupied, all the time believing that they were effecting the essential work. This development builds upon the theme that has run through the whole story; Christian was the chosen one whose visionary experiences taught him what was really happening in the work, while the others were fooled by the appearance of things. Very clearly, the author of the tale believed that without true vision the alchemist could never achieve the great work.

Greatly relieved that he has not been punished, Christian set to work with the others. They are given the ashes of the bird, with which they combine their prepared water to form a paste. This they heat over a fire and then pour into two small molds. At this point, they steal a glance at the other alchemists, who are taking turns blowing a fire with a pipe, exhausting themselves. This is probably a reference to the contemptuous term "puffer and blower" that alchemists used for those who did not understand the true nature of the alchemical process.

The ashes of the bird form the material used in the process at this point. Ash was a very powerful substance in alchemy, and was a symbol of great importance. In Hindu alchemy, the reduction of mercury to ash symbolized a return to perfection, to divinity before manifestation.[36] As one Western alchemist wrote, "the ferment of this divine water is ash, which is the ferment of the ferment."[37] Another calls ash a pigmy that is able to destroy giants.[38] Dr. von Franz called the ash "[a] most precious thing and a great mystery." She believed that it referred to the objective substrate of the self, as well as to the substance out of which the resurrected body will be formed.[39]

---

36. David Gordon White, *The Alchemical Body* (Chicago: University of Chicago Press, 1996), p. 282.

37. Patricia Tahil, trans., *The Alchemical Engravings of Mylius* (Edinburgh: Magnum Opus Hermetic Sourceworks, 1984), p. 81.

38. E. J. Langford Garstin, *Theurgy: or the Hermetic Practice* (London: Rider, 1930), p. 91.

39. M.-L. von Franz, *Aurora Consurgens*, Bollingen Series LXXVII (New York: Bollingen Foundation, 1966), pp. 344–345.

In many ways, the ash symbolized the purest residue left when something was purged by fire. It was the core, the essence, and that aspect of the divine that is found in both physical and psychic centers. It was the body in which spirit was placed, but a body that was transmuted and purified into its highest form. Earlier in the story, the king and queen had also been reduced to ashes, and their ashes were used to make the bird. Now the bird is reduced to ashes and used to create a new being.

I have discussed the bird as an image or an inner figure, born out of the interaction of the ego with the unconscious, and embodying in itself the first *coniunctio*. That image had to die so that the next phase of the work could be accomplished. The image that carried the self has been reduced to the purest essence of the self. It has no form as yet, nor any individuality. The level of the self that has been reached in the ashes corresponds to the pure center of the inner divine, before any manifestation. It is the pure and undefiled essence of the self, the very core of being. In this sense, it is what von Franz called an "irreducible and indissoluble substrate of physical and psychic facts which everyone has from birth and out of which individuation is accomplished."[40] The core of the self is a mystery, but the reduction of the image of the self to its purest essence means that the next image that is formed will carry that essence within it.

With the death of the inner figure, the ego encounters the self as it exists in a formless state. Such experiences do not last very long, but they offer the ego insights into the enigma that the inner figure will embody. They provide a glimpse into the mystery that the image has held for them, and they insure that the next inner figure to

---

40. M.-L. von Franz, *Aurora Consurgens*, p. 345.

emerge will carry an even deeper level of the self. The ash holds the divine essence, which often cannot be directly perceived, but can be known only as it appears in the imaginal realm. For this reason, the ash was mixed with the mercurial water in a new solution. This process indicates that the alchemist must introduce the divine essence into the imaginal realm in order to experience it.

Mystics of all times are familiar with the imageless experience of the vast and cosmic, experiences often called "oceanic." They are formless and often hold no content, for they are direct experiences of the divine spirit itself. One knows bliss in such states, but engages in no dialogue or interaction. For some individuals such experiences comprise the goal itself, but the alchemist wishes to do more than experience the divine as cosmic bliss. He wishes to ground the divine in the psyche, itself, and form with it an ongoing partnership that includes not only the vast, but the small and the ordinary, as well. In order to gain these goals, the alchemist unites the divine with an image in which it may then incarnate. In our tale, the alchemists add the imagination to pure Divine Essence in order to create a new inner figure.

In fact, Christian pours the solution into a mold, thereby giving form to the formless. The unknown is given imaginal shape when it is introduced into the imagination, and out of the union of the Divine Essence, and the imaginary experience of it, emerges a new personification of the self. The mold Christian uses is, in some ways, the most important part of the process, for it is through the mold that the paste takes on shape once more.

The self may be experienced in its formless and universal aspect, but it almost immediately creates imaginal experiences through which it takes on form. It propels itself into form, as an artist seeking his proper canvas. And the canvas on which it captures itself is the imagination.

The process presented at this point in the allegory might be summarized by saying that we must experience the very essence of the universal self, the divine at the center of the human soul, and mix it with the imagination, in order to create an inner figure who will embody this essence.

The next step in the process is the emergence of the new figure. From this point on, there are two figures, referring to the king and queen. It is important to keep in mind, however, that these two were in union, and together formed the self. Though they were kept distinct, they are a single whole. Recall the last image of the *Book of Lambspring*, which portrayed the union as three individuals. Each of these individuals represented a different aspect of the manifest self, which may be experienced as a single inner figure.

After allowing the solution to cool, the alchemists open the molds to discover "two beautiful, bright and almost transparent images such as human eyes have never seen, of a little boy and girl, each only four inches long."[41] These tiny beings are so beautiful that Christian and the others are struck dumb in amazement. They can hardly tear their eyes away from them in order to carry out their work, but at last they do so. Though beautiful, the two little creatures remain lifeless and tiny. The alchemists begin to feed them the blood of the bird, and as they do, the little beings grow until they are fully-grown.

The tiny humans who have emerged from the molds are the first appearance of the self in its new personification. The tiny size relates these beings to the image of the *homunculus*, the diminutive human being that appeared from time to time in alchemical writings. Paracelsus wrote extensively about the *homunculus*, which he believed was a magical being that could actually be created from human sperm

---

41. *The Chemical Wedding*, p. 92.

left to putrefy in a vessel. These Lilliputian humans had magical abilities and great wisdom. According to Paracelsus, the *homunculus* first appeared in a transparent way, almost without form. The alchemist must then feed it human blood, and allow it to grow for forty weeks, at which point it emerges as a perfect human being, only very small. The imagery that Paracelsus used closely resembles that found in the present allegory, and may have served as a model for it. For Paracelsus, the *homunculi* could reveal great secrets, and knew all the mysteries of life.[42]

The *homunculi* symbolize the emergence of an inner figure that will personify the deepest aspects of the self. They are magical beings, filled with wisdom and power. Christian attempted to bring them to full size by feeding them the blood of the bird. The blood is the essential nature of the being from which it comes, and symbolizes the energy and power that had been in the bird as the image of the self. Though the previous image has been lost, the energy and essence of it has been preserved. Once this is added to the new image, it undergoes transformation and rapid growth. It is as if all the work and effort that had gone into the interaction with the first image is not lost when it disappears, but is transferred to the new entity. This transferal stimulates the new image into quick development so that it is not necessary to repeat the previous work.

If I have spent years interacting with an inner figure, it has grown and developed because of that work. If that figure must be sacrificed, so a new figure capable of embodying more of the self is produced, that effort is not lost. It is preserved and shifted into the new image as it appears. None of the labor of the ego is wasted.

---

42. Paracelsus, "Concerning the Nature of Things" in A. E. Waite, *The Hermetic and Alchemical Writings of Paracelsus the Great*, vol. 1, p. 125.

All the energy of the self, as it appeared in the first *coniunctio,* is preserved and embodied in the self as it appears in the second level union. As I mentioned earlier, the essence of the self is the same at every level so that its blood or essential core is never lost, but fed to the center as it emerges at the next level. The personification of the self as it emerges into the next level is thus a very powerful figure. It embodies the new center born within the psyche at this stage of the work.

The *homunculi* possessed unearthly beauty and produced in Christian an almost rapturous state. Such beauty symbolizes spiritual beings, and in this case indicates how much of the self has been embodied in the new image. The ecstatic state also indicates how numinous the personified form of the self is. The beauty and the rapture are accurate descriptions of the experience an individual will have when facing the figure that personifies the manifest self. Gazing on such a figure in the imaginal world creates the deepest ecstasy, and the distinct feeling that one is glimpsing into the essential beauty of the universe. The inner figure carries paradise within itself, so that an individual in relationship with it perceives heaven on earth. Moreover, the beauty and mystery of the self appears in a human form, one with which the ego can create a relationship of intimacy, love, and trust. The human form has nothing of the wildness or capriciousness of the bird, nor does it require a leash to form a relationship with it. Appearing in human form, the self presents itself to the ego—with whom it cultivates a rapturous union forever.

Still, despite their rapid growth, the two beautiful figures remain lifeless. The missing souls have to be added to the bodies for the work to be complete. Once again the two guides, the Virgin and the old man, try to trick the alchemists into missing the essential nature of the process. The three alchemists who accompanied Christian in the work are deceived, and miss seeing the real incarnation of the souls, but Christian (largely because of his earlier visions) is able to detect the souls reentering their bodies.

The guides have done their best to confuse and mislead the alchemists. One might wonder about this theme—and its meaning in inner alchemy. After all, guides are supposed to guide and not confuse. If one cannot trust one's guides, who may one trust? The answer given in this work is clear; one must trust one's own vision and perception of things, and not anyone else's, not even one's guides. One of the hardest parts of imaginal work is to develop the necessary trust in one's experiences. Typically, one always doubts and is afraid to trust, for trusting means taking full responsibility for one's own choices, and not being able to rely on others. Moreover, since one's own visions are usually unique, they force one to accept such differences, which is not easy. But—as the story of Christian indicates—failure to trust one's own vision means losing the opportunity to gain true wisdom and insight. Christian does not boast of his visions, nor even insist on being recognized for having them. He has them quietly and privately, and yet they consistently reveal to him the truth of what is happening. One may certainly elicit help in understanding what one has seen, but at some point, the inner vision must be the true and trusted guide.

Christian alone notices that the roof of the room is very strangely constructed. It consists of seven concave hemispheres. The middle one is higher than the others and has a closed hole at the top. At the right moment, this hole opens and the souls enter. The two guides have brought six large trumpets into the room, which are now used to bring the souls into the bodies. While distracting the other alchemists by lighting foliage on fire, the old gentleman places one end of the trumpet in the mouth of the lifeless body of the young king, while the upper end reaches to the hole in the roof. When the hole in the roof opens, the soul enters, passing into the trumpet and through it into the mouth of the young king. This is repeated three times for the king and three times for the queen. The souls of all the kings are thus placed in the body of the young king, and the same is true for the young queen. The king and queen come to life, but remain sleeping. Cupid, the trickster and mercurial figure of the tale, comes in and wakes them up. He then "introduces them to one another again."[43] Finally, the king and the queen are clothed in beautiful crystal garments. The work is now accomplished and there is a general celebration at dinner. Though there is still one more day in the allegory, there are no more reference to the process, for the stone has been created.

The body having been thoroughly prepared, the souls are reincarnated. The soul has a great many meanings in alchemy, and is a very rich and complex symbol. There are three ways of understanding it that are most relevant to our story. It is the life principle that bestows animation and vitality on the body. Without a soul there can be no life, and clearly in *The Chemical Wedding* the new forms of the royal couple are inanimate until the soul is restored to them. Secondly, it is the ferment. As Edward Kelly wrote, "the ferment is the soul, because it gives life to the body and changes it into its own nature."[44] The soul not only animates the body; it changes it in such a way as to make it reflect its own nature. The soul thus alters the body that it animates, and forms it into an image or reflection of itself. Finally, and clearly related, the soul bestows individuality onto the body and is, in essence, the individual being that inhabits the body.

---

43. *The Chemical Wedding*, p. 94.
44. Edward Kelly, *The Alchemical Writings of Edward Kelly*, A. E. Waite, trans., p. 43.

I have indicated that the *homunculi* form the personified inner figure that embodies the newly created manifest self. However, if the soul is not added to that inner figure it will remain a more or less collective image, lacking the essential individuality of the person to whom it appears. Any image that emerges from the unconscious has a collective aspect to it, for the same image may appear to anyone. If I dream of a king who is the reflection of the self, that image is still a universal one, for anyone can dream of a king who represents the self. For the inner figure of the king to truly embody *my* self, as opposed to *the* self, it must incarnate my own uniqueness and individuality. When it does this, it ceases to be a universal image and becomes particular to me.

The soul in this case is something akin to what in Zen is called the original face, the essential and unique individual nature of a human being that transcends the ego, and possibly even death. It is my core essence, and one of the great mysteries of life. For anyone to discover his or her own individuality is rare indeed, but without discovering it, the self can never come alive. Until the soul is added to the image of the self, that image remains half dead and without real power. When the soul is added to the image, it acts as ferment, converting that image to its own nature. That is to say, if one can experience his or her own deepest individuality, it is added to the image of the self, so that image comes to embody it fully. One's uniqueness colors the inner figure, so that it ceases to be a universal image, and takes on the unique aspects of the soul. The soul aspect of the self is the essence of its individuality as manifested in a particular human being.

The experience of one's own soul is often a visionary event that carries one into the psychoid. There is an objective and transcendent quality to the soul that makes of it something that is transpsychic and immortal in its own right. Hence the imagery in the tale of the hole in the roof and the trumpet. There is a hole in the psyche, through which the psychoid may be experienced. At the right time, and in the right place, this hole can be opened to allow one to experience other levels of imaginal reality. It is on these other levels that the true nature of the individual may be discovered.

The soul, having been liberated from the body earlier in the work, experienced a *sublimatio* in which it discovered and integrated the higher spiritual powers, and at the same time discovered its own nature. Only when the soul separates from the body and is able to contemplate its own eternal nature and uniqueness can it gain true self-knowledge. This treasure having been found, the soul returns to the body, animating and transmuting it into its own nature. When the soul is united with the inner figure of the self, that inner figure transmutes, and becomes the living embodiment of the unique individuality of the person. Since this individuality belongs to both the ego and the unconscious as well, it must be embodied in the personification of the self, and not in the ego, for only the self is strong enough to house it.

The psychoidal nature of the soul is not to be confused with the self of the psychoid. The psychoidal self is an image of the divinity that appears in a unique way to match the individuality of the person relating to it. The soul is psychoidal in the sense that it exists in a realm beyond the ordinary world, and is eternal in its own right. When the eternal aspect of the self is united with the image of the self, one has passed to the second *coniunctio*, and the manifest self comes to life.

The trumpet is the means by which the soul comes into the body. This is a very ancient image of incarnation, with a definite reference to the incarnation of Christ. As Jung pointed out, "there are . . . medieval paintings that depict the fructification of Mary with a tube or hose-piping coming down from the throne of God and passing into her body, and we can see the dove or the Christ-child flying down it."[45] This tube of the trumpet along which the soul descends, is like the tube along which Christ descends from God to the Virgin Mary. Both are symbols of the process by which the soul descends into matter.

The trumpet (or horn) appears in a number of alchemical emblems. In figure 22 (page 216) the angel Gabriel appears to be waking the sleeping sun and moon by blowing on his horn. The title of the emblem is *fermentatio,* and the connection of the soul to the ferment suggests that this process is the incarnation of the soul, which awakens the lifeless body.

The stages described in this part of the allegory point to the opening of the hole to the other world, or the development of the imaginative capacity to see into other levels of reality. When this ability is sufficiently powerful, one must use it to see what and who one really is. The discovery of the soul as an eternal truth is a great awakening, but it must be followed by the incarnation of the truth within one's own psyche. This can be accomplished through the imaginal experiences by which one's deepest individuality colors the inner figure that personifies the self, so that it incarnates that individuality. Always keeping in mind that such individuality transcends the ego, one can see that only an inner figure can fully incarnate it. When this incarnation occurs, the body and the soul are reunited in the second *coniunctio,* and the manifest self is the result.

---

45. C. G. Jung, *The Archetypes and the Collective Unconscious,* Collected Works, vol. 9i, R. F. C. Hull, trans., Bollingen Series XX (Princeton: Princeton University Press, ¶ 108). Future references will be to CW 9i.

The crystal clothes that adorn the king and queen are a reference to the stone, which is compared to crystals in a number of texts.[46] They symbolize the purity and power of the new royal couple as they emerge into life. It is Cupid who awakens and reintroduces the couple to each other, as if they have forgotten who the other was in some way. Cupid acts as a trickster figure in this tale, but is symbolically related to his mother Venus, and through her, to the principle of love. The power of love informs part of alchemy, though students of the alchemical work often neglect it. As Dorn wrote, "we take the characters of Venus, that is, the shield and buckler of love, to resist manfully the obstacles that confront us, for love overcomes all difficulties. . . ."[47] Love awakens the marriage pair to the final consummation of their union.

As I mentioned at the beginning of this chapter, the alchemist does not control the processes he attempts to initiate, and in fact is never quite sure that they will take place at all. Processes such as the ones I have been discussing occur naturally and organically within the imaginal realms, operating through the transcendent function that binds the opposites together. These processes accomplish the great work, and though the ego must witness them as deeply as possible, it can do little else. Over and over again, in our tale, Christian's ability to see connects him to the deepest aspect of the processes that are unfolding. Though the others are always misled or confused, Christian correctly perceives the nature of the work. This capacity to "see" is the requirement of anyone who truly wishes to experience

---

46. C. G. Jung, CW 14, ¶ 642.
47. Quoted in C. G. Jung, CW 13, ¶ 214. From Gerald Dorn, *Devita Longa* (1583).

Figure 22. The wise old man, or perhaps the alchemist, watches as the angel Gabriel blows his horn to awaken the sleeping sun and moon. Just as in *The Chemical Wedding* the king and queen remain asleep until the trumpet is blown and their souls return, so here the trumpet summons the souls of the sun and moon to awaken them to union. The emblem is called *fermentatio* and, as Edward Kelly says, the ferment is the soul. The illustration depicts the rejoining of the soul to the body with the consequent animation and transformation of the body. The soul's return causes the body to reflect the indiviso duality and uniqueness of the self. (From J. D. Mylius, *Philosophia reformata*, Frankfurt, 1622.)

the alchemical procedures and operations, and one can develop this skill only through extended work with the imagination. As the mercurial power, imagination allows the processes to occur, and is the medium through which they can occur. The ego relaxes all control and must be content to witness the manner in which the self dies and is reborn into its new, glorified state.

CHAPTER 5

The
NATURE
of SPIRITUAL ALCHEMY

Even the most practical of alchemical texts can teach one a great deal about the nature of imaginal undertakings. Certain texts are more concerned with inner experience, and what may be called the spiritual side of alchemy. These texts have a certain tone, and an emphasis that marks them as different from the others especially in the ways in which they deal with the role of the divine and the spirit in the alchemical work. Though they, too, speak of processes and procedures, they nevertheless are more obviously interested in the spiritual nature of the work than other, more practical writings. The more spiritual texts portray the *opus* as a mystical and magical endeavor to channel the universal power (or force) found in nature into a hidden center in order to create a stone of marvelous efficacy. Having examined practical processes in the last chapter, we shall now examine the spiritual context and perspective in which many alchemists place those processes.

The model that informs spiritual alchemy has much in common with the essential model of all alchemy; a stone may be prepared from the union of certain opposites, such as sulfur and mercury. The stone may then perform transformative and healing feats. To one degree or another, the very concepts and goals that motivate the alchemists are spiritual. When the spiritual element dominates, there are four attributes of the alchemical enterprise that stand out.

There is a spirit or divine force hidden in nature. In the alchemical processes this spirit may be isolated, strengthened, and used to empower a material object. This spirit is latent, and much of its power is lost in the material world in which it finds itself. The alchemist must find a way to release it from its prison and, having fortified it, locate it in a physical form that is suitable. Placed in the proper physical container, the spirit does not lose its efficacy. In the struggle to release this divine force, the alchemists engaged in the spiritual work of redeeming God, or at least one aspect of God.

Since the spirit must be located in an appropriate container, the physical side of the stone is just as important as the spiritual side. This, too, is true of all alchemists, but the more spiritually oriented among them emphasize the spiritual nature of the matter, often comparing it to the body of resurrection, or even the body of Christ after the crucifixion. I am inclined to think that this side of alchemy points to a mysticism of matter, a spiritual perspective on the body and the material world that deserves much more study.

Many of the more spiritually inclined alchemists clearly indicate that the work takes place in the imaginal realm, and relies on the power of the imagination for its accomplishment. In cases where this is not mentioned, the special qualities of the matter and spirit with which the alchemists worked revealed that they did not feel themselves involved in the ordinary world of material objects. If, for example, an alchemist is creating a body of resurrection he or she is not working with ordinary matter, but with subtle or psychoidal matter.

Finally, the spiritual alchemists reject the search for gold and hardly speak of healing. For them the stone creates mystical experiences and ecstasy, and offers a door that leads to the celestial world. Their goal in the creation of the stone is direct encounter with divinity. These four points of view give spiritual alchemy its peculiar flavor.

THE CENTER OF NATURE CONCENTRATED

The first text to consider from this perspective is a tract titled *The Center of Nature Concentrated* by a writer who called himself Ali Puli. The author purported to be an Arab alchemist, and claimed that the work was first written in Arabic, though this all seems highly unlikely. The work was published in 1682, and shows definite influence from Jacob Boehme.

The writer begins with an attack on alchemy and those alchemists who pursue it for a love of gold, rather than for a sincere desire for truth. Gold-oriented alchemists have wasted their lives and neglected their wives and children; all to no good end. He reminds his readers that life is short, and that they should "seek to discover your own true self and seek the presence of your soul, now as hard as iron, as cold and dirty as lead. . . ."[1] The spirit of God that is continuously present could penetrate and transform the soul, and this transformation is of far greater importance than seeking the philosopher's stone. The author quite consciously distinguishes himself from the puffer and blowers, and makes it clear that alchemy is about the transformation of the soul, and not about metals. Having said all that, he seems to reverse course. For those who practice all the virtues, and pray with humility for wisdom, the practice of alchemy should not be discouraged.

Almost every alchemist urges his readers to be devout and lead a virtuous life, which includes the earnest prac-

---

1. Ali Puli, *The Center of Nature Concentrated* (Edmonds, WA: The Alchemical Press, 1988), p. 9.

tice of prayer. It seems at times almost a formulaic rendition without much energy or import. Ali Puli, however, not only gave the formula with sincerity, he also set the stage for understanding alchemy as the science of the transformation of the soul. He certainly has in mind the natural world as well as the soul, but he conceives of the natural world as belonging to the transcendental spiritual world.

For example, the work of creation itself is part of the struggle between Lucifer and God. The central substance is salt, and before the fall of Lucifer, salt is the center of a void, but it burst into flames as Lucifer attempted to exalt the light and radiance that came from himself, and to thereby create a realm similar to God's—one which exalts Lucifer himself. The "elementary substance was thereby changed from the bright light of Nature to murky darkness and then became ether."[2] Creation thus resulted from a battle between Lucifer and God, and in true gnostic fashion Ali Puli believes that Lucifer's act of rebellion corrupts nature and the central salt.

Nature would have forever been corrupt and impaired had not God sent a beam of His light into the center core of salt, causing it to awake. Lucifer turned his light to darkness through the heat of his imagination, and God redeemed his world by sending His light into it.

Everything in the physical world of Nature could be understood only through this mythic contest between God and Lucifer. The act of redemption is thus the true work of the alchemist, as he discovers and purifies the spirit that God implanted in the natural world. This gnostic element is as old as alchemy itself, but receives a special emphasis in the mystical writing of Ali Puli. The struggle to increase

---

2. Ali Puli, *The Center of Nature Concentrated*, p. 12.

the light at the expense of darkness is the true work of the alchemist who works with the magical substance that most embodied the light—the salt.

The salt is the secret of the work and is the quasi-physical apotheosis of the light. Salt has become an important element in alchemy at least since the time of Paracelsus, who makes it equal in significance with mercury and sulfur. Salt is part of the alchemical world before Paracelsus, but receives more emphasis as a result of his studies. Following Paracelsus, writers such as Sendivogius, Nolle, and Le Febre find in salt one of the great secrets of nature, the substance in which matter and spirit seemed to come together. Jung summarizes the meaning of this image when he writes that salt as a cosmic principle was "the spirit, the turning of the body into light (the *albedo*), the spark of the *anima mundi*, imprisoned in the dark depths of the sea."[3] Most especially salt was connected to the center. One alchemist writes that "salt is the center of life"[4] and for Ali Puli, salt as a center is most significant.

Within the slimy water which results from Lucifer's darkening, there exists a "concentrated focal point" which was the salt. This salt is the "World of the Luminary," and wherever it spreads, it forms centers by a "circumambient pulsation, to which the Salt clings together with the Divine Spirit of Nature, and the Invisible Breath of the Divine Injunction."[5] The salt is a concentrated focal point of the Divine light, and it operates efficiently in Nature, and

---

3. C. G. Jung, *Mysterium Coniunctionis*, Collected Works, vol. 14, R. F. C. Hull, trans., Bollingen Series XX (Princeton: Princeton University Press, 1970), ¶ 328.

4. Sigismond Bacstrom, *Alchemical Anthology*, J. D. Hamilton-Jones, ed. (Kila, MT: Kessinger, n.d.), p. 91.

5. Ali Puli, *The Center of Nature Concentrated*, p. 14.

in the Word of God that created Nature. Salt, then, is the embodiment of the light that God sends into the world, but it exists in the darkness created by Lucifer. When activated, this focal point, through its own pulsation, creates centers, which united into one the salt, the natural spirit, and the Divine Word.

Salt is related to the self, both because salt symbolizes the arcane substance lost in the murky material world, and thus resembles the latent self, and because it is the center of all things, just as the self is the center of the psyche. But the salt is not just the center; it creates centers through its pulsation, which then unites within themselves a trinity of divine forces. Such a center contains the salt which "clings" to it, as well as the divine force of nature, and the Word of God, which created nature. The salt will symbolize the power that creates the self, and then is embodied in the self. The divine light of Nature is the divine core found in the human being that forms part of the self, while the Word of God, existing outside of the nature it creates, is the psychoidal self. The psychoidal self exists outside the natural world of the psyche, and yet incarnates in it at the very center, which has come into being through the manifestation of salt.

The salt is the power that moves the self from the latent to the manifest state. At the same time it unites within itself the two aspects of divinity—that found in the psyche and that found outside the psyche. The salt is thus the power that creates the manifest self. In that center the human being finds not only his or her own nature, but achieves the union between the light of nature and the Word of God, unifying the God within the soul and the psychoidal God. The salt creates the second and third *coniunctios*.

The spiritual alchemy of Ali Puli found the hidden divine germ within the Luciferian darkness and redeemed it. Through the processes of its redemption, the salt created a center that unites the human soul and God within itself. Since the salt contained the center and the Divine Word, even when lost in the darkness, its transformation is at the same time redemption of God and a multiplication of His light. Man was redeemed, and so was God.

Ali Puli next elaborates further on the nature of salt. It is the power that manifests in all the natural processes, and so explains the conception and birth of human beings and animals, but its main role is still as the center. As the center it is "the middlemost point, to which cling both the uppermost and the nethermost."[6] It thus takes on the power of the upper and lower worlds, uniting nature and spirit in itself. It is the source of all life and the means by which life is sustained, for without it all would die. It is thus related to the notion of the *anima mundi* and is the influx of God's power that nourishes all life. It is also the *prima materia*, for from salt could be made the magical instrument, the "Glorious and Splendid Thing"[7] which is the image of resurrection and immortality, clearly revealing the celestial Father and all the mysteries of nature and spirit. The philosopher's stone is thus created from the salt.

The quest for the proper salt is important as well. Salt is found in all things, but the salt most suitable for the creation of the stone is found in one thing above all others. Ali Puli states that he would speak without the usual "embellishments," and would reveal the truth quite clearly. The salt is found in man himself. Man is the great mystery and the crown of creation, and man "is the universal focal point."[8] Ali Puli has already stated that salt is the focal point, so that

---

6. Ali Puli, *The Center of Nature Concentrated*, p. 14.
7. Ali Puli, *The Center of Nature Concentrated*, p. 15.
8. Ali Puli, *The Center of Nature Concentrated*, p. 19.

human beings and salt were equated in this passage. Though he never states the identity of human beings with salt in so many words, he goes on to describe the human in the same way he speaks of salt earlier. Human beings are not only a focal point, but are "in the middlemost point between the uppermost and the nethermost."[19] Ali Puli uses the same words to describe the salt. More than this, human beings united within themselves the eternal Word of God as It existed in eternity, and the Word of God as It existed in nature. Clearly, human beings as self are the salt which is the focal point, and which unites not only higher and lower, but the two aspects of divinity, the Word in time and the Word in eternity. The human self is the center that unites God and all creation within itself. It is the center, therefore, in which the second and third *coniunctios* are attained.

The salt creates a center whenever it is activated, and it has now been made clear that this center is within the human being. In this alchemical mysticism, every human being holds within the latent center lying under the muck of unconsciousness and Luciferian darkness. So long as the human lives in darkness and. supports the Luciferian inflation of the ego, the self cannot be created. Leaving behind the identification with illusion and fantasy, the ego may turn within and activate the pulsating power of the latent center, which initiates the processes by which it becomes manifest. The manifest center unites in itself the two aspects of God and, as well, the human soul. It becomes unique and able to unite with the psychoidal world in the third *coniunctio*.

The spirituality of Ali Puli places the greatest value on human beings, who are the arcane salt itself. We are the crown of all creation and the potential redeemer of ourselves

---

9. Ali Puli, *The Center of Nature Concentrated*, p. 20.

and of God. We are the center of the universe. Imagine, if you can, what it means to be the center of the universe! To recognize within yourself the magical power to unify human and divine worlds, to incarnate the uppermost and the nethermost, and to join together the two aspects of the Divine Word. There is no greater power, no higher majesty than the human self. Nor is this just true of one type of human, one race, or one religion. Every human being is the center of creation, at least potentially. Though this center must be created through the processes of inner alchemy, every man, woman, and child is the core of all of life. Imagine living in a world that treated every human being as the center of life, and that afforded to the human self the respect which it is due. It is no wonder that the greatest struggle of the modern world is to liberate the individual from the masses, and to restore to the individual the dignity and honor each person deserves. If our society would recognize the potential lying within the darkness of every human soul and would expend its resources toward the development of that potential, our world would be far different indeed. This is, of course, not likely to occur, but those who study psychology and attempt to guide human development would do well to consider the miraculous nature of the psyche with which they are working.

Alchemical spirituality sees the human being as the center of existence, human and divine, and seeks to develop its potential. Ali Puli now reveals the influence of Jacob Boehme when he writes that Lucifer rebelled through the force of his imagination as did Adam and Eve. In the chapter on imagination I wrote about Boehme's understanding of imagination's great power for good and bad. Through it Adam and Eve fall from grace, but the power of imagination remains hidden in the soul. In fact, Ali Puli next writes that imagination is "the focal point of everything." This phrase should by now be familiar to the reader. Salt is the focal point, the human being is the focal point, and imagination is the focal point. Through the focal point of imagination, "all things in the world must obey him [the human being]."[10]

The human being possesses the true salt from which the stone is created. The stone is the center, which unites the soul with the Divine Word. The salt, as the process by which the center emerges, and the power of the center when it has emerged, is the imagination. Salt, as the incarnation of the divine, is both the center and the imaginative power of the center through which all things may be accomplished. All things in the universe obey the imagination of the self. So powerful is the imagination that it is through it that the fall occurs, but likewise it is through the imagination that redemption might be had. Once the center has been redeemed, the power of imagination may shine through, unimpaired, to reveal the secrets of life.

Alchemical spirituality unites the power of the imagination with the center of the soul to envision a human self that has dominion over all that is, and that has united not only the human and the divine, but the two aspects of the divinity as well. The ultimate mystery of such spirituality is the human being itself:

> I say to you, my disciples in the study of Nature, if you do not find the thing for which you are seeking, in your own self, much less will you find it outside your self. Understand the glorious strength resident in your own selves. Why trouble to enquire from another? In Man, named after God, there are things more glorious than are to be found elsewhere in the whole world. Should anyone desire to become a master, he will not find a better material for his achievement anywhere than in himself.[11]

---

10. Ali Puli, *The Center of Nature Concentrated*, p. 21.
11. Ali Puli, *The Center of Nature Concentrated*, p. 23.

The human being has within the greatest power and mystery found anywhere in creation. We contain the center of the universe, and the imaginative power to know and experience all things. The masterpiece of alchemical, as well as of Jungian spirituality, is the human self. The self has the capacity to awaken as the center of the psyche, and of the psychoid worlds as well, for it may marry the twin poles of the Godhead: the Word within the psyche and the Word outside of it. The salt by which this work is performed is the human imagination, the focal point of life.

TRUTH'S GOLDEN HARROW

There is another theme often found in alchemy that might be termed the spirituality of the body. The alchemist always believes that the work must not only liberate the spirit, it must embody it in a physical form that transforms so profoundly that its physicality becomes of a different order. Not only does the nature of the body alter; it gains immortality or at least longevity:

> *The body will rejoyce with the Soul, and the Soul will rejoyce with the Body and Spirit, and the Spirit will rejoyce with the Body and Soul and they will be fixed together, and dwell one another, in which Life they will be made perpetual and immortal without separation for ever.* [12]

The complex interaction between body and spirit in alchemical spirituality deserves far greater study than it has received, but I can only review it here. The touchstone of alchemical spirituality is its insistence on the partnership between the body and the spirit. The alchemists understand this partnership in a variety of ways, but they uniformly insist upon it.

---

12. Calid, "Secret of Secrets" in Stanton J. Linden, ed., *The Mirror of Alchemy* (New York: Garland, 1992), p. 113.

In one of the more interesting texts asserting the physicality of the stone, Robert Fludd, a well-known esoteric writer and visionary of the 17th century, presented his case against taking the stone metaphorically. In *Truth's Golden Harrow*, he presents the spiritual view of the stone, while at the same time insisting that the stone has a body. He terms the stone the "castle of love and the temple of wisdom, the earthly sonne of the philosophers which is as well the tabernacle of the divine emanation as the heavenly."[13] At the same time, he compares it to the body of resurrection, the miraculous body that appears at the end of days. Moreover, it is like the very body which Christ has after the crucifixion, and which he wears when he briefly returns to the world. The resurrected Christ is, in fact, the image for Fludd of the stone as physical substance. In the risen Christ, body and soul are woven together into a whole by which means death is vanquished.[14] What, asked Fludd, are we to call such a body? Is it not material because it is spiritual? Rather, he answers, it is both at the same time. Moreover, he argues that the body and the spirit are not so different, but only differ as to their refinement and purity. If, therefore, we are to deny the physicality of the stone, it would be the same as rejecting the risen Christ. Rather, the stone consists "of a divine and plusquamperfect spirit and a body exalted from corporeality unto a pure and spiritual existence, from morality into immortality, and being the patterne of Christ risen again, it must needs have the power to multiply infinitely."[15]

---

13. Robert Fludd, "Truth's Golden Harrow" in C. H. Josten, "Truth's Golden Harrow: An Unpublished Alchemical Treatise of Robert Fludd in the Bodleian Library," *Ambix: The Journal of the Society for the Study of Alchemy and Early Chemistry*, vol. 3, April, 1949, p. 108.

14. Robert Fludd, "Truth's Golden Harrow," p. 110.

15. Robert Fludd, "Truth's Golden Harrow," p. 111.

The body does not remain corporeal, but has attained a new level of being, a pure and spiritual existence, and yet still remains a body. The Sufi alchemists discuss this body of resurrection as well. Shaikh Aḥmad Aḥsā'ī argues that alchemical operations never occur with physical substances, but with bodies that are spiritual:

> *This is why the Philosophers affirm: it is certainly a* body, *but its virtue and operation are* spiritual. *So be sure you understand the sign, the marvel here described. For this kind of corporeality is exactly the marvel that characterizes the spiritual body of those who live in Paradise.*[16]

He relates such bodies to imaginal forms, and places them within the imaginal realm. Thus, the body of the stone is not physical in the ordinary sense of the word, but a body with form and corporeal attributes, and yet at the same time a spirit.

Fludd goes on to express the spiritual alchemical view that spirit has become lost in the darkness of matter and requires redemption. The redemption occurs when the alchemist releases the spirit hidden in matter and unites it with the pure spirits of the air. He next joins the transformed spirit with the purified body, creating a union of body and spirit. The body is now not only physical, but spiritual as well. This he terms a resurrection, the result of which is that matter is "transmuted into the nature of incorruptibility and immortality."[17]

Jung is interested in the relationship between body and psyche, not only as a physician concerned with the problems of healing, but also as a theoretician struggling to un-

---

16. Henry Corbin, *Spiritual Body and Celestial Earth*, Nancy Pearson, trans. (Princeton: Princeton University Press, 1989), p. 209.
17. Robert Fludd, *Truth's Golden Harrow*, p. 120.

derstand the nature of reality. To my knowledge, he never proffers a clear statement of his own views, but he raises the possibility that, in another sphere of experience, the body and the psyche might be the same:

> We do not know whether what we on the empirical plane regard as physical may not, in the Unknown beyond our experience, be identical with what on this side of the border we distinguish from the physical as psychic. . . . Precisely because the psychic and the physical are mutually dependent it has often been conjectured that they may be identical somewhere beyond our present experience.[18]

Jung used the word "psyche" where the alchemists would say "spirit," and the two are not always interchangeable. From my own perspective, which views the spirit as imaginative power and expression, the union of the physical with the spiritual world means the unification of the physical and the imaginal, and the creation of an imaginal body. The alchemists' concern with healing leads them to the exploration of the imagination as a restorative force. Their study of the ways in which spirit and body overlapped and interacted also leads them to formulate theories of the imagination as a subtle body.

Alchemy aims at the union of matter and spirit, with the result that the body becomes spirit and the spirit becomes body, creating a union of opposites, which liberates the body from the bonds of death. The stone, as the union of opposites, most assuredly is a body, and yet as body is not corporeal. There is no one word used for this new type of body, but it has been called the body of resurrection and the subtle body. I would term it the psychoid body, for it is, by definition, the union of body and spirit.

---

18. C. G. Jung, CW 14, ¶ 765.

Applying the notion of the psychoid body to the self and to the imagination opens up many possibilities for exploration. I wrote in an earlier chapter about an experience in which I was simultaneously in bed in my physical body and on top of a mountain. When I was on the mountain, I felt myself in a body, one that was as real as my body lying on the bed. In other experiences I came to understand that this body was different than the physical body, in that it was not subject to the normal physical limits or barriers of ordinary life. It could float, change locations instantly, and so forth. Yet in all other ways I felt embodied. In such experiences it is the psychoid body, the body of the manifest self that one inhabits. It seems to me perfectly possible that at death one would be able to move from the ordinary body into the psychoidal body.

As I mentioned, there has been very little study of such things. To even speak of them garners one projections that are uncomfortable to say the least. It takes a great deal of courage to speak of the psychoidal and of the body as psychoid in our society, and the complete resistance to such ideas makes such discussion difficult. However, there have been a few people who have spoken and written of these concepts from the Jungian perspective.

Dr. von Franz wrote an interesting work on dreams and death, in which she speculates that the manifest self might survive death. Moreover, she entertains the possibility that the souls of the dead could appear in dreams as well. In his introduction to this work, Emmanuel Kennedy-Xypolitas explains that such dreams, which might be called. psychoidal, "have an intense emotional impact on the dreamer and are characterized furthermore by a unique, indescribable feeling—a touch of eternity."[19] Anyone who has ever had such

---

19. Emmanuel Kennedy-Xypolitas, Introduction to *On Dreams and Death*, by M.-L. von Franz (Chicago: Open Court, 1988), p. ix.

a dream knows that they have a unique feel about them, which is unlike any other dream.

In her study, Dr. von Franz reached the conclusion that the manifest self has the power to survive death intact:

> *Only a conscious realization of the Self—which, as spiritus rector of all biological and psychological occurrences, represents the eventual unity of all archetypes—seems to represent a possession which cannot be lost, even in death.*[20]

The creation of the manifest self, which unites all of the archetypes in a single unity, opens the door to eternity, for the self so created is of such power and durability that not even death itself can diminish its consciousness. It is as if the self, on manifesting, gains a psychoidal dimension. It might be that it gains a psychoidal body as it manifests. The ego, since it is part of the manifest self, experiences this stage as coming into its own immortality.

Barbara Hannah, a student of Jung's and a close friend of von Franz's spoke shortly before her death about the nature of the subtle body. She conjectured that the unconscious is concerned with building a subtle body of a spiritual nature. She spoke of a number of dreams that indicated life goes on beyond death and argued that—through close attention to the self—one could experience one's "own specific death which will crown and not tear apart our life."[21]

These two Jungian analysts wrote on death and immortality late in their lives, after living with the self for many, many years. It should be heartening to all of us that their lifetime of experience with the individuation process gave them such a firm sense of the immortality of the self. Such a conviction would not surprise the alchemists, for they see

---

20. M.-L. von Franz, *On Dreams and Death*, p. 142.
21. "The Beyond," private transcript of a taped lecture presented by Barbara Hannah in 1962 at the Second Bailey Island Conference.

in the stone the key to immortality and in its creation the secret of eternal life:

> *Approach, ye sons of Wisdom and rejoice; let us now rejoice together; for the reign of death is finished and the son doth rule, and now he is invested with the red garment, and the purple is put on.*[22]

Spiritual alchemy perceives the body as something that can be transmuted through its union with the spirit, and believes firmly that such a transmutation can create the body of resurrection, the eternal subtle body through which the power of death is broken forever. The possibility that our own selves could enter a level of being that generates a new and immortal body should stimulate our interest and encourage us to explore these imaginal experiences more deeply.

THE GOLDEN TREATISE OF HERMES

Since the alchemists can experience the stone as an inner figure, a living entity of some kind, the question naturally arises regarding the relationship between themselves and the stone. The stone is a figure possessed of great magical power, and whenever there is such power involved in relationships one of the problems that arises is about who is to control that power. For the most part, the alchemists view the relationship with the stone as being one of partnership, with no firm and fixed rules of conduct, nor with either partner established in a superior position. Love is an important element in the alchemical process, and one that should not be overlooked. There are many references to Cupid, Venus, and the principle of love that both represent. There is

---

22. "The Golden Treatise of Hermes" in Israel Regardie, *The Philosopher's Stone* (Saint Paul: Llewellyn Publications, 1978), p. 37.

no question that the alchemists love the stone, and it is likely that much of their sexual and marriage symbols point to this emotional bond with the stone. This relationship is an important part of spiritual alchemy. One alchemist portrayed the stone speaking of this relationship as follows:

> *Protect me, and I will protect thee; give me my own, that I may help thee. My Sol and my beams are most inward and secretly in me. My own Luna, also, is my light, exceeding every other light; and my good things are better than all other good things; I give freely and reward the intelligent with joy and gladness, glory, riches, and delights; and what they ask about I make them to know and understand and to possess divine things.* [23]

The stone asks for the help from the alchemist and promises help in return. It specifically asks for protection, which points to an interesting dynamic in the relationship between the ego and the self. I recall one analyst in Zurich referring to the ego as the bodyguard of the self. He meant by this that there are times when the ego must safeguard the self from injurious influences, or the self may actually be damaged. There are, in fact, at least three periods during which the self is extremely vulnerable and requires the protection of the ego.

At the beginning of the work, the self is in a latent condition. It will remain in that state indefinitely without the intervention of the ego. The self requires the ego's aid in order to transform, and without the ego it never realizes its potential. The protection of the ego in this case means the attention that the ego pays to the self and its processes, as well as its willingness to steadfastly undergo the required experiences. Though the ego cannot make the

---

23. "The Golden Treatise of Hermes," p. 37.

transformative operations occur, they most certainly will not occur without the ego's ceaseless effort and vigilance. The ego must protect the self, and initiate and maintain the procedures it desperately requires.

There are times when the external world is hostile and critical, and if the ego identifies with such outside opinion, it may reject its self, or allow the opinions of others to prevent self-development. It may even jettison work that has been accomplished if the results do not meet with external approbation. In childhood, outside influences are so dominant that if a child is living in a hostile or abusive environment the self disappears. It is as if it goes into hiding, because the ego of a child is not strong enough to defend it. I have often heard of dreams of people entering analysis that show them discovering corpses in refrigerators, or children hidden in drawers or attics. The self that hid in order to protect itself may come out of hiding if the ego takes over the job of guaranteeing its safety.

There are also times when the internal world of an individual is hostile. If a complex is out of control, or an archetype has constellated, the ego must insure that they do not overcome or injure the self. If, for example, an individual is just beginning to connect with an inner figure that personifies a small part of the self, such as a creative talent, and a complex arises denigrating and dismissing this talent, the inner figure may be driven back into the unconscious. It may never reemerge—or may do so only much later. In such a situation, the complex blocks the manifestation of that aspect of the self. I have known many talented clients who never develop their abilities because their inner critic is so severe that they are afraid of producing inferior products. The critic prevents the self from emerging. It is up to the ego to protect the self from such inner attacks, which it must do by insulating itself from the influence of the complex. Though the critic attacks with ruthless ferocity, the ego must go forward regardless. If the ego is courageous enough to continue its creative work, despite the critic's endless carping, the self gains strength. Eventually, it finds the strength to undermine the critic.

At other times, an archetype may assimilate an image of the self to it, thereby contaminating it and preventing the personification of that which is unique in the personality. I recall a case in which a person received an important insight about her own spiritual life, and wrote a lot in her journal about the spiritual path presented to her. As almost always happens, the archetype of the redeemer was activated within her and immediately assimilated the new content that had emerged. The client felt herself compelled to teach the world about her great insight, even though she had never even tried to live it herself. All of the energy that should have gone into her own development went, instead, into devising ways to teach others. Teaching is quite a good thing, but only at the right time. One's own insight and knowledge must first be integrated, or the work the self requires may never occur.

The ego must develop certain skills that allow it to protect the self. It must learn to trust its own inner vision and sense of things. It needs to develop such a deep relationship with the self that it is prepared to resist any suggestion or pressure to forfeit the connection that has grown between them. At the same time, it must develop such sensitivity that it can detect the slightest attacking or inhibiting force from either the inner or outer world. Such skills and attitudes take time to develop, and are most easily engendered through active imagination work with the inner figure that embodies the self. At some point in one's individuation process, one must reach the firm and clear decision that one must honor the self no matter what the consequences are, and that its protection and expression are more important than anything else, even than life itself.

The stone promised that it would provide protection as well. There are times when the self becomes the protector of the ego, and returns the favor the ego has granted it. There are many ways this protection might occur. In the first place, and perhaps most importantly, the ego finds in the self a friend and confidant, an inner partner whose encouragement and support never flag. There are times in life when an individual must go out on a limb, or risk all in order to develop, and feeling an inner encouragement and friendly presence can make all the difference in making the attempt or turning away from it. When the self has grown and the ego has established a relationship with it, the self can instill in the ego such feelings of love and security that no hazard appears too great. Imagine all those times in your life when a kind word and a loving gesture permitted you to face defeat courageously, or risk condemnation of those you cared for in order to be yourself. When the self has manifested as an inner figure with which one can relate, the kind word and the loving gesture are readily available. I have never seen the self take away one's pain, or minimize one's risk, for such experiences are the raw material of individuation, but I have seen it repeatedly accompany the ego through its dark passage. Having such a companion makes even the deepest turmoil bearable, and the darkest night appear just a little brighter. The self's love and its companionship are the primary way it offers its protection to the ego.

There are other forms in which protection may appear as well. The ego faced with a challenging and difficult situation may have an insight just when it is needed, or experience a synchronicity that opens the door hitherto thought shut for good. A dream may come—or a vision bringing the sought for solution. In a thousand ways, the ego may experience the miraculous turn of events that makes the path passable once more. It would not be correct to say that the self causes these things to happen, for causality may be a concept that does not apply to such situations, but it certainly appears that it *arranges* things in such a way that they turn out for the good of the ego. The more deeply the relationship with the self has been forged, the more frequently fortuitous synchronicities occur. This does not mean that the ego always gets what it wants, but it gets what is best for it and what it needs for individuation.

Once in Zurich I had reached the point where all of my funds were dried up. I did not know if I would be able to stay, or even if I had enough money for food. I had 10 francs left and I told my analyst about my untenable situation. He asked me to hand the money over to him and proceeded to set it on fire. "Now," he said, "you are really free." I wasn't quite sure how I felt about such freedom, but knew there wasn't much else I could do but trust. The next day I received three calls from individuals, all of whom wanted to start analysis with me. The money crunch disappeared and has never returned. Coincidence? It would be impossible to prove that it was not, but it certainly did not feel like a coincidence. It felt like the self was protecting me as I continued my quest for self-knowledge.

The stone next proclaims that it possesses its *Sol* and its *Luna* within itself, whose lights are wondrous. It possesses glories and riches that exceed all other good things and its rewards are unlike anything else. As the unifier of opposites, the self contains its own bright consciousness and awareness, and the powers and creativity of the imagination. It offers its gifts freely to the ego that is in relationship with it. Other alchemists also joyously proclaim the gifts of the self. At the same time, they struggle to express the exact nature of the relationship with the stone. In the *Rosinus ad Sarratantam Episcopum* an alchemist calling himself Rosinus wrote:

The stone is below thee, as to obedience; above thee, as to dominion; therefore from thee, as to knowledge; about thee, as to equals. . . . This stone is something which is fixed more in thee . . . created of God, and thou are its ore, and it is extracted from thee, and wheresoever thou art it remains inseparably with thee.[24]

This passage paints a complicated and intricate image of the relationship between ego and self. The self obeys the ego, and yet rules the ego, for it obeys the wishes of the ego and yet has dominion over the ego. This is paradoxical, for though the self has power that far exceeds the ego's, it most often is content to follow the lead of the ego, if that lead proceeds from the heart. There are many situations in which the ego must make decisions that will impact its life profoundly, and often it prefers to wait to find out what to do from a dream or an active imagination. But those are the very situations in which the self clams up and refuses to answer. Recently I saw a client who had retired in order to pursue a more inward life. His old company decided it could not survive without him and asked him to return on very generous terms. He did not know what to do, feeling obligated to his old friends and associates, but drawn to the new life he was creating. He could get no information from his dreams or his actives, and finally the inner figure that carried the self for him said simply, "You must lead." He finally decided to refuse the offer and stay with his new interests. Months later it became apparent that this decision was the turning point in his inner work. It not only marked a whole new level of com-

---

24. "Rosinus ad Sarratantam Episcopum" in *Artis Auriferue*, I, pp. 198–200, quoted in Johannes Fabricius, *Alchemy* (London: Diamond Books, 1989), p. 208.

mitment to it on his part, but also ushered in a time when his experiences of the self increased in frequency and depth.

The ego must accept responsibility for its own life and choices. There are times when it must give up the lead and willingly follow the inner voice, but those times usually come when it is too controlling or has not yet learned what partnership with the self means. More often, once that partnership has been established to one degree or another, the ego finds itself in the position of having to make its own choices. The self generally is content to follow. The requirement, however, is that the ego truly follow its heart and not its head, or the urgings of others. In the example above, the client knew quite clearly that he did not wish to return to work, but he felt obligated. Choosing to follow his feelings was the most important part of the decision, for the self always supports true feelings. Had he chosen to return to work in disregard of his real wishes, the self might then have resisted. The paradox is that the true feelings that the ego must consult in its decision-making probably originate from the self anyway. Still, the act of choosing is terribly significant, and a responsibility the ego must come to accept.

The ego must make choices, but the self has dominion. I have sometimes heard the self called the ruler and the ego the minister that carries out its commands, but this is too simplistic an image. As I have just mentioned, the ego often must make the choice with the self gladly supporting and following that choice. The self's dominion is more like that of a lover or close friend for whom we would do anything. The lover does not control us or make demands, but there is nothing we would not do for him or her. The dominion of the self is that of love, not power, and it establishes an authority of love and joy, based on mutual cooperation. Nevertheless, it is also true that an ego that refuses to follow the inner promptings of the self, or to seek its own individuation, often experiences adverse

Figure 23. The union of the sun and moon into one being denotes the creation of the philosopher's stone. The ego and the unconscious unite so completely as to form the manifest self, which is one person with two heads or centers of consciousness. It stands upon the dragon, vanquishing the chaos that existed at the beginning of the work. The winged sphere is the awakened and vital center, the self in its own mysterious essence, which the king and queen personify. The five crowns refer to the quintessence, the number of absolute unity. (From J. D. Mylius, *Philosophia reformata*, Frankfurt, 1622.)

reactions. If love is refused too long, power may well assert itself. At the deeper stages of union, the ego and the self are so in harmony that it is almost impossible to determine who wills what, or who accomplishes what.

Figure 23 depicts the union attained when *Sol* and *Luna* are united. The stone in the quote (on page 240) referred to his inner *Sol* and *Luna* shining within him. The self is the union of the king and the queen, of consciousness and the unconscious. It stands on the vanquished dragon, representing the chaos at the beginning of the work. The five crowns refer to the quintessence, the image of absolute unity, and also symbolize the dominion of the self. The winged sphere on which the double-headed being stands is the awakened and vital center, the self in its own essence that the king-queen being personifies. The scene of absolute unity that this emblem conveys includes the ego. One could as easily take the head of the king for that of the self, and the queen that of the ego, or vice versa, for the self and the ego are in union. The ego never loses its own sense of identity and separateness; it retains its own head, but its feels itself at one with the self. The self never loses its own separateness either, so it retains its own head, but together they stand on the center, which is the common ground out of which they both emerge.

The self stands apart from the ego in terms of knowledge, but in all else is equal. The self, in retaining its own identity, exists as an inner figure with which the ego may interact. This inner figure embodies the power and the felt sense of the center on which it stands; it also incorporates all the wisdom of the unconscious. Since the collective unconscious is a vast reservoir of knowledge, the ego may consult the self on any topic and expect to be well informed. The self is the animated personification of absolute knowledge. The store of learning that the self possesses is not only intellectual, however. It is rare that the self lays forth some theoretical explanation; it knows in a visionary and feeling way, and it conveys its knowledge through direct experience. If I have a question about the meaning of life, or a question about a specific relationship in which I feel stuck, I may ask the self for help. Sometimes that help will take the form of a dialogue in which the ego and the inner figure discuss aspects of the issue, but the deeper explanation almost always comes in either a direct flash of knowing or in an imaginal experience that uncovers the hidden solution to the problem.

Since the self, no matter how deeply I am in union with it, stands apart from me, I may always dialogue and relate with it. That places its wisdom at my disposal. But the author of *The Rosinus* pointed out that the alchemist and the stone are also equals. The equality of the self and the ego refers to the need that each partner has for the other. The ego, whether it knows it or not, is always hungry for the companionship of its inner friend, and will never find any true satisfaction without some form of union with it. The same is true for the self, not only because it will never manifest without the ego, but because it, too, hungers for partnership. The self not only seeks its own expression; it seeks its lover as well. Neither the ego nor the self can ever be complete alone, for each finds totality in the embrace of the other.

The ego does not serve the self, nor does the self submit to the control of the ego. They are equal partners who function as two heads with one heart. They help each other to find ways to express the bidding of that heart, and are joined by the feelings that it creates. The inner figure who is the self, and the ego view each other as two halves of the same whole, and interact as such. Though the inner figure is the self in the imaginal world, and therefore has power and wisdom far exceeding that of the ego, it still treats the ego as its equal, for in the great adventure of living life as a whole person, the ego is coequal with the self.

The Rosinus also declares that the human being is the ore out of which the stone emerges. This is a principle doctrine of spiritual alchemy, and concerns the human being that is the beginning and end of the work, and that transmutation of the human soul which is an essential part of the *opus*. Moreover, the stone never stands apart from the alchemist, but "remains inseparably with thee." Once the self has arisen from the dark waters of the unconscious, it struggles to maintain its central position, to become a fixed and undiminished inner presence. Once an individual reaches the second level of union, the self is always present and never leaves the ego. The ego can focus on the self at will, and never loses the feeling that the self is with it inseparably.

What I am saying about the self is also true of the ally. When the third *coniunctio* is attained, the ego finds an equal partner, and a lover, in the self of the psychoid, the individual form of the divinity that enters union with the center of the psyche. The personified form or Name of God has dominion in the psyche as the manifest self previously did, and adds its power to that of the human center. When incarnation occurs in the third level of union, the divinity has become an inner figure who relates to the ego with the same degree of familiarity, love, and partnership as did the manifest self. From the perspective of the ego, the self, at the third level, has become the living God, and the mystical nature of the alchemical work shines forth in all its glory. It is especially at this stage of the work that the alchemists experience the ecstasy of divine incarnation:

> *Now is the stone shaped, the elixir of life prepared, the love-child or the child of love born, the new birth completed, and the work made whole and perfect: O wonder of wonders!*[25]

---

25. Johannes Fabricius, *Alchemy*, p. 190.

The ecstatic tone of this quote is quite obvious. The alchemists created and experienced the third *coniunctio* in states of ecstasy which are almost impossible to describe. When the spirit of the divine enters the psyche—not as a visitor but as a permanent resident—psychic life is altered forever. Whenever the ego turns its gaze on its new guest, it instantly enters altered states of consciousness and perception, and feels an abiding joy and ecstasy that nothing diminishes. Though I must acknowledge the futility of capturing the essence of this state in words, it is nevertheless important to try, if only to present a possibility that rarely occurs in the life of most people. As I mentioned earlier in this chapter, each human being is the center of the cosmos. Each individual has the capacity to attain some degree of union with the self, and each has at least the potential to reach the third level. The following discussion should be viewed as a discussion of a conceivable, if little known, state of the human psyche.

The writer ecstatically proclaims the birth of the love-child or child of love, and this is a reference to the important role of love in creating the union with the self at whatever stage of the work one has achieved. But that work results in the birth of the child, who as an inner figure embodied the divine spirit and the manifest self as one in the third union, and this child is created through and out of love. Spiritual thought often emphasizes the love between the human and the divine partners, and alchemical mysticism is no exception. Despite the often dry references to processes and vessels, alchemy is also about love and the union that it engenders.

The author of this quote went on to discuss the child of love in greater detail. It has soul, body, and spirit. It unites within itself the quality of the Father, the Son, and the Holy Ghost, "even all these three, in one fixed and eternal essence and being."[26] The references to the number 3 and the variety of three aspects that the son possessed indicates the importance that this number plays in alchemy. The allusion to the Trinity is quite specific in this and other alchemical texts, as the writer establishes the comparison between the stone and God. The stone is a divine being which incarnates the Son, the Father, and the Holy Ghost.

In discussing the last picture in the series from the *Book of Lambspring*, I pointed out that the three figures—the king, his son, and the angelic being—symbolized three aspects of the self that came into being at the third *coniunctio*. The current quotation uses the exact same imagery to denote this state. In the mind of the alchemist the stone embodies every aspect of the divinity, and is in itself a living personification of the Trinity. From the point of view of the Jungian model, the father would symbolize the manifest self, the son the *filius*, or the personal expression of God that unites with the self, and Holy Spirit is the transcendent function, or the imaginative power of the spirit, to create more growth and transformation.

The text also states that the three were united in one form, "in one fixed and eternal essence and being." Just as the mystery of the Trinity lies in its being three and yet only one, so the stone unites the three aspects of the divinity in one fixed essence. The self is one, yet unites in itself the human center and the divine center, as well as the imaginative power that has multiplied greatly with its formation. One inner figure, produced by the self, may therefore come to incarnate the manifest self and the divine ground of being. When this inner figure comes into being, it unites within itself human and divine centers, and

---

26. Johannes Fabricius, *Alchemy*, p. 190.

has the spiritual capacity to present itself to the ego in one imaginative experience after another. The individual ego which does active imagination with such a figure finds itself in a world of ecstasy and profound vision, for the eternal and infinitely diverse self depicts its own nature in myriad forms. The only work remaining at this stage is to know the million faces of God as they reveal themselves in the imaginative realm, and to deepen forever the bonds of relationship and love that join ego and self.

Spiritual alchemy sees in the creation of the stone the incarnation of God and the transmutation of the human soul. The text next states that the "man of paradise is become clear as transparent glass, in which the divine sun shines through and through, like gold."[27] The transformed soul is likened to clear glass through which the divine essence shines, so that the soul has become opened to God, and no barriers exist between them. This is the gold that the alchemist strives to create—the purified and regenerated human soul that has been rectified to the point of crystal clarity, and become a home for the divine radiance. Moreover, the human being has become the "man of paradise," for with the attainment of the third level of union we find ourselves in paradise, for paradise is where the light of God shines without hindrance. The paradise of the soul is within, and the soul participates in that reality, whatever else is occurring in the outside world.

The alchemists have no better way to express the attainment of the third *coniunctio* than to compare it to paradise. Nicholas Flammel, for example, writes that the stone carried a person up to the imperial heaven,[28] while Sendi-

---

27. Johannes Fabricius, *Alchemy,* p. 190.
28. Nicholas Flammel, *Alchemical Hieroglyphics* (Berkeley Heights: Heptangle Books, n.d.), p. 88.

vogius poignantly remarks that he no longer wondered "as once I did, that the true sage, though he owns the stone, does not care to prolong his life; for he daily sees heaven before his eyes, as you see your face in a glass."[29] When the self has fully awakened and united with the divine center, there is such bliss and ecstasy within the human soul that no further idea of paradise could be entertained. Paradise is union with the living self.

The text goes on to state that the soul living with the self in this way "can make herself whatsoever she will, and do and have whatsoever she will. . . . And this same one will is God's eternal infallible will." The soul is liberated from any limitations that previously bound her in, for she has gained full access to imaginative power. In union with the self, which at this point has concentrated within itself an immense imaginative capacity, the ego can participate in unlimited imaginal experiences.

I do not know what bounds may be placed on the power of the imagination. It can heal the body, reveal the secrets of divine truth, transform the personality, incarnate God, and open up worlds of infinite diversity and potential. There are possibly limits to what it can achieve, but I have not discovered them. The ego in union with the self has the power with which it can play, create, mold and instruct its life. The will of the ego is no different at this point than the will of God, for so deep is the union that what one wills, the other wishes for as well. It should not be assumed that the ego uses this power for its own aggrandizement and material gain, for such is the stuff of fantasy and not true imagination. The ego has tasted the wonders of paradise and thirsts no more for outer recognition or

---

29. Michael Sendivogius, *The New Chemical Light* (Alchemy Website, Database online), p. 41.

influence. It wants to know more of the inner wonders, and to embody them in its outer life. It wills to live its mythic life, as does the self with whom it shares this adventure.

The text concludes that "the divine man is in his own nature become one with God."[30] The man of paradise is also the divine human being, for his own center has taken on the divine being so that the psyche itself is divinized. The center, the self, is now as much divine as it is human, and when the ego turns its gaze within, it beholds the godhead. Nicholas Flammel wrote about this state as well when he said of the stone:

> [It] is incapable of Alteration or change, over which the heaven itself nor his Zodiac can have no domination nor power, whose bright shining rays, that dazzle the eyes, seem as though they did communicate unto a man some super-celestial things, making him (when he beholds and knows it) to be astonished, to tremble, and to be afraid at the same time.[31]

The stone is unchanging and fixed, and the individual who once attains it may never lose it. Nor is it subject to the workings of fate or destiny, but grants freedom to the person with whom it is in union, so that he or she may live life from his or her own center without external control or hindrance. Finally, it creates visionary and imaginative states of blinding intensity in which the ego beholds the nature and power of God face-to-face.

Such then are the goals of spiritual alchemy. It aims high, and settles for nothing less than the transformation of the soul and the union with the divinity. Moreover, it seeks

---

30. Quoted in Johannes Fabricius, *Alchemy*, p. 191.
31. Nicholas Flammel, *Alchemical Hieroglyphics*, p. 89.

union with the divine and its incarnation within the psyche. Increasing ecstasy, bliss, and joy marks the states by which it moves toward the attainment of these goals, as paradise— once lost—is regained. It may be impossible for most of us to imagine what these states would feel like, but it is important to at least grasp that such states exist, and that we may legitimately aim for their attainment. In effect, within the context of alchemy, there are no limits to what we may achieve or what the power of the imagination might create for us. The only limitations are those imposed by our own failure of vision, and by a refusal to do the work as it presents itself to us. Though it is true that the ultimate goal lies beyond the reach of most, the journey itself is rich and joyful enough to invite us to make the effort, for whatever level is attained is itself of value. Rather than being discouraged by the immensity of the task, we should be stimulated by the fruitfulness of the journey. Though it passes through death and destruction more than once, it leads to a richness and potency of life that no other journey can promise.

The alchemical imagination dares to dream of paradise, of immortality, and of union with God so intimate that one can hardly tell where the human stops and the divine begins. It envisions freedom and bliss, the unceasing exploration of the inner world, and it anticipates a human being and a human existence that knows no limits. It imagines neither in metaphors nor in wished-for possibilities, but in real experiences that create the processes by which the goal might be attained. Every step of the way toward paradise is marked by experience, and the experiences are so profound and rewarding in themselves that we often forget that they are only preliminary steps leading to a more permanent state.

In the grandeur of its vision and the profundity of its hope and optimism, spiritual alchemy is a corrective to the prevalent view of life and of the individual. For the alchemists, the individual is the center of the universe, and carries within the seeds of paradise. The human being is a mysterious creature with the power to redeem the universe, and to bring God to self-awareness. The value of the individual has been undermined for the past century, as collective movements and standards, united with the rise of totalitarian governments, have denied the importance of one woman or man alone. As Winston Churchill noted with great prescience before the turn of the century, the coming century would witness the "great war for the existence of the Individual."[32] War continues unabated, and the rekindling of the old alchemical view of the individual is one way to fight it. It was one of Jung's greatest achievements to rediscover the value of the individual self, and to see in it the means for the attainment of life's greatest goals. In this he was in complete agreement with the alchemist.

---

32. Martin Gilbert, *Churchill* (New York: Henry Holt, 1991), p. 115.

CONCLUSION

In this book I have followed two major themes through the writings of the alchemists. I have focused on the power and importance of the imagination, as well as on the ways the self comes to manifest at different stages of inner work. In doing so I have built upon the writings of Jung and on his concepts of the self, active imagination, and the transcendent function. In these three constructs lies the key for understanding alchemy and its wealth of images.

Throughout I have taken the position that the symbols of alchemy depict actual experiential states and processes. Alchemy is not just a metaphor for psychological life, but the insightful portrayal of imaginal experiences that create profound transformations of the psyche. Not only does alchemy present these experiences symbolically, it is a practical system that offers ways to facilitate and produce these inner encounters. Alchemy is not just a guide for inner work, but a map of the way. The series of images show this, and I have tried to present something of the practical side as well, so that readers might fully appreciate the fact that alchemy is a system of pragmatic procedures.

The study of alchemy is not an easy undertaking, yet the rewards are great. As a system that evolved within Western culture, it represents itself in ways that are most suitable to the Western mind. As Westerners, we do not need to seek our truths in the systems of other cultures, but may find it in our own cultural heritage. But so great has been the split with the past, we cannot simply rely on our traditions to sustain us in our inner work. Most people do not feel connected to our ancient traditions, and must first work on creating bridges that reunite them to the old ways. Jung's theories serve as bridges of this kind, for, though written for the contemporary individual, his writings nevertheless turn to the images of the past to find spiritual truths and insights. Though Jung's work is masterly and no one could ever hope to equal his accomplishments in understanding alchemy, much work remains to be done.

Jung has created a model that modern individuals can use to find self-knowledge while studying older models of thought and learning from them. One of the greatest truths the present culture can discover in alchemy is the incredible worth and power of the individual. An equally valuable lesson to be drawn from the alchemist is the richness and efficacy of the imagination. I have tried to indicate the ways in which the imagination plays a central role in all levels of self-creation. We can also learn from alchemy about actual processes we may expect to experience within the imaginal realm: what they mean, the states they create, and the transformations they produce. In this last regard I have only been able to hint at some of the lessons alchemy can offer, but there remains a tremendous amount to discover from it about the nature of the inner journey.

I have speculated throughout these pages that there exists a state beyond the psyche that I have termed the psychoid. It seems to me that the true range of the alchemical imagination cannot be discerned without including this dimension of experience. When we attempt to understand the third *coniunctio*, for example, it is necessary to imagine a self beyond the center of the unconscious. I am very cognizant of the fact that I have probably not convinced the skeptical readers that such a realm exists. It is a very hard task to prove the reality of the psychoid to those who have not experientially encountered it for themselves, but I must admit that my ultimate goal is not to prove the existence of this transpsychic world. Rather, I have presented it to the reader as a guide might discuss a tricky turn in the road to one who has not yet arrived at that juncture. I want readers who might experience the psychoid to be aware of what it is that they have encountered so that they might work with their own adventure in a wise and informed fashion.

Furthermore, I have observed the experiences of hundreds of individuals. Applying the concept of the psychoid to my work with others has yielded rich rewards. To interpret psychoidal experiences correctly opens up a dimension of growth and possibility that most find energizing and challenging. At any stage of the individuation process, correct interpretation is essential. Understanding that is too limited or reductive interferes with the free development of the psyche. Explanation that takes the psychoid into account assures at least the possibility that we can reach the third *coniunctio*. An interpreter must always be careful to understand other people's experiences in terms of where on the map they find themselves. To view experiences of the first level in terms of the third level is a mistake, but so, too, is taking experiences of the third level as belonging to the first. Those who guide others in inner work should have as full and inclusive a map to work with as possible. In my opinion, that requires consideration of (and respect for) psychoidal experiences.

At the same time I would argue that including such experiences and the possibilities they present in my work with alchemy has deepened my understanding and appreciation for the alchemical vision. As my chapter on spiritual alchemy hopefully made clear, the goal included not only the individuation of the human being but the union with the divine worlds as well.

Is it possible that the experiences of God carry us beyond the psyche to the psychoid world where God exists in

Its own realm? Is it possible that God lives outside the human soul but that the human soul can experience It in transpsychic states? Mystics of every age have answered yes to these questions, as do I. The psyche, vast in itself, borders on a realm even more vast, and though the human center may unite with the center of this wider world, it never comes to contain it. I also believe that the alchemist would answer these questions in the affirmative as well. If we say yes to them, we must allow that psychoid experiences exist.

In line with this thinking I have also postulated that there exists a self of the psychoid. By this term I indicate an aspect of God that seeks individual expression and union with a human partner, and that—in the final states of the individuation process—incarnates in the human center. The self of the psychoid would correspond to what in other work I have termed the ally, or what the Sufis have called the Name of God. The psychoidal self presents itself in the imaginal realm as an inner figure created through the imaginal power of God, which may come to embody God in ever-increasing depth and complexity. The idea of God incarnating in the human soul is astounding enough, but that it does so in an inner figure with which we may dialogue and relate may seem fantastic indeed. Yet such is the case. The alchemists present this idea in their more ecstatic writings and in some of their more profound symbols.

The addition of the psychoid and the self of the psychoid to our ways of understanding the alchemical imagination not only deepens our insights, it opens up new ways of comprehending inner experiences and the work of self-creation that individuals are engaged in today. I entertained such ideas for a decade before daring to lecture on them, for I wanted to prove to myself that I was not the only one having such experiences. I am quite sure of that fact now, for literally dozens of people have shared experiences of the psychoid with me. The new frontiers that these ideas point to are yet to be fully studied, and the nature of the psychoid and its center are still not understood. As more and more people turn to such study, they will note, as I did, how helpful alchemy can be. In meditation on the alchemical images we can encounter and create imaginal states that open the psychoid for deeper understanding.

In this work I have also emphasized the role of the inner figure and active imagination with such figures. There are certainly other ways in which spiritual experiences may be had, but there are few better than active imagination work for the Western individual. The teaching and study of active imagination states and practices is of the greatest importance in the world today, for in the imaginal realm, individuals find the images which lead them to the experience of human wholeness and divine incarnation, without endangering the role of the ego. Above all else, the ego must be preserved and strengthened if inner alchemy is practiced. The ego must give up its fantasies to be sure, but it must remain healthy and vital, or the self will never manifest.

It is little short of tragic that at a time when new frontiers are opening in the study of the imagination, the Jungian community seems bent on abandoning the inner world. At the moment when analysts must more than ever be psycho-pomp to souls in travail, the lure of the ordinary, the collective, and the clinical have become irresistible. Jungians, like all other people, wish to be accepted, but to be welcomed in a world gone mad is scant comfort indeed. Rather than turn our backs on the inner, rather than proclaim the demise of analysis, we must accept the challenge of deepening our own experience of the inner world so that we may truthfully present ourselves as guides to and teachers of the self.

This work is by no means easy. It demands everything that we have, and sometimes more. There are forces of illusion and delusion that make the work impossible to achieve without the greatest discrimination. I have stressed, however, that the goals outlined in this book, even in the third *coniunctio*, are not beyond our reach. The ecstasy of manifesting the self and uniting with the ally are not idealistic and unattainable utopic stages, but real experiences that we can sample for ourselves, providing the effort is made.

All too often I see people convinced of the impossibility of reaching God, or of finding a way to express their own inner truths. I wish to make it plain that such things are in fact obtainable. I have worked with individuals for over 20 years and am quite aware of how difficult it is to create change. Despite this, I am also quite aware that we can taste something of the inner truth for ourselves and that striving for just a morsel of it is enough to invest any life with meaning and richness.

Jung saw in alchemy a map for the processes of individuation and psychic growth. That map is as valid today as it was in his day, but in addition, we are beginning to recognize in alchemy a blueprint for psychoidal transmutation, and an invaluable aid in the quest for the longed-for goal of human and divine union. As we move into the new millennium, it is possible that the myth of the coming age will deal with the discovery and exploration of the psychoid, and the creation of new levels of union with the self of the psychoid. If so, alchemy will lead the way for questing individuals in this new era, as it has so often done in previous ones.

BIBLIOGRAPHY

Abraham, Lyndy. *Marvel and Alchemy.* Brookfield, Aldershot, England: Scholar Press, 1990.

Altus. *Mutus Liber.* La Rochelle, 1677. See Adam McLean for modern edition.

Agrippa, Henry Cornelius. *Three Books of Occult Wisdom,* Donald Tyson, ed., St. Paul: Llewellyn, 1995.

Anonymous. *Lives of the Alchemystical Philosophers.* London: John M. Watkins, 1955.

Ashmole, Elias. *Theatrum Chemicum Britannicum.* Kila, MT: Kessinger, n.d.

Bacstrom, Sigismond. *Alchemical Anthology.* J. D. Hamilton-Jones, ed. Kila, MT: Kessinger, n.d.

Boas, George, trans. *The Hieroglyphics of Horapollo.* Princeton: Princeton University Press, 1993.

Boehme, Jacob. *The "Key" of Jacob Boehme.* William Law, trans. Grand Rapids, MI: Phanes Press, 1991.

―――. *The Three Principles of the Divine Essence.* Chicago: Yoga Publication Society, n.d.

Broddle, S. Merrow, ed. *Alchemical Works: Eirenaeus Philalethes Compiled.* Boulder: Cinnabar, 1994.

Calid. "Secret of Secrets," see Stanton J. Linden.

―――. "The Secrets of Alchimie," see Stanton J. Linden.

Chevalier, Jean and Alain Gheerbrant. *The Penguin Dictionary of Symbols.* John Buchanan-Brown, trans. New York: Penguin Books, 1996.

Chittick, William. *Imaginal Worlds: Ibn al-'Arabi and the Problem of Religious Diversity.* Albany: State University of New York Press, 1994.

Corbin, Henry. *Spiritual Body and Celestial Earth,* Nancy Pearson, trans. Princeton: Princeton University Press, 1989.

Craven, J. B. *Doctor Heinrich Khunrath: A Study in Mystical Alchemy.* Glasgow: Adam McLean, 1997.

de Rola, Stanislas Klossowski. *The Golden Game.* New York: Thames and Hudson, Inc. 1997.

Dobbs, Betty Jo Teeter. *The Janus Face of Genius.* Cambridge: Cambridge University Press, 1991.

Edinger, Edward. *Anatomy of the Psyche.* La Salle, IL: Open Court, 1994.

The Emerald Tablet. Alchemy Website (Database Online).

Evola, Julius. *The Hermetic Tradition.* E. E. Rhemus, trans. Rochester, VT: Inner Traditions, 1995.

Fabricius, Johannes. *Alchemy.* London: Diamond Books, 1989.

Faivre, Antoine. *The Eternal Hermes: From Greek God to Alchemical Magus.* Joscelyn Godwin, trans. Grand Rapids, MI: Phanes Press, 1995.

Faivre, Antoine and Jacob Needleman, eds. *Modern Esoteric Spirituality.* New York: Crossroad, 1995.

Figulus. *A Golden and Blessed Casket of Nature's Marvels.* Kila, MT: Kessinger, n.d.

Flammel, Nicholas. *Alchemical Hieroglyphics.* Berkeley Heights, CA: Heptangle Books, n.d.

Fludd, Robert. "Truth's Golden Harrow," in C. H. Josten, "Truth's Golden Harrow: An Unpublished Alchemical Treatise of Robert Fludd in the Bodleian Library," in *Ambix: The Journal of the Society for the Study of Alchemy and Early Chemistry,* vol. 3, April 1949.

von Franz, Marie-Louise. *Alchemy.* Toronto: Inner City Books, 1980.

————. *Aurora Consurgens.* Bollingen Series LXXVII. New York: Pantheon, 1996.

————. *On Dreams and Death.* Chicago: Open Court, 1988.

von Franz, Marie-Louise and James Hillman. *Lectures on Jung's Typology.* Dallas: Spring, 1984.

Gilbert, Martin. *Churchill.* New York: Henry Holt, 1991.

Godwin, Joscelyn, trans. *The Chemical Wedding of Christian Rosenkreutz.* Grand Rapids, MI: Phanes Press, 1991.

Hannah, Barbara. "The Beyond." Lecture given at the Second Bailey Island Conference, 1962.

Haq, Syed Nomanul, *Names, Natures and Things.* Boston: Kluwer Academic Publishers, 1994.

Van Helmont, Joan Baptista. *The Image of God in Man or Helmont's Vision of the Soul.* Walter Charelton, trans. London: James Flesher, 1650.

Ibn 'Arabi, Muhyi-D-Din. *The Seals of Wisdom.* New York: Concord Grove Press, 1983.

————. *The Wisdom of the Prophets.* Titus Burckhardt and Angela Culme-Seymour, trans. Aidsworth, Gloustershire, England: Beshara Publications, 1957; and New York: Concord Grove Press, 1983.

Jung, C. G. *Aion.* The Collected Works, vol. 9ii, R. F. C. Hull, trans. Bollingen Series XX. Princeton: Princeton University Press, 1968.

————. *Alchemical Studies.* The Collected Works, vol. 13, R. F. C. Hull, trans. Bollingen Series XX. Princeton: Princeton University Press, 1970.

————. *Analytical Psychology: Its Theory and Practice.* New York: Pantheon, 1968.

————. *The Archetypes and the Collective Unconscious.* The Collected Works, vol. 9i, R. F. C. Hull, trans. Bollingen Series XX. Princeton: Princeton University Press, 1969.

————. *Man and His Symbols.* Garden City: Doubleday, 1964.

————. *Memories, Dreams, Reflections.* New York: Vintage Books, 1963.

————. *Mysterium Coniunctionis.* The Collected Works, vol. 14, R. F. C. Hull, trans. Bollingen Series XX. Princeton: Princeton University Press, 1970.

————. *Psychology and Alchemy.* The Collected Works, vol. 12, R. F. C. Hull, trans. Bollingen Series XX. Princeton: Princeton University Press, 1977.

————. *Psychology and Religion.* New Haven: Yale University Press, 1938.

————. *Psychology and Religion: West and East.* The Collected Works, vol. 11, R. F. C. Hull, trans. Bollingen Series XX. Princeton: Princeton University Press, 1969.

————. "On the Psychology of the Concept of the Trinity," G. V. Hartman trans., in *Quadrant* XXXVII:I. Winter, 1998.

————. *The Structure and Dynamics of the Psyche.* The Collected Works, vol. 8, R. F. C. Hull, trans. Bollingen Series XX. Princeton: Princeton University Press, 1969.

Kelly, Edward. *The Alchemical Writings of Edward Kelly.* A. E. Waite, trans. New York: Samuel Weiser, 1976.

Kelly, L. G. *Basil Valentine: His Triumphant Chariot of Antimony with Annotations of Theodore Kirkringius.* 1678. Reprint: New York: Garland, 1990.

Langford Garstin, E. J. *Theurgy: Or the Hermetic Practice.* London: Rider, 1930.

Linden, Stanton J., ed. *The Mirror of Alchemy.* New York: Garland, 1992.

Lindsay, Jack. *The Origins of Alchemy in Graeco-Roman Egypt.* New York: Barnes and Noble, 1970.

McLean, Adam. *A Commentary on the Mutus Liber.* Grand Rapids, MI: Phanes Press, 1991.

————. *Compendium on the Rosicrucian Vault.* Edinburgh: Hermetic Research Series, 1985.

Mindell, Arnold. *Dreambody.* Boston: Sigo Press, 1982.

Morienus. *A Testament of Alchemy.* Lee Stavenhagen, ed. and trans. Published for the Brandeis University Press by the University Press of New England, Hanover, NH, 1974.

Newman, William R. *Gehennical Fire.* Cambridge: Harvard University Press, 1994.

Pagel, Walter. *Joan Baptista Van Helmont: Reformer of Science and Medicine.* London: Cambridge University Press, 1982.

Patai, Raphael. *The Jewish Alchemists.* Princeton: Princeton University Press, 1994.

Puli, Ali. *The Center of Nature Concentrated.* Edmonds, WA: The Alchemical Press, 1988.

Regardie, Israel. *The Philosopher's Stone.* St. Paul: Llewellyn, 1978.

Roob, Alexander. *Alchemy & Mysticism: The Heremetic Museum.* Shaun Whiteside, trans. Koln: Taschen, 1997.

Rulandus, Martinus (Martin Ruland). *A Lexicon of Alchemy or Alchemical Dictionary* (1893). York Beach, ME: Samuel Weiser, 1984; Reprint: Kila, MT: Kessinger, n.d.

Sandner, Donald and Steven Wong, eds. *The Sacred Heritage.* New York: Routledge, 1996.

Schuler, Robert M., ed. *Alchemical Poetry: 1575–1700.* New York: Garland Publishing, 1995.

Scott, Walter. *Hermetica.* Boston: Shambhala, 1983.

Sendivogius, Michael. "The New Chemical Light." Alchemy Website, Database on Line.

———. "Treatise on Salt." See Zbigniew Szydlo.

Smith, Pamela. *The Business of Alchemy: Science and Culture in the Holy Roman Empire.* Princeton: Princeton University Press, 1994.

Szydlo, Zbigniew. *Water Which Does not Wet Hands: The Alchemy of Michael Sendivogius.* Warsaw: Polish Academy of Sciences, 1994.

Tahil, Patricia, trans. *The Alchemical Engravings of Mylius.* Edinburgh: Magnum Opus Hermetic Sourceworks, 1984.

Trismosin, Salomon. *Splendor Solis.* Grand Rapids, MI: Phanes Press, 1991.

Urban, Hugh. "Imago Magia, Virgin Mother of Eternity: Imagination and Phantasy in the Philosophy of Jacob Boehme," in *Alexandria,* vol. 2, 1993.

Valentine, Basil. *Triumphant Chariot of Antimony: With Annotations of Theodore Kirkringius (1678).* L. G. Kelly, ed. New York: Garland Publishing, 1990.

Vaughan, Thomas. "Coelum terrae." See A. E. Waite, trans.

Waite, A. E., ed. *The Hermetic and Alchemical Writings of Paracelsus the Great.* Reprint: Kila, MT: Kessinger, n.d. Originally published in London in 1894 by James Elliott.

———. *The Hermetic Museum.* Reprint: York Beach, ME: Samuel Weiser, 1973.

———. *The Magical Writings of Thomas Vaughan.* Reprint: Kila, MT: Kessinger, n.d.

————. *The Turba Philosophorum.* New York: Samuel Weiser, 1976.

White, David Gordon. *The Alchemical Body.* Chicago: University of Chicago Press, 1996.

Yates, Frances A. *The Rosicrucian Enlightenment.* London: Routledge, 1996.

Zadrobilek, Vladislav, ed. *Opus Magnum.* Prague: Trigon Press, 1997.

INDEX

Jeffrey Raff received his BA from Bates College, a Master's in Psychology from the New School for Social Research, and a Ph.D. in Psychology from the Union Graduate School. He attended the C. G. Jung Institute in Zurich from 1972 to 1976, graduating as a diplomate Jungian analyst. He's written several articles on both shamanism and alchemy from the Jungian perspective, and has been in private practice as a Jungian analyst in Littleton, Colorado since 1976. He also teaches classes, seminars, and workshops all over the country on Jungian psychology and alchemy. In 2002 he published, with Linda Bonnington Vocatura, *Healing the Wounded God*, which goes in depth into active imagination and work with the ally. Readers may contact him and get information about his schedule and books through his Web site: http://www.jeffraff.com.